Microsoft® Word

for the Apple® Macintosh®

THE
APPLE®
MACINTOSH®
BUSINESS
LIBRARY

Covers
Version 4

Microsoft® Word
for the Apple® Macintosh®

Michael Boom

PUBLISHED BY
Microsoft Press
A Division of Microsoft Corporation
One Microsoft Way, Redmond, Washington 98052-6399

Library of Congress Cataloging in Publication Data

Boom, Michael.
    Microsoft word for the Apple Macintosh. Michael Boom.
       p.   cm. -- (The Apple Macintosh business bookshelf)
    Includes index.
    ISBN 1-55615-275-2

    1. Microsoft Word (Computer program).   2. Macintosh (Computer) --
Programming.   3. Word processing. I. Title. II. Series.
Z52.5.M52B66   1990   90-6447
652.5'536--dc20   CIP

Printed and bound in the United States of America.

1 2 3 4 5 6 7 8 9   MLML   4 3 2 1 0

Distributed to the book trade in Canada by General Publishing Company, Ltd.

Distributed to the book trade outside the United States and Canada
by Penguin Books Ltd.

Penguin Books Ltd., Harmondsworth, Middlesex, England
Penguin Books Australia Ltd., Ringwood, Victoria, Australia
Penguin Books N.Z. Ltd., 182-190 Wairau Road, Auckland 10, New Zealand

British Cataloging in Publication Data available

Acquisitions Editor: Marjorie Schlaikjer
Project Editor: Nancy Siadek

To my mother, Diana, and my father, Ken,

for two widely diverging views of life.

I'm grateful for them both.

Contents

Acknowledgments

I'd like to express my appreciation of the perspicacious staff at Microsoft Press who oversaw this project from rough drafts through printed pages. Thanks in particular to Marjorie Schlaikjer, who first suggested this book; to Wally Parker, Mark Dodge, Jerry Joyce, and Mary DeJong, who alternated in the devil's advocate chair as technical editors; to the Microsoft Press Proof department, particularly Jean Zimmer, who worked above and beyond the call of proofing duty; and to Nancy Siadek, who boldly slashed and tweaked where slashing and tweaking did the most good. I appreciate their good judgment and counsel—if any of the sample documents in this book elicits groans, it's not their fault.

Finally, I'd like to thank my wife, Lynn, who never once said anything rude to me as I wandered, mumbling, around the house trying to gather my constantly straying thoughts into cogent explanations of Word features. Thanks, honey. I just want you to know that many of those stray thoughts were of you.

Introduction

If you bought Microsoft Word version 4 because you wanted the most powerful and popular word processor available for the Macintosh, you did the right
thing. Word offers traditional word processing features such as full editing
and text-formatting capabilities, graphics support, and a spelling checker; but
Word also goes far beyond the basics. Word's advanced features let you
create document outlines, arrange information in tables, manage footnotes,
and create your own form letters. Word also offers features that sort lists,
hyphenate text, perform calculations, and complete a variety of other tasks
that can make your work easier.

Word is designed to help beginning users. It offers fundamental features
that are easy to find and use, and it keeps more advanced and potentially confusing features tucked away where novices are less likely to stumble on them.
The trick to getting the most out of Word is to find the advanced features that
can help you the most and then learn to make the best use of them. This book
shows you Word's most used and useful features and teaches you how to use
them well so you can get straight down to business.

How to Use This Book

This book begins with the basics of Word and then moves to more advanced
topics. Although the first chapters don't require that you know anything about
Word, you should already know how to perform fundamental Macintosh
tasks—such as turning the Mac on and off, inserting and ejecting disks,
opening and closing folders and disk icons, and dragging files to new
folders—before you read this book. These are skills you can master by following instructions in the documentation that comes with your Macintosh or
by getting help from your computer dealer, computer administrator, or local
Macintosh users' group.

The book is divided into four sections and an appendix. Each section
addresses a different level of experience:

- Section One, "Beginnings," addresses users who are completely
  new to word processing. It describes how to install Word and its
  associated programs (if they aren't already installed) and how to
  start Word. After a brief tour of Word's features, it describes how
  to enter, edit, format, and print a standard letter.

- Section Two, "Basics," teaches beginning Word users how to get the most from Word's fundamental features. It covers how to enter and format characters, how to import graphics, how to edit text with Word's editing tools, and how to apply formatting to paragraphs. Next it describes how to handle tabs and how to create headers and footers. The last chapter of this section describes how to save, open, and print finished documents.

- Section Three, "Beyond Basics," is for users who want to create more complex documents. It offers information about editing tools such as the glossary, thesaurus, and spelling checker. It teaches how to create footnotes, use styles (an advanced formatting feature), format full documents and sections of documents, and create document templates. The last chapter of this section offers information about advanced printing techniques, including printing with a laser printer, and exporting documents to page-layout programs.

- Section Four, "Power Tools," is for users who want to try some of Word's most advanced features. It shows how to use Galley View, Page View, and Outline View, how to create and edit tables, and how to customize Word to include your own menus and keyboard shortcuts. It ends with a chapter about printing form letters.

- The appendix is for fleet-fingered Word users who want to work faster without moving their fingers from the keyboard. It offers a complete list of Word's keyboard shortcuts.

Each section of the book begins with chapters about text entry, followed by chapters about editing and formatting, followed by chapters about printing and document-file management. Find the section that sounds appropriate to your level of experience and begin there. If you have trouble understanding the material there, simply move back to a previous section.

Each chapter offers practical examples that illustrate the main concepts presented in that chapter. A sample document that appears at the beginning of most chapters shows you what you will accomplish by following the exercises within. Try the exercises! You'll learn more quickly if you teach your fingers as well as your mind. And finally, take some time to experiment with Word as you read—you'll become a more proficient and knowledgeable Word user.

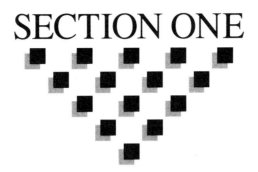

SECTION ONE

Beginnings

This section gets you started on Word 4 for the Macintosh: You verify that your computer is set up to run Word, you learn Macintosh system and environment fundamentals, and you create your first Word document.

Chapter 1

Setting Up Word 4

If you recently bought Microsoft Word version 4 and want to set it up to run on your Macintosh, this chapter is for you. In it you'll find an explanation of the computer equipment and system software you need to run Microsoft Word as well as some recommendations for additional hardware and software that can make Word run even better. You'll also find instructions for installing Word and its related files on either a hard-disk drive or on floppy disks, whichever is appropriate for your Macintosh system.

You'll find instructions here for installing some of the additional pieces of software that come with Microsoft Word, such as AutoMac III and Word Finder. Once installed on your system disk, you can use these programs to add utility to Word's own features. Later chapters of this book show you how to use both programs.

If you have already installed Word on your Mac or have had someone install it for you, you might want to skip this chapter and move on to the next chapter, which shows you how to start Word. If you haven't installed Word, you want to check that Word is correctly installed on your Mac, or you're simply curious about the installation procedure, you should find the material in this chapter to be quite useful.

REQUIRED HARDWARE

Microsoft Word version 4 runs on any current models of the Macintosh and can run on older Macintosh models if they've been updated. The following list of Macintosh computers tells which models run Word and whether they require modifications:

- *The Macintosh 128* (also called the "Skinny Mac"): This is the original Macintosh. In its original form it can hold 128 KB of RAM (Random Access Memory) and an internal drive for single-sided floppy disks. To run Microsoft Word, this machine must be updated to include at least 512 KB of RAM, a new set of operating-system ROM chips, an internal drive for double-sided floppy disks, and an added external drive for double-sided floppy disks.

- *The Macintosh 512K* (also called the "Fat Mac"): This is the successor to the Mac 128. It can hold 512 KB of RAM and includes an internal drive for single-sided floppy disks. To run Microsoft Word, this machine must be updated to include a new set of operating-system ROM chips, an internal drive for double-sided floppy disks, and an added external drive for double-sided floppy disks.

- *The Macintosh 512KE:* This is an enhanced version of the Mac 512K. It can run Word unmodified if it has two drives for double-sided floppy disks OR one drive for double-sided floppy disks as well as a hard-disk drive.

- *The Macintosh Plus:* Currently sold as the beginner-level Macintosh, this machine can hold 1 MB of RAM. It can run Microsoft Word unmodified if it has two drives for double-sided floppy disks OR one drive for double-sided floppy disks as well as a hard-disk drive.

- *The Macintosh SE family:* The SE family—both the Macintosh SE and the SE/30—are the most full-featured Macintoshes in a single case with a monochrome monitor. The newer SE/30 uses a powerful 68030 CPU (Central Processing Unit) and operates at 16MHz (that is, 16 million cycles per second). The standard SE uses the older 68000 CPU and runs at 8MHz. Each SE can hold up to 4 MB of RAM and can run Microsoft Word unmodified if the machine has two drives for double-sided floppy disks OR one drive for double-sided floppy disks as well as a hard-disk drive.

■ *The Macintosh II family:* This group of Macs currently includes the II, the IIx, the IIcx, the IIci, and the IIcfx. These Macs are enclosed in a large, flat, rectangular case that can be opened easily so that plug-in cards can be added. Users can add any of a variety of monitors, all of which are larger than and can display more information than the standard monitors of the earlier Mac families. Mac IIs use a 68020 or 68030 CPU and are faster and more capable than the 68000-based Macs. A Macintosh in the II family can run Microsoft Word unmodified if the Mac has two drives for double-sided floppy disks OR one drive for double-sided floppy disks as well as a hard-disk drive.

■ *The Macintosh Portable:* The Portable is a battery-powered Mac with a fold-down LCD screen, a built-in keyboard, and a trackball instead of a mouse. It has much the same operating power as a Mac SE, but the Portable is faster, has a larger screen, and does not have a numeric keypad. A Macintosh Portable can run Microsoft Word unmodified if it has two drives for double-sided floppy disks OR one drive for double-sided floppy disks as well as a hard-disk drive.

Printers

To print the documents you create with Microsoft Word, you must have a printer connected to your Macintosh. Most Macintosh systems use printers made by Apple. Two of them—the ImageWriter and the ImageWriter II—are 9-pin dot-matrix printers that use a print head with nine pins to hammer characters and graphics onto paper by pressing against inked ribbon. The ImageWriter LQ is a dot-matrix printer that prints much higher-quality characters than the ImageWriter or ImageWriter II because of its 24-pin print head.

The Apple LaserWriter family of laser printers use a laser, toner, and print drum to impress images and characters onto paper. These laser printers are generally much faster than dot-matrix printers, and their print quality is much higher.

Some non-Apple printers also work with the Macintosh—they're usually sold as ImageWriter-compatible or LaserWriter-compatible printers. If they are compatible with Apple printers, you can connect them in the same way you would the Apple printers.

OPTIONAL HARDWARE

Although Microsoft Word *can* run on a system consisting of a Mac with two floppy-disk drives and an ImageWriter printer, some additional hardware can help Word perform faster and more efficiently.

If your system has only floppy-disk drives, the best investment you can make for running Word is to add a hard-disk drive, which offers additional file-storage space and faster access to Word and document files. Because a hard disk can store so much data, you can create a much larger System file on a hard disk than you can on floppy disks, and because the System file stores fonts, you can thereby gain access to a much larger collection of fonts in Word.

Adding RAM to your Mac allows Word to load all its parts into memory at one time so it won't need to pause during operation to load its parts from the disk drive as they're required. Additional memory also allows more of a long document to be stored directly in RAM so that Word doesn't need to pause intermittently to load more of the document from the disk. If you're a MultiFinder user you'll need a system with at least 2 MB of RAM to run Word simultaneously with other Macintosh programs.

Word users who frequently add graphics to their documents might want to invest in a scanner, a device that turns printed black-and-white or color pictures into digitized images that you can easily insert into a document. Scanners run the gamut from simple, slow, and inexpensive hand-held models to expensive desktop models that can quickly digitize large images.

REQUIRED SOFTWARE

In order for you to run Word on your Macintosh, your Mac must have up-to-date system software. Part of this software is included in the ROM (Read-Only Memory) chips within your Mac—you needn't worry about the ROM chips' being inadequate unless you have an old Mac 128 or Mac 512K, in which case you should update your machine at your Mac dealer. The remaining system software is included in files you must store on your startup disk.

The Startup Disk

If you're new to the Mac, it's important that you know what a startup disk is. Simply put, a startup disk is a disk that contains the computer's operating system; it must be present in the Mac when you first turn the Mac on. If you have a hard-disk drive, the hard disk is commonly your startup disk; it provides the Macintosh system software when you turn your Mac on. If you don't have a hard-disk drive, you use a floppy disk, possibly labeled "System Tools," "System," or "Startup," as a startup disk. You can insert it into any floppy-disk drive before you first turn your Mac on. If you insert a disk that isn't a startup disk, the Mac ejects it and displays a flashing question mark on the screen, asking for another disk. If you insert a startup disk, a smiling Mac icon appears on the screen and is soon replaced by the desktop. The desktop is part of the Macintosh's visual interface—it acts as your home base. The icons on the desktop represent places for finding, storing, and discarding information.

The System Folder on your startup disk, shown in Figure 1-1, stores all the system files that the Mac must read when you first turn it on. It is the System Folder's presence on a disk that makes it a startup disk.

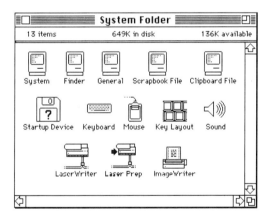

Figure 1-1. *The System Folder on the startup disk contains the System and Finder files.*

The System and Finder Files

The System and Finder files are the two most important system files in the System Folder. The Mac can't run without them. The System file contains system software that helps the Mac keep track of data in memory and perform other necessary functions; the Finder file contains software that creates the desktop, runs programs, displays windows, and keeps track of files on disks.

Both the System and the Finder have been periodically updated and improved by Apple. To identify the different versions as they are released, Apple assigns a version number to each. The higher the number, the more recent the version. It's important that you use a version of System and Finder that is recent enough to run Word and also compatible with your equipment.

To run Word on an updated Macintosh 128, an updated 512K, or a Mac 512KE or Mac Plus, you need to have System version 3.2 or later and Finder version 5.3 or later installed. To run Word on a Mac SE or II, you need System version 4.1 or later and Finder version 6.0 or later. The Mac SE and Mac II work well with more recent versions of the System and Finder because these machines' ROM chips contain more extensive system software to support later versions. If you use a 128 or 512 Mac, you might want to use a system version earlier than 4.1 and a Finder version earlier than 6.0 because later versions might not work well with your machine's ROM chips.

The instructions for installing Word that appear later in this chapter tell you how to check the version number of the System and Finder files on your startup disk.

Printer Files

To print your Word documents, the System Folder (on your startup disk) must contain a printer file that matches the printer connected to your Mac. Each printer file is named after the printer it controls, as follows:

- The ImageWriter file controls the ImageWriter and ImageWriter II dot-matrix printers.

- The LQ ImageWriter file controls the ImageWriter LQ dot-matrix printer.

- The LaserWriter and Laser Prep files (you need both) control all the LaserWriter laser printers with the exception of the LaserWriter II SC printer.

- The LaserWriter II SC file controls the LaserWriter II SC laser printer (Apple's low-end LaserWriter). You don't need the Laser Prep file to run this laser printer.

Your System Folder can contain more than one printer file, but you must activate the printer file that matches your connected printer in order to use that printer. You'll learn to activate printer files later in this chapter.

OPTIONAL SOFTWARE

You don't need any other Macintosh software in order to run Microsoft Word, but several programs and system software files in particular can make working with Word more convenient. Some of these programs and files come with your Mac; others come with Word.

MultiFinder

The Finder file in your System Folder is responsible for the way your Mac runs programs and loads files. If your machine holds more than 1 MB of RAM and you want to run Word simultaneously with other programs such as SuperPaint or HyperCard you can use MultiFinder instead of Finder. Multi-Finder allows you to run several programs at once and easily switch back and forth among them. Without MultiFinder, you must quit Word each time you want to run another program. The DA Handler (Desk Accessory Handler) helps programs in MultiFinder keep track of fonts and desk accessories and should be in the System Folder with MultiFinder in order for MultiFinder to function properly. Installation instructions later in this chapter describe how to run MultiFinder.

Control Panel Files

Several system files let you set the way the Mac operates as you use Microsoft Word. These files must be located in the System Folder if you want them to appear in the Control Panel, a desk accessory located in the Apple menu. To use the files, first double-click on the Control Panel icon to open its window. The following system options appear:

- *General* allows you to set the desktop pattern, sound volume, cursor blinking rate, current time and date, and other characteristics.

- *Keyboard* allows you to set the key repeat rate, repeat delay time, and other keyboard characteristics.

■ *Mouse* allows you to set the double-click rate and the distance the pointer moves on the screen in relation to mouse motion.

Useful Utilities

Font/DA Mover and HD Backup (Hard Disk Backup) are two useful utility programs for Word users. Font/DA Mover is a necessary tool for adding new fonts to your system so you have a wider variety of typefaces available in Word. HD Backup is an essential hard-disk tool for making backup copies of the Word documents you keep on your hard disk, a practice that can prevent catastrophe if the hard-disk drive should fail for any reason.

These utility programs come on disks with your Macintosh and need not be stored on your startup disk. Your Macintosh manual contains instructions for using them.

Other Useful Software

Microsoft Word comes packaged with three extra pieces of software that you can use to improve and enhance your Word documents. The programs are:

■ SuperPaint 1.1, a painting and drawing program you can use to create images and insert them in Word documents;

■ Word Finder, a thesaurus program that helps you find the word on the tip of your tongue; and

■ Auto Mac III, a macro program that records your actions on the keyboard and mouse so you can play them back later. Each recording is called a *macro;* you can use a macro of a repetitive action to save yourself the time and effort of repeating a sequence of keystrokes or mouse movements over and over.

SuperPaint is, like Microsoft Word, an application. You run it independently to create images and then transport the images to Word via the Clipboard or the Scrapbook, a process described in Chapter 3, ''The First Session.'' Word Finder is a desk accessory, a type of program you can run from the Apple menu while you work on a Word document. And AutoMac III is an INIT (short for ''initialization'') program, a type of program that begins running when you turn on the Macintosh and remains available as long as the Mac is turned on.

INSTALLING WORD ON YOUR MACINTOSH

Now that you know what your system requires in order to run Word, the steps you take to install Word on your Macintosh should make sense to you. This section briefly describes how you should physically set up your Macintosh to run Word and then continues with specific instructions for installing Word on your system. You'll find one set of installation instructions for users with a hard-disk drive and a second set of instructions for users with two floppy-disk drives and no hard-disk drive.

The Equipment Setup

To install Microsoft Word on your Macintosh successfully, your system components must be connected correctly and the correct system software must be installed. Chances are you're working on a Macintosh that's already been set up and that runs well, but if you aren't, you must be sure that AC power cords run to the Mac, the printer, an external monitor or hard-disk drive, and any other components of your system that require power. You must also be sure that each component is connected to the Mac with a data cable.

The instructions that come with your Mac show you how to make necessary connections; most are very simple and require only a few minutes to make. If you have a Mac II, you might need to take a little extra time to set up and connect the monitor and install any plug-in cards that are included with your system, according to accompanying instructions. Figure 1-2, on the following page, shows a typical Macintosh system with a printer, keyboard, and mouse connected.

Because you might spend hours at a time in front of the computer, take some time to arrange the keyboard and monitor screen for comfort. If you position the monitor at eye level so you can look at it without bending your neck, you can avoid neck and back pain. Lower the keyboard (or raise your seat) so you can drop your elbows to your side and extend your forearms at a 90-degree angle to place your fingers on the keyboard. If you don't need to raise and lower your forearms, you'll have less wrist, elbow, and shoulder strain. Finally, avoid using lights that reflect on your monitor screen because screen glare can tire your eyes. Lighting above and slightly behind your monitor illuminates your keyboard and surroundings without producing glare.

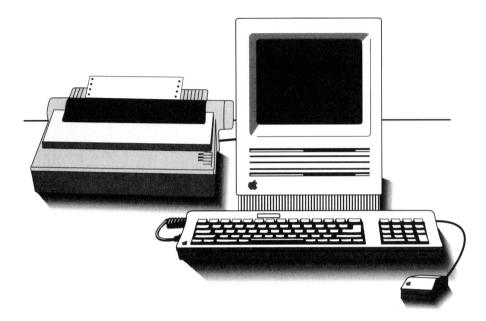

Figure 1-2. *A Macintosh SE with a keyboard, a mouse, and an ImageWriter II printer.*

Turning Your Macintosh On

To turn your Macintosh (except a Mac II) on, trip the rocker switch on the back of the main unit. If you have a Macintosh II, first turn your monitor on (the AC power switch is in a different location on different monitors) and then press the key labeled with a left-pointing triangle in the upper right corner of the keyboard. If you have a hard-disk drive with correctly installed system software, you'll soon see a smiling-Mac icon (the happy Mac!), followed by the desktop. If no software has yet been installed on the hard disk, you need to start your Mac with a floppy startup disk and then follow the instructions in your Mac manual to install the system software on the hard disk and make the hard disk your startup disk.

If you have floppy-disk drives and no hard-disk drive, the Mac screen displays a question mark when you first turn it on: It's requesting the startup disk. Insert the System Tools disk (any disk that contains the System Folder will work), and the system software begins loading. You'll soon see the happy-Mac icon, followed by the desktop.

Checking System and Finder Version Numbers

Once the Mac is running, you can easily check the version number of your System and Finder files by choosing *About the Finder* from the Apple menu. A dialog box like the one shown in Figure 1-3 appears, showing the version number for both System and Finder. You need System 4.1 or later and Finder 6.0 or later if you have a Mac SE or a Mac II. If you have a Mac Plus, 512K, or 128, you need System 3.2 or later and Finder 5.3 or later. If you don't have the correct versions of System and Finder, ask your Macintosh dealer for updated system software.

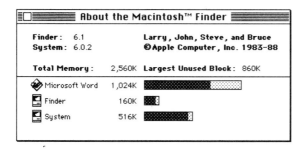

Figure 1-3. *The About the Finder dialog box displays the version number of System and Finder.*

Protecting Your Original Disks

Before you install Microsoft Word, take a minute to protect the floppy disks you'll use in installation. They are Word's three disks and, if you're installing Word onto floppy disks, also two of the system disks that come with your Mac: the System Tools (or System Tools 1) disk and the System Utilities (or Utilities 1) disk.

First write-protect the disks so you can't accidentally erase data while the disks are in a floppy-disk drive. To check for write-protection, hold a disk so you can read its front label, and then look at the small square hole in the disk's upper right corner. If you can see through the hole, the disk is write-protected. If the hole is covered by a sliding tab, the disk isn't write-protected. To write-protect the disk, turn the disk over and slide the tab up with your thumbnail or a pen tip to open the hole.

Next copy each disk and store the original disks in a safe place. If you've never copied disks before, refer to the instructions in your Macintosh manual.

After you copy the disks, label each copy and use the copies as your working disks. If anything were to go wrong with a working disk, you could easily make a new copy from your write-protected, original Microsoft Word disks.

Installing Microsoft Word on a Hard-Disk Drive

If you have a Macintosh with a hard-disk drive, read the following instructions for installing Word on your hard disk. If you don't have a hard-disk drive, skip to the next section, which covers installing Word on floppy disks.

1. Double-click on the hard-disk-drive icon to open its window if it's not already open.

2. Choose *New Folder* from the File menu to add a new folder to the hard-disk-drive window. You will load Microsoft Word and its associated files into this folder.

3. Rename the new folder (labeled ''Empty Folder'') by typing a new name and pressing the Return key. ''Word'' and ''Word 4'' are appropriate names—but of course, you can give this folder whatever name you want.

4. Insert the Word disk labeled ''Program'' into a disk drive and double-click on the Program disk icon to open its window if it's not already open.

5. Using your mouse, drag the icon labeled ''Microsoft Word'' from the Program disk window and onto your new Word folder icon. The Macintosh will copy the Word program into the folder on your hard disk.

6. Eject the Program disk by dragging its icon onto the Trashcan icon.

7. Insert the Word disk labeled ''Utilities 1'' into a disk drive and double-click on the Word disk icon to open its window.

8. Drag the icons labeled ''Standard Glossary,'' ''Word Hyphenation,'' and ''Word Help'' from the Utilities 1 disk window onto your Word folder icon.

9. If you want Word to check spelling in your documents, using American English spellings, drag the icon labeled ''MS Dictionary'' from the Utilities 1 window onto the Word folder icon.

10. Eject the Utilities disk by dragging its icon onto the Trashcan icon.

11. If you want Word to check spelling in your documents, using British English spellings, insert the Word disk labeled "Utilities 2" into a floppy-disk drive and double-click on the disk's icon to open its window if it's not already open. Drag the icon labeled "UK Dictionary" from the Utilities 2 window onto the Word folder icon. Open the Word folder, select the UK Dictionary icon, and rename it "MS Dictionary."

You have now installed Microsoft Word on your hard disk and you are ready to run. The file labeled "Microsoft Word" contains Word itself. The other files contain supporting Word features: Standard Glossary contains a set of glossary entries you can use with Word's glossary feature (which you'll learn to use in Chapter 12, "Writing Tools"); MS Dictionary contains a list of words that Word uses to check spelling in a document; Word Hyphenation contains a list of hyphenation guidelines that Word uses to hyphenate words; and Word Help contains the text you view when you use Word's help feature to find information about different parts of Word.

The other Word-disk files that you didn't copy to the hard disk are sample documents and glossaries that you can browse through when you know how to run and use Word. You can copy them onto the hard disk, but you might want to keep them on a floppy disk, from which you can always gain access to them later for viewing. Keeping them on the floppy disk also saves valuable space on the hard disk for your own documents.

Installing Microsoft Word on Two Floppy-Disk Drives

If you have a Macintosh with two floppy-disk drives and no hard-disk drive, read the following instructions to learn how to create three working floppy disks for using Word. The first disk is a slimmed-down startup disk that contains the essential system files needed to start up your Mac. (You can use this startup disk with other applications as well.) The second disk is a program disk that contains Word itself. And the third disk is an auxiliary-files disk that supports Word's features.

The following instructions describe how to make each disk. To make your slimmed-down startup disk, take the following steps:

1. After first checking that you have a *copy* of the System Tools disk and not the original, insert the copy of the System Tools disk into a floppy-disk drive.

2. Double-click on the System Tools disk icon to open its window.

3. Drag every icon except the System Folder icon out of the System Tools window onto the Trashcan icon.

4. Double-click on the System Folder icon to open its window.

5. Drag every icon except those listed below out of the System Folder window and onto the Trashcan icon. The following icons must remain in the System Folder:

    ☐ Clipboard File

    ☐ Finder

    ☐ General

    ☐ ImageWriter (if you're using an ImageWriter or ImageWriter II printer)

    ☐ LQ ImageWriter (if you're using an ImageWriter LQ printer)

    ☐ LaserWriter and Laser Prep (if you're using a LaserWriter IINT or IINTX printer)

    ☐ II LaserWriter (if you're using a LaserWriter II printer)

    ☐ Keyboard

    ☐ Key Layout

    ☐ Mouse

    ☐ Startup Device

    ☐ System

6. Rename the disk ''Microsoft Word startup disk'' or whatever name you think is appropriate, and eject it.

You now have a startup disk to use when you start your Mac to use Word.

To create the Word program disk, take the following steps:

1. Insert a new disk into the floppy-disk drive, initialize it, and then name it ''Word program disk'' or whatever name you think is appropriate. (If the disk has never been used in a Mac, the Mac will ask whether you want to initialize it when you first insert the disk, at which point you can initialize it and then give it a name. If the disk has been used previously, you must select the disk's icon and then choose *Erase Disk* from the Special menu. After initialization, you can select the disk icon and rename it.)

2. Insert the Word disk labeled ''Program'' into the second floppy-disk drive, and then double-click on its icon to open its window.

3. Drag the Microsoft Word icon from the Program window onto your Word program disk's icon to copy the file to your Word program disk.

4. Eject the Program disk.

5. Eject the Word program disk.

To create the Word auxiliary disk, take the following steps:

1. Insert a new disk into the floppy-disk drive, initialize it, and then label it ''Word auxiliary disk'' or a similar name.

2. Insert the Word disk labeled ''Utilities 1'' into the second disk drive, and then open Utilities 1's disk icon when it appears.

3. Drag the following icons from the Utilities 1 window onto the Word auxiliary disk's icon to copy files onto your Word auxiliary disk:

   ☐ Standard Glossary

   ☐ Word Help

   ☐ Word Hyphenation

   ☐ MS Dictionary (but only if you want Word to check spelling in your documents, using American English spellings)

4. If you want Word to check spelling in your documents, using British English spellings, eject the Utilities 1 disk and insert the Utilities 2 disk. Double-click on the Utilities 2 icon to open its window and then drag the UK Dictionary icon from it onto the Word auxiliary disk icon. Double-click on the Word auxiliary disk icon to open its window, click on the UK Dictionary icon to select it, and then rename the file "MS Dictionary."

5. Eject the Word auxiliary disk from the Mac.

To run Word on your Macintosh, insert the startup disk in a floppy-disk drive before you first turn your Mac on and then insert the Word program disk in the other drive when the Mac is running. Because the startup disk contains the system software the Mac needs to run Microsoft Word, it should remain in the drive whenever possible as you work with Word. If it's removed, you're likely to get messages asking you to reinsert the disk. Because you removed unnecessary system files in creating your startup disk, the disk contains extra space for storing your Word documents. It's a good idea to keep the system files on this disk as few and as small as possible to leave room for your documents. (System files include fonts and desk accessories, so in order to maintain adequate document storage space, you'll need to resist adding too many to your System file.)

The program disk in the second drive contains the Word program, to which Word needs to have access as it runs. Again, you should try to keep the Word program disk in the drive as you work with Word or you're likely to get messages asking you to reinsert the disk whenever Word needs to consult the program file.

You should keep the Word auxiliary disk readily available, as well. You'll need it if you use Word's spelling checker or hyphenation features or if you ask for help using Word. When you do, Word prompts you to tell it where to find the Dictionary, Hyphenation, or Help files. You then swap the auxiliary disk for the program disk and proceed until Word asks for the program disk again (which might not be for a long time).

As you work with Word you can, of course, eject any of the startup, program, or auxiliary disks as necessary to read documents on other disks, to save your own documents to other disks, or simply to check the contents of other disks. You should try to keep the startup and program disks inserted in your floppy-disk drive as much as possible, however, to keep your disk-swapping and time delays to a minimum.

An important note for owners of newer Macintoshes: Apple now includes FDHD floppy-disk drives on most SEs, Portables, and IIs. These drives can store 75 percent more data than the standard drive for double-sided floppy disks can. If your Mac has two FDHD floppy-disk drives, you can forgo creating the third Word disk—the auxiliary disk—and include all its files on your Word program disk. With only two disks—the startup and program disks—you'll do much less disk swapping when you use Word's auxiliary features. You'll also have much more room on your startup disk for fonts and desk accessories.

CHOOSING A PRINTER

If your Macintosh isn't already set up to print, you can use the Chooser desk accessory to tell the Macintosh how your printer is connected and, if you have more than one printer connected to your Mac, which printer you want to use. To do so, take the following steps:

1. Choose *Chooser* from the Apple menu to run Chooser. The Chooser window, shown in Figure 1-4, appears.

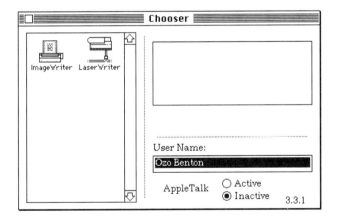

Figure 1-4. *Use the Chooser desk accessory to tell your Macintosh how your printer is connected and which printer you want to use.*

2. If your Macintosh is connected to an AppleTalk network, click on the AppleTalk Active button. If you're not connected to AppleTalk, click on the AppleTalk Inactive button. (If you are using a Laser-Writer, it's connected via AppleTalk. If you are using an Image-Writer, chances are it's connected to your Mac by a simple cable that does not use the AppleTalk communications-management program.)

3. If you're sharing a printer via AppleTalk with other Mac users, you should enter a name to identify yourself in the User Name text box. AppleTalk identifies your printing jobs with this name so other users know who's printing.

4. The scrolling list on the left side of the window shows an icon for each type of printer file you have in your System Folder. Click on the icon that represents the type of printer you'll use to print.

5. If you choose a printer icon while AppleTalk is inactive, the upper right box in the window displays a choice of two output ports, the normal printer port and the modem port. Select the icon that matches the icon etched in plastic above the port to which your printer's connected on the back of your Macintosh.

6. If you choose a printer icon while AppleTalk is active and more than one printer is available on the AppleTalk network, the upper right box in the window lists a choice of printers. Select the name of the printer you want to use.

7. When you're finished choosing printers and connections, click on the close box in the upper left corner of the window. The Chooser box closes.

The printer settings you create in Chooser remain in effect until you open Chooser again and create new settings.

USING MULTIFINDER

If your Mac has more than 1 MB of RAM and you want to run MultiFinder so you can run Word simultaneously with other programs, you must first set the desktop to run MultiFinder and then restart your Macintosh. To do so, follow the steps that begin at the top of the next page.

1. Choose *Set Startup* from the Special menu. The startup dialog box, shown in Figure 1-5, appears.

Figure 1-5. *The startup window offers a choice between Finder and MultiFinder.*

2. Select the Multifinder option, and then click on the OK button to close the dialog box.

3. Choose *Restart* from the Special menu to restart your Macintosh. The Mac reloads its system software from your startup disk, this time running MultiFinder instead of Finder. A small Macintosh icon appears in the upper right corner of the screen.

Note that if your Mac doesn't have enough RAM, you won't be able to run Microsoft Word under MultiFinder. MultiFinder will display a message saying your machine doesn't have enough memory. If so, follow the directions above—this time selecting Finder instead of MultiFinder—to turn Finder back on.

Installing the Word Finder DA

Word Finder is a desk accessory that offers you an online thesaurus. You'll learn how to use it in Chapter 12, ''Writing Tools.'' To install it, use the utility program named Font/DA Mover included on the Utilities disk that came with your Macintosh system. Follow the steps that begin at the top of the next page to install Word Finder.

1. Insert the Utilities disk in a floppy-disk drive. (If you're using a Macintosh system that has two-floppy-disk drives and no hard-disk drive, eject your Word program disk and insert the Utilities disk into that drive.)

2. Double-click on the Utilities disk icon to open its window.

3. Double-click on the Font/DA Mover icon to run Font/DA Mover. The Font/DA Mover window, shown in Figure 1-6, appears.

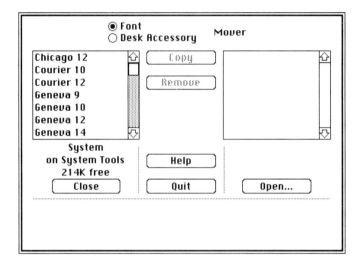

Figure 1-6. *Use the Font/DA Mover to install Word Finder in your System file as a desk accessory.*

4. The Font/DA Mover is set to move fonts. Select the Desk Accessory button if you want to move desk accessories. The scrolling-list window on the left changes to show all the desk accessories contained in your currently active System file; the scrolling-list window on the right is empty.

5. Select the Open button below the scrolling-list window, which is displayed on the right. The file-opening dialog box appears on top of the Font/DA Mover window.

6. Click on the Drive button until the dialog box shows the contents of the Utilities disk and then click on the Eject button to eject the Utilities disk.

7. Insert the Word disk labeled "Utilities 2" into the floppy-disk drive. The dialog box, shown in Figure 1-7, will display the contents of the Utilities 2 disk.

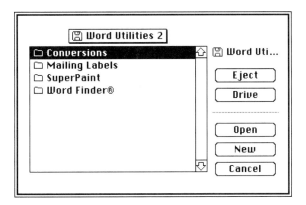

Figure 1-7. *The file-opening dialog box shows files available in different folders stored on different disks.*

8. Double-click on *Word Finder®* in the scrolling list to open the Word Finder folder.

9. Double-click on *Word Finder® DA* in the scrolling list to open the Word Finder DA for moving. The dialog box disappears and uncovers the Font/DA Mover window, where *Word Finder®* appears in the scrolling list on the right.

10. Choose *Word Finder®* from the scrolling list on the right and then click on the Copy button to copy Word Finder into your System file. (If you have too many desk accessories in your System file, you might not be able to copy Word Finder. If so, you'll need to remove one of them before you can add Word Finder to your System File. See your Macintosh and system software manuals for more information about removing desk accessories.) If you don't have a hard-disk drive, you'll need to reinsert the Macintosh Utilities disk when the system prompts you to do so.

11. When the Font/DA Mover has finished copying Word Finder, click on the Quit button. If you don't have a hard-disk drive, you'll need to reinsert the Word Utilities 2 disk when the system prompts you to do so. The Font/DA Mover window disappears from the screen.

12. Double-click on the Utilities 2 disk icon to open its window.

13. Double-click on the Word Finder folder icon to open its window.

14. If you have a hard-disk drive, drag the Word Finder Thesaurus file icon from the Word Finder folder into the Word folder on your hard disk. Storing the Thesaurus file in the Word folder means you won't need to insert the Utilities 2 disk every time you use Word Finder.

15. If you have a system that has two floppy-disk drives and no hard-disk drive, copy the Word Finder Thesaurus file from the Utilities 2 disk to your Word auxiliary disk by dragging its icon from its home folder onto the Word auxiliary disk icon. (Insert the Word auxiliary disk into a floppy-disk drive to see its icon.) FDHD drive owners can copy the Thesaurus file to the Word program disk instead of to the auxiliary disk.

Word Finder is now a part of the System file stored in the System Folder on your startup disk. When you restart your Mac, you'll find Word Finder available in the Apple menu as a desk accessory. Keep in mind that adding Word Finder has added about 44 KB to your System file, a fact to consider if you're working with two floppy-disk drives and are worried about the size of the system files on your startup disk. If your System file is now too large, you can use the Font/DA Mover to remove Word Finder from the System file.

INSTALLING AUTOMAC III

AutoMac III allows you to use macros with Word. Because AutoMac III is an INIT program, a program that starts up when you first turn on your Mac and runs in the background as you work with other programs, you must copy its files into the System Folder on your startup disk.

1. Insert the Word disk labeled "Utilities 1" in a floppy-disk drive. (If you're running a system that has two floppy-disk drives and no hard-disk drive, eject the Word program disk from one drive and insert the disk labeled "Utilities 1" into that drive.)

2. Double-click on the Utilities 1 disk icon to open its window.

3. Double-click on the AutoMac III Folder icon in the Utilities 1 window.

4. Drag the icons labeled "AutoMac III," "MacroEditor," and "MacroEditor.help" from the AutoMac III Folder window into the System Folder on your startup disk.

AutoMac III is now installed on your startup disk but won't appear until you restart your Macintosh. When you restart, you'll know that you installed AutoMac successfully if you see a small "A" in the upper left corner of the screen.

Only one of the three files you moved to the System Folder is necessary to run AutoMac III: the AutoMac III file. The MacroEditor file adds an advanced editing feature to AutoMac III, and the MacroEditor.help file offers some explanatory text about macro editing features as you use them. If you want to keep the size of your system files to a minimum, you can remove the MacroEditor and MacroEditor.help files from your startup disk. (MacroEditor requires 22 KB of memory, and MacroEditor.help files require 12.5 KB of memory.)

Now that you've set up your Macintosh system to run Microsoft Word and its associated programs, you're ready to start Word and take a look around—a tour you'll begin in the next chapter.

Chapter 2

A Tour of Word

In this chapter, you'll start Microsoft Word version 4 and take a look at its environment. You'll see the different parts of a Word document window and take a peek inside Word's menus to see the types of commands the program offers. Most importantly, you'll be introduced to the vocabulary and features that will become familiar to you as you continue to use Word.

STARTING MICROSOFT WORD

To start Microsoft Word, you must first turn your Mac on and run the system software so that the desktop appears on screen. You then double-click on the Word program icon to start the program. From this point, the steps differ depending on whether you're starting Word from a hard disk or floppy disks. If you're working with floppy disks, skip to the next section, "Starting Word from Floppy Disks." Instructions for starting Word from a hard disk follow.

Starting Word from a Hard Disk

To start Microsoft Word when it's installed on a hard-disk drive, take the following steps:

1. Turn your Macintosh on. The system software begins to load itself from the hard disk, and after a short delay, the desktop appears.

2. Double-click on the hard-disk icon to open its window if it's not already open.

3. Find the folder that contains the Word program in the hard-disk window (it's probably named "Word" or "Word 4"), and double-click on its icon to open its window if it's not already open. Figure 2-1 shows a typical open Word folder.

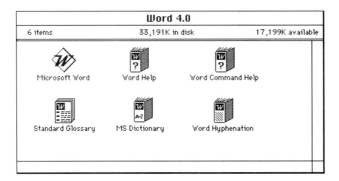

Figure 2-1. *The Word folder on a hard disk contains Word and its associated files.*

4. Double-click on the Word icon (it's labeled "Microsoft Word") to start Word. Word is loaded from the hard disk.

Starting Word from Floppy Disks

If you run Word from three floppy disks (as set up in the previous chapter "Setting Up Word 4"), start the program by taking the following steps:

1. Turn your Macintosh on.

2. Insert your slimmed-down startup disk in any floppy-disk drive. The system software begins to load itself from the startup disk, and after a short delay, the desktop appears.

3. Insert the Word program disk in the remaining floppy-disk drive. A floppy-disk icon labeled "Word" (or a similar label) appears on the desktop.

4. Double-click on the Word program disk icon to open its window if it's not already open. Figure 2-2 shows a typical open Word program disk window.

5. Double-click on the Word icon (labeled "Microsoft Word") to start Word. Word loads from the Word program disk.

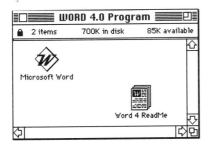

Figure 2-2. *The Word program disk contains Word and its associated files.*

Word's First Appearance

If this is the first time you've run Microsoft Word, a dialog box appears asking you to personalize your copy of Word by entering your name and, optionally, the name of an organization, as shown in Figure 2-3. The information you enter here appears briefly in a notice on the screen each time you start Word. To fill it in, type your name in the Name box (press Delete to correct any mistakes as you type), and then press Tab to move the cursor to the Organization box. Type an organization name here if you want. Check that the information is correct (press Tab to switch between the two text boxes if you need to revise text), and then click on the OK button to close the dialog box. After the dialog box closes, the notice showing your name and organization appears briefly.

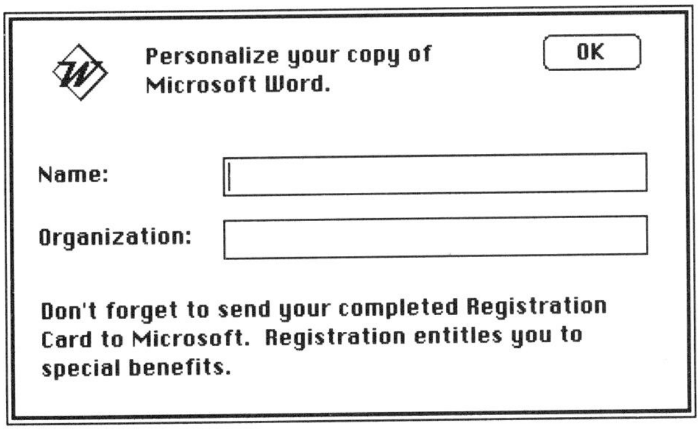

Figure 2-3. *The first time you run Word, a dialog box asking you to personalize your copy appears.*

WORD'S PARTS

Once you start Word and the name notice makes its brief appearance, a Word document window, shown in Figure 2-4, appears on the desktop and Word's menus appear in the menu bar at the top of the screen. If you're running Word under MultiFinder, a small Word icon appears at the right end of the menu bar, indicating you're now working with Word.

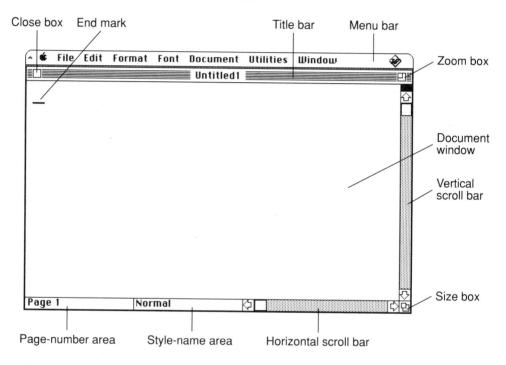

Figure 2-4. *A Word document window and the Word menus appear when you start Microsoft Word.*

Full and Short Menus

The first time you start Microsoft Word, it appears with *short menus*, a limited set of menu commands. This simple command set contains Word's most commonly used features and does not display more advanced features; therefore, beginning users can't venture into unfamiliar territory. To see all the commands, set Word to show full menus by choosing *Full Menus* from the bottom of the Edit menu.

When you quit Word at the end of this session, Word retains the full menus setting. The next time you start Word, you'll see full menus. Leave the setting at full menus—you'll use full menus for all the examples in this book.

The Document Window

The document window on the screen contains a single Microsoft Word document. It's empty and untitled when you first start Word because you have yet to fill it with text and give it a name. The window fills the screen on standard Mac monitors; on other monitors, it's larger to take advantage of the larger screen, usually filling the screen from top to bottom but leaving a strip of open space on the right side of the screen.

The document window shares many of the elements common to other Macintosh windows. It contains the following:

- A *title bar* on top showing the name of the document (currently "Untitled1"). You can click on and hold the mouse button while pointing to the title bar to drag the window to a new location.

- A *close box* in the upper left corner that you can click on to close the window.

- A *zoom box* in the upper right corner that you can click on to quickly shrink or enlarge the window.

- A *size box* in the lower right corner that you can drag to resize the window.

The document window also contains elements that are unique to Word. These elements perform word processing tasks.

The Insertion Point and the End Mark

The large, white expanse filling the document window is the *text area* where text appears as you type. In the upper left corner of the text area is a small, blinking vertical line called the *insertion point*. It marks the spot where you enter text. Try typing something now, and watch the insertion point as you type. It moves across the text area from left to right, inserting characters as it moves.

The short, thick horizontal line at the left edge of the text area, immediately below the text you enter, is the *end mark*. It marks the end of the document and moves downward as you fill the text area with text.

The Ruler

Microsoft Word can show a *Ruler* along the top of the document window, as shown in Figure 2-5. You can use the Ruler to control the appearance of paragraphs of text.

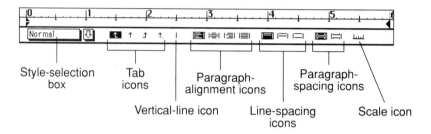

Figure 2-5. *The parts of the ruler control the appearance of paragraphs of text in a document.*

You can see the Ruler and its parts by choosing the menu command *Show Ruler* from the Format menu. The Ruler appears at the top of the document window.

The *measure* is the line that shows inch markings along the Ruler. It measures the width of the page you're typing. Notice the three markers along the measure, two on the left (a split wedge) and one on the right (a solid wedge). They show the left and right indents of the paragraph you're typing. The upper triangle of the left marker controls the first-line left indent. The lower triangle controls the left indent. The right marker controls the right indent. Dragging the markers in and out (as you'll learn to do in Chapter 7, "Paragraph Formatting") changes the paragraph indents.

The box in the lower left corner of the Ruler is the *style-selection box*, a Word control that mixes a menu and a text box. You can type your selection in it or click and hold on the arrow to its right to display a list of styles. The style-selection box puts one of Word's most powerful features at your command: the ability to control the general appearance of one or several paragraphs by choosing a single style name. You'll learn more about styles in Chapter 15, "Styles Made Simple: Formatting with Speed and Power."

The four *tab icons* to the right of the style-selection box set tab stops along the measure. By clicking on different tab icons, you can align columns of words on their left or right edge, center columns of words, or align columns of numbers on their decimal point. The single icon to the right of the tab icons is the *vertical-line icon*, which extends a vertical line from the top to the bottom of one or several paragraphs. You'll learn much more about tabs in Chapter 8, "Tabs."

Following the tab and vertical-line icons to the right are four *paragraph-alignment icons*. These icons control the way Word displays text in conjunction with the selected paragraph indents. They can align text on the left indent (leaving a ragged right indent), center text halfway between the indents, align text on the right indent (leaving a ragged left indent), or display the text with both the left and right indents justified.

The *line-spacing icons* follow the paragraph-alignment icons; they control the amount of space between lines. You can choose single-line spacing, one-and-one-half-line spacing, or double-line spacing. Next to the line-spacing icons are the *paragraph-spacing icons*, which control the amount of space between paragraphs. You can choose no blank lines or one blank line.

The last icon is the *scale icon*, which you can click on to display three views (scales) of the Ruler—normal scale, page scale, and table scale. Normal scale displays tabs and paragraph indents; page scale displays text margins; and table scale displays table columns and the table's column boundaries when the insertion point is in a table.

You'll learn to use most of the ruler features in Chapter 3, "The First Session," and in Chapter 7, "Paragraph Formatting."

The Scroll Bars

The document window contains two scroll bars: the *vertical scroll bar* and the *horizontal scroll bar*. The vertical scroll bar, at the right side of the window, serves two purposes: it shows you roughly where you are in a document, and it lets you move your viewpoint quickly from one place in the document to another. The horizontal scroll bar, at the bottom of the window, lets you move the view of the document window from left to right so you can see all the text on a page that is wider than the document window.

Both of Word's scroll bars work like standard Macintosh scroll bars: the location of the scroll box (the white square box) along the scroll bar shows your relative location in a document—toward the top, the middle, or bottom of the document in the vertical scroll bar; at the right, middle, or left of a document in the horizontal scroll bar. You can change the view by dragging the scroll box or by clicking on the scroll arrows or the gray part of the scroll bar on either side of the scroll box. In Chapter 3, "The First Session," you'll learn how to use the scroll bar to choose a new viewpoint location.

The Page-Number Area and the Style-Name Area

The *page-number area* and the *style-name area* share the bottom of the document window with the horizontal scroll bar. Both areas display information about the document displayed in the window.

The page-number area shows your page location in a large document. Word documents can comprise hundreds of pages and can be divided into many different sections. The page-number area shows the section number (if there are sections) and the page number of the current view location. The page-number area can also display messages from Word about current status, such as its progress in saving a document, and can prompt you to type information when you use a keyboard shortcut to change the font, apply a style, or perform another Word action.

The style-name area shows the name of the style applied to different paragraphs or text blocks. You'll learn more about its use in Chapter 15, "Styles Made Simple: Formatting with Speed and Power."

USING WORD'S MENUS

Word's menus work like menus in any other Macintosh program—you open a menu by pointing with the mouse pointer, clicking and holding on the menu, and dragging downward; you choose a command by releasing the mouse button when the command you want becomes highlighted.

The following sections offer a few more facts that you might not know about Word's menus.

Choosing Menu Commands with the Keyboard

For Word users who don't like to move their fingers from the keyboard, Word offers an alternate method of choosing menu commands: You can press keys to open menus and choose commands. Pressing the period key on the numeric keypad of the keyboard highlights the menu bar so you can open a menu. Each press of the left-arrow or right-arrow cursor key opens the menu to the left or right along the menu bar. Once you open a menu, pressing the up-arrow or down-arrow cursor key highlights a different command, and pressing Return chooses the highlighted command. If you want to abandon the menus without choosing a command, simply press Esc.

If your keyboard has a numeric keypad, try using the keyboard method now to select a menu command. Take the following steps:

1. Press the period key at the bottom of the numeric keypad. The menu bar is highlighted.

2. Press the right-arrow cursor key. The File menu opens.

3. Continue to press the right-arrow cursor key. At each press, the current menu closes and the menu to its right opens. Stop pressing as soon as the rightmost menu closes and the Apple menu at the far left of the menu bar opens.

4. Press the down-arrow cursor key once to highlight the About Microsoft Word command.

5. Press Return to choose the highlighted command. The menu closes and the About Microsoft Word dialog box appears.

6. Press Esc to close the dialog box.

Navigating MultiFinder Menu Sets

If you run Word under MultiFinder, you can run several programs at one time, and you might find that the menus in the menu bar belong to a program other than Microsoft Word. To see Word's menu set, simply click on one of Word's document windows. Word then becomes the active program, and its menus appear in the menu bar. If you're unsure about which menu set you're using, open the Apple menu. You'll see at the bottom of the menu a list of all the programs currently running; a check mark indicates the active program, whose menu set now appears in the menu bar.

WORD'S MENUS

You'll find most of Word's features offered as families of commands within Word's menus. By opening each menu and looking at its contents, you can get a good overview of what Word offers.

The Apple Menu

The Apple menu is displayed at the far left of the menu bar; its icon is an apple with a bite taken out of it. The Apple menu displays a list of desk accessories (DAs) available to you while you work with Microsoft Word. Each DA is a small program that runs simultaneously with Word. If you installed Word Finder (the thesaurus DA) by following the instructions in the previous chapter, you'll find ''Word Finder'' listed in this menu. You're also likely to find other DAs, such as Calculator, Chooser, and Control Panel.

The Apple menu also contains commands that give you information about Word (including help about its features) and let you switch between programs if you're using MultiFinder.

The File Menu

You'll find four sections of commands in the File menu. The first section includes document control commands—commands that save your documents to disk, recall them later, start new documents, and delete saved documents. The second section includes printing commands—commands that show, before you print, how your document will look on paper, control page size, and send a print command to your printer when you're ready. The third section includes mail commands—commands that allow you to send and receive electronic mail through Word if you're connected to a Microsoft Mail server and other computers via a network. And the last section, Quit, quits Word and returns you to the desktop.

The Edit Menu

The commands in the Edit menu remove, copy, and move blocks of text and graphics in your document. They also help you edit tables, insert blocks of text and graphics from a collection of blocks, and make visible the characters that are usually invisible in the document window. The link commands work under MultiFinder to link information in another application—such as figures from an Excel spreadsheet—to a Word document so the information changes in Word as you change it in the other application. The commands at the bottom of the menu help you customize Word's performance by changing the arrangement of menu commands, setting the way Word loads into the Mac's memory, changing the units of measure the Ruler uses, and setting other Word operating standards.

The Format Menu

The Format commands turn the Ruler in the document window on and off. They control the appearance of groups of characters, paragraphs, document sections, and full documents, and they apply and set styles (Word's powerful tool for controlling the appearance of paragraphs and the text that they contain). They also control types of character emphasis (bold, italic, and others) that you can add to or remove from text in a document.

The Font Menu

The Font menu offers a collection of type styles you can use for the characters in your document. It also offers a choice of sizes for character sets.

The Document Menu

The Document menu contains four sections of commands. The commands in the first section set the contents of the header and footer that appear at the top and bottom of each document page, and the commands in the second section create footnotes and repaginate a document after changes have been made. The commands in the third section offer alternate views of a document, one showing each page in full detail with page borders and margin contents, the other showing the bare bones of the document as a condensed outline. And the fourth section includes commands that insert in a document items that you can't insert as simple text from the keyboard. These items include tables designed to align text as you type, graphics, and entries that help Word create its own tables of contents and indexes.

The Utilities Menu

The Utilities menu offers a set of tools that can assist you in creating a Word document. Use them to search through a document and replace words or strings of text, to check spelling, or to break up a long word at a line's end with hyphenation. Use them to add an index or a table of contents to a document, to count the number of characters, words, lines, and paragraphs in a document, and to calculate the results of combined values and operators in your text. Two of the utilities number paragraphs and sort lists in alphabetic and numeric order.

The Window Menu

The Help command at the top of the menu displays a dialog box from which you can access help text about most of Word's features. The commands in the middle section display the contents of the Clipboard (a tool that holds blocks of text and graphics being cut and pasted) and create a new window for an existing document. The bottommost section lists all the documents currently open in Word. You can click on any one of the document commands listed (if you have more than one document open) to place that document's window on top of the other document windows.

Menu Variations

Word's menus aren't set in stone—you can change their contents to fit your needs as you did earlier in this chapter by setting long menus. You can also remove commands that you don't need from menus, add commands currently not listed in a menu, and customize menus by adding, deleting, and moving commands. You'll learn how to change menus in Chapter 22, "Customizing Word." In the meantime, all the menu descriptions in this book follow the default menu setups, as shown in this tour.

QUITTING WORD

When you finish using Microsoft Word, choose *Quit* from the File menu to quit Word. If you added text to any open documents or revised their contents in any way, Word displays a message that asks whether you want to save your changes. Click on the Yes button to save the document changes and then quit Word; click on the No button to quit Word without saving changes; click on the Cancel button to return to Word without quitting. Once you quit Word, you return to the desktop, where you can start another application or turn off your Macintosh.

Note that if you're using MultiFinder and you have several programs running, quitting Word might take you to another program instead of returning you to the desktop. To return to the desktop, simply choose *Finder* from the list of programs in the Apple menu.

Now that you're familiar with Word's terrain, it's time to move on to the next chapter, where you'll learn how to create and print a Word document.

Chapter 3

The First Session

In this chapter you'll do your first real work with Microsoft Word 4—you'll create and print a document. In the process, you'll learn how to use the scroll bar, the Clipboard, the Ruler, the dialog boxes, and the Mac keyboard. You'll also learn how to save a document, how to begin a new document, and how to open a document you worked on previously.

THE FIVE STAGES OF DOCUMENT CREATION

You create a Word document in five stages, as follows:

- *Enter*—type the text
- *Edit*—correct mistakes and revise the text
- *Format*—set the style of characters and paragraphs and design the printed pages of your document
- *Save*—capture your document on disk
- *Print*—send your document to a printer to be output

You won't necessarily follow the stages in the above order. You might print the document before you go back to edit it; you might set formatting as you enter text; and you might (and should) save a document many times as you work on it.

Look closely at the document in Figure 3-1, on the following page. The paragraph indents vary; some text lines are centered; and some words are boldface, italic, or underlined. In this chapter you'll use the five stages of document creation to re-create this sample letter.

9/9/90

Mr. Orloff Petruchio
General Manager
Typecast, Inc.
4526 Ardentia Lane
Heater, CA 93265

Dear Mr. Petruchio:

I just received the first shipment of 10,000 videotape packages you printed for us. We have a problem. The first paragraph on the back of the package should read:

Helltax!

A Horror Film for the Entire Family...

When IRS auditor Nicholas Axolotl is possessed by demons, a week of terror begins for the hapless Trunhill family. As blood oozes from stones, each family member must endure merciless and probing questions from disembodied voices about recent spending habits. Realistic portrayals of disallowed deductions and dire fiscal consequences will raise hairs on the back of every viewing adult while putting the kids to sleep. A perfect film for families with overactive children. Rated PG-13.

You mistakenly printed "A perfect film for families with radioactive children" in the last sentence. This severely limits the market for this movie, so we must have the entire run reprinted with corrections at your expense. I've tried to contact you by phone, but have had no luck. Your secretary tells me you're negotiating contracts at the Fresno Film Festival. Please call me immediately. We *must* fix this problem now.

Yours sincerely,

Pieter Geestliefde
Marketing Director
Goretax Films
Oakland, CA 94601

Figure 3-1. *This document illustrates Word's ability to format text and paragraphs.*

ENTERING TEXT

You enter text from the keyboard of your Macintosh. As you type, characters appear in the text area at the insertion point, which moves from left to right. Your keyboard has a standard set of character keys as well as extra keys that you use to perform special functions.

The Keyboard Layout

Figure 3-2, on the following page, shows the keyboards most commonly used with Macintosh computers. The Plus keyboard comes with the Macintosh Plus, and the Portable keyboard comes with the Macintosh Portable. The remaining keyboards—the regular keyboard and the extended keyboard—are optional keyboards for the SE and II families of Macs; you'll usually find one or the other with a Mac SE or II. Notice that the extended keyboard offers a row of function keys and other keys not found on the other keyboards.

Different groups of keys on the keyboard perform different functions. Learning what each group does will help you become more efficient as you enter text in Word.

The character keys

When you press a character key, you enter a character in your document. Typical characters are uppercase and lowercase letters, numerals, and symbols. A space is also considered a character; to enter it, press the space bar.

The Tab key

To move the insertion point to the next tab stop to the right, press the Tab key. When you first start Word, tab stops are set at half-inch intervals. (You'll learn to set tab stops in Chapter 8, ''Tabs.'')

The Shift, Caps Lock, Control, Option, and Command keys

The Shift, Caps Lock, and Control keys are labeled on the keyboard as they are named. The Command key is labeled with an Apple symbol and a clover symbol on all keyboards except the Mac Plus keyboard. The Mac Plus command key is labeled with only the clover symbol. The Option key on an extended keyboard displays a small *alt* label in addition to a full-size *option* label. The Option key on the other Apple keyboards displays only a full-size *option* label.

(A) The Macintosh Plus keyboard

(B) The Macintosh Portable keyboard

(C) The regular keyboard

(continued)

Figure 3-2. *Keyboards typically used with different Macintosh systems.*

Figure 3-2. *continued*

(D) The extended keyboard

These five keys work in combination with other keys. For example, to produce capital letters and the symbols above the numerals in the top row of keys, hold down Shift and press a letter or number key. If you press Caps Lock once, all letters you type will be capitalized. (You must hold down Shift to produce the symbols above the numerals, however.) To turn off the Caps Lock feature, press the Caps Lock key a second time.

To use the Control, Option, or Command key, hold down the key while you press the combination key. In this book, keyboard combinations are shown with a hyphen between the key names. For example, Command-O indicates that you hold down Command and press O. Shift-Option-K indicates that you hold down Shift and Option and press K. In effect, keyboard combinations are shortcuts in Word; you can use them instead of choosing a command from a menu.

The Esc key

Press the Esc key to leave (escape from) a process you started but don't want to finish. For example, if you open a menu with a keyboard command and then decide you don't want to choose a command, simply press Esc.

The Delete and Del keys

Use the Delete and Del keys to correct errors as you type. (Del is found only on the extended keyboard.) Pressing Delete deletes the character to the left of the insertion point and moves the insertion point one position to the left.

Pressing Del erases the character to the right of the insertion point; the insertion point remains in place.

The Return key

Pressing the Return key moves the insertion point to the beginning of a new line. In Word, you press Return only to begin a new paragraph, not to begin a new line. Word begins a new line when you type to the right edge of the page. You'll see how this works later in the chapter as you enter the text of the sample document.

The cursor keys

Cursor keys are marked with arrows. When you press a cursor key, the insertion point moves in the direction of the arrow: up, down, left, or right.

Cursor-movement keys (available only on the extended keyboard) move the insertion point in larger jumps, as follows:

- *Home* moves the insertion point to the left of the first character in the text area (usually at the top of the window).

- *End* moves the insertion point to the right of the last character in the text area (usually at the bottom of the window).

- *Page Up* scrolls the document down one screen (moving your view farther up the document) so that you can see old text. It also places the insertion point in the top line of text.

- *Page Down* scrolls the document up one screen (moving your view farther down the document) so that you can see new text. It also places the insertion point in the bottom line of text.

Cursor keys move the insertion point only through text already entered, not out of text and into blank areas of the screen.

The numeric keypad

The numeric keypad, shown in Figure 3-3, is a collection of number and operator keys that function one way if the Num Lock feature is turned on and another way if Num Lock is turned off. When you first start Word, Num Lock is turned off. To turn it on, press Clear (also labeled *num lock* on the extended keyboard) in the upper left corner of the keypad. The message *Num. Lock* appears in the page-number area at the bottom left of the document

Figure 3-3. *The numeric keypad.*

window to show that Num Lock is turned on. To turn Num Lock off, press Clear once again. The *Num. Lock* message disappears from the page-number area.

While the Num Lock feature is turned on, pressing the number keys of the keypad (0 through 9) will display numerals on the screen, pressing the operator keys (=, /, *, −, and +) will display operator characters on the screen, pressing the decimal-point key will display a decimal point on the screen, and pressing the Enter key will begin a new paragraph in the same way that the Return key does. (In later chapters, you'll learn that when the Enter key is used in key combinations, it doesn't produce the same results that the Return key does.)

While Num Lock is off, the keypad keys perform the same functions as the cursor keys, moving the insertion point through text in a document. They also open menus and change the document-view position. The keypad keys function as follows:

- *4* moves the insertion point one character to the left (as does the left-arrow cursor key).

- *6* moves the insertion point one character to the right (as does the right-arrow cursor key).

- *8* moves the insertion point one line up (as does the up-arrow cursor key).

- *2* moves the insertion point one line down (as does the down-arrow cursor key).

- *7* moves the insertion point to the immediate left of the first character in the text area (as does the Home key).

- *1* moves the insertion point to the immediate right of the last character in the text area (as does the End key).

- *9* scrolls the document down by one screen and places the insertion point in the top line of text (as does the Page Up key).

- *3* scrolls the document up by one screen and places the insertion point in the bottom line of text (as does the Page Down key).

- *0* moves the insertion point back to its previous location (useful when you jump around in a document and lose your last place).

- . (decimal point) selects the menu bar so you can open a menu by using a keyboard command (as described in Chapter 2, ''A Tour of Word'').

- * (asterisk) scrolls the document view one line up.

- + (plus sign) scrolls the document view one line down.

- - (hyphen) extends the selection to a specified character. (You'll learn more about selection in Chapter 6, ''Editing Text.'')

The function keys

The function keys, included only on the extended keyboard, perform functions with a single keystroke—for example, a single function key can insert text or print a document. Because function keys initiate actions that can alter your document, it's best not to press a function key unless you know what it does. A complete list of function-key operations and keyboard shortcuts appears in the appendix, ''Keyboard Shortcuts.''

The Help key

The extended keyboard also contains a Help key (grouped with the cursor-movement keys). Pressing it turns the pointer into a question mark. If you use the question-mark cursor to click on a feature or to choose a menu item for which you want more information, Word displays the Help dialog box, which contains help text for that feature. If you have a non-extended keyboard, you can produce the same results by pressing the key combination Command-? (question mark).

The Restart key

The Restart key (only on the extended keyboard), labeled with a left-pointing wedge, turns the computer on or restarts it. The Restart key works only with the Macintosh II family of computers.

Entering the Sample Text

Try your hand at entering the text in the sample document. First turn your Mac on and start Microsoft Word. When the document window appears, be sure the ruler appears at the top of the window. If it doesn't, choose *Show Ruler* from the Format menu to activate the ruler. When the insertion point appears in the upper left corner of the text window, take the following steps:

1. Type the date and address as shown in Figure 3-4, on the following page. Press Return at the end of each line. (Pressing Return twice creates a blank line.)

2. Type *Dear Mr. Petruchio:*. Now press Return twice and stop. If you make mistakes as you type, press the Delete key to delete the incorrect characters, and then type the correct text. Notice that the text you type doesn't look the same as the finished document shown in Figure 3-1—you'll edit and format later to make them match. Now continue with your letter.

3. Type the first paragraph of the letter body, and then press Return twice at the end of the paragraph. (Don't press Return to end lines within the paragraph.)

Notice that when you type to the end of a line, Word moves the insertion point and the word you're typing to the beginning of the next line. This feature is called *wordwrap*; it lets you type without worrying about either running off the edge of the page or splitting words.

When you press Return, Word moves the insertion point to the beginning of the next line—whether or not you're at the end of a line—and interprets your pressing Return as marking the end of a paragraph. For example, the first lines of the letter you typed are each separate paragraphs because you pressed Return at the end of each line.

The content of a paragraph is anything you've typed since the last time you pressed Return (or since the beginning of the document). For example, the first paragraph of your document is "9/9/90." The second paragraph has

9/9/90

Mr. Orloff Petruchio
General Manager
Typecast, Inc.
4526 Ardentia Lane
Heater, CA 93265

Dear Mr. Petruchio:

I just received the first shipment of 10,000 videotape packages you printed for us. We have a problem. The first paragraph on the back of the package should read:

Helltax!

A Horror Film for the Entire Family...

When IRS auditor Nicholas Axolotl is possessed by demons, a week of terror begins for the hapless Trunhill family. As blood oozes from stones, each family member must endure merciless and probing questions from disembodied voices about recent spending habits. Realistic portrayals of disallowed deductions and dire fiscal consequences will raise hairs on the back of every viewing adult while putting the kids to sleep. A perfect film for families with overactive children. Rated PG-13.

You mistakenly printed "A perfect film for families with radioactive children" in the last sentence. This severely limits the market for this movie, so we must have the entire run reprinted with corrections. I've tried to contact you by phone, but have had no luck. Your secretary tells me you're negoshiating contracts at the Film Fresno Festival. I can't believe you did this to me, you poltroon! Please call me immediately. We must fix this problem now.

Yours sincerely,

Pieter Geestliefde
Marketing Director
Goretax Films
Oakland, CA 94601

Figure 3-4. *Enter the text as it appears in this example.*

no content: It's a blank line you created by pressing Return twice. This definition of a paragraph is an important word processing concept. This will be clear later when you format paragraphs in a document.

Note: Word's line breaks on your screen might not match the line breaks shown in Figures 3-4 and 3-5. This is because a LaserWriter printer can fit fewer characters in a line than an ImageWriter printer can, and Word adjusts its screen to match whatever printer you have set up. If your Mac is set up to use an ImageWriter, it won't show the same breaks as Figures 3-4 and 3-5, which were created with a LaserWriter setup.

Continue now with your letter.

4. Type the rest of the document through the end of the line "Yours sincerely." Be sure to include any misspellings in the text (you'll correct them later), and remember not to press Return until the end of each paragraph.

5. To create blank space for a signature, enter four blank lines.

6. Type the name and address of the sender.

As the text window fills up, text at the top of the screen disappears, so you can enter new lines at the bottom of the screen. In the next section, you'll learn how to scroll back to see the text at the beginning of your document.

EDITING TEXT

After you finish typing your document, you can correct spelling and typing errors. You can also change wording or rearrange ideas. A simple way to change text is to move the insertion point to the characters you want to change, press Delete (or Del) to erase characters, and then type new text. Another way is to select a block of text and use menu commands to edit it.

Moving the Insertion Point

You can use the cursor keys or the mouse to move the insertion point. To use the mouse, point to a new position in the document window and then click the mouse button. If you click on a spot outside the text, the insertion point goes to the text nearest the pointer. You can't use the mouse to point to text not visible in the text window. Instead, use the scroll bar to move to the section of the document you want, and then point and click.

Using the Vertical Scroll Bar

Word keeps your entire document in memory, including the sections that are out of sight above and below the text window. You see only one part of the document at a time. You might find it useful to think of the portion of the document you see in the document window as a viewport that shows a single portion of a document contained on a single, long page. The page grows as you enter more text. To change your view of the document, you can use the cursor keys or the vertical scroll bar, shown in Figure 3-5, to scroll the long document page upward or downward.

Dragging the scroll box upward in the scroll bar scrolls your view to a preceding part of the document; dragging the scroll box downward scrolls the view to a following part. The length of the scroll bar represents the length of the entire document. To move the view to any section of the document, drag the scroll box to the location on the scroll bar that corresponds to the section's approximate location in the document.

If you haven't changed the view since you finished typing the sample document, the bottom part of the letter appears in the text window. Because Word always follows the end of a document with one screenful of blank

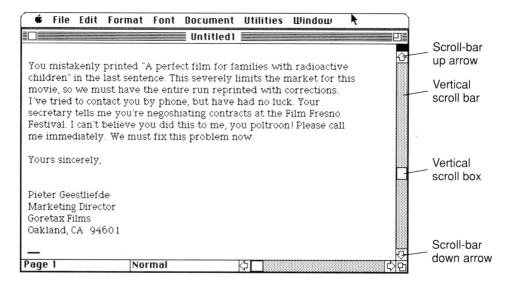

Figure 3-5. *Use the vertical scroll bar to move your view of the document.*

space, the view you see now is actually the middle of the document, and the vertical scroll bar reflects this: It shows the scroll box vertically centered in the bar. Use the vertical scroll bar to move to the top of the document:

1. Move the pointer to the scroll box.

2. Hold down the mouse button.

3. Drag the scroll box to the top of the scroll bar's shaded area.

4. Release the mouse button.

The scroll box moves to the top of the vertical scroll bar, and the text window shows the top of the document.

You can use the vertical scroll bar in two other ways, as follows:

■ Click on the up arrow or down arrow of the scroll bar to scroll the view upward or downward by one line.

■ Click on the shaded section of the scroll bar above or below the scroll box to scroll the view upward or downward by a full screen.

When you use the scroll bar to move the view, the insertion point doesn't move with it. To move the insertion point into the document window, point to a character in the window and click with the pointer. If you begin to type with the insertion point out of sight, Word switches the view to the location of the insertion point and changes the scroll-box location in the scroll bar to match.

A quick word about the horizontal scroll bar: It works in much the same way as the vertical scroll bar but moves the view horizontally across the document rather than vertically. Most documents created for printout on 8½-by-11-inch paper don't show any text beyond the right edge of the text area, so you usually won't need to use the horizontal scroll bar. If you create documents that have wide text margins or you shrink the size of the window, you might then need to use the horizontal scroll bar to scroll from side to side as you view text.

Making Simple Text Corrections

If you typed the letter exactly as it is shown in Figure 3-4, it contains several mistakes. Move the insertion point to correct them, beginning with the misspelled word ''negoshiating.'' Follow the steps on the next page.

1. Use the cursor keys or the vertical scroll bar to move the view to the end of the letter. You must be able to see the last full paragraph before the closing paragraph.

2. Place the insertion point between the "h" and the "i" of the word "negoshiating," in the last paragraph.

3. Delete the "s" and the "h" by pressing Delete twice.

4. Type *t* to replace the "sh."

The text moves to the left to fill in when you delete characters, and it moves right to give more space when you type new characters. You can insert as much text as you want; Word pushes following text to the right and then to the beginning of the next line if necessary. Insert the phrase *at your expense* at the end of the second sentence as follows:

1. Place the insertion point between the letter "s" and the period in the sentence that ends with the words "with corrections."

2. Type a space followed by *at your expense*.

The rest of the text in the paragraph moves to the right and then downward to following lines to accommodate the inserted phrase.

Selecting Text

Moving the insertion point in this way is an effective way to correct small mistakes, but it's not an easy way to delete or move large sections of text. Word's editing commands are more efficient. To use them, you must first *select* the block of text you want to work on. The easiest way to select text is to indicate both ends of the text by using the insertion point.

Selecting text by using the mouse

Move the pointer to the beginning (or end) of the text you want to select, and then drag the pointer (by holding down the mouse button) to the other end of the text. Word highlights the text as you drag. When you release the mouse button, the text remains highlighted. This highlighted text is called a *selected text block*. To drag the text selection into an area preceding or following the current view, move the pointer to the top or bottom border of the document window; Word scrolls upward or downward in the indicated direction.

If you want to select a block of text without dragging the pointer, you can move the pointer to one end of the text block and click, and then move the pointer to the other end of the text block, hold down the Shift key, click, and then release the Shift key. Word then highlights the text block. This process is called *extended selection*, and it allows you to select a very long text block by using the vertical scroll bar between selecting the beginning and end of the text block.

Selecting text by using the keyboard

First use the cursor keys to move the insertion point to the beginning (or end) of the text you want to select. Next hold down the Shift key and move the insertion point to the other end of the text, and then release the Shift key. As you move the insertion point, Word highlights the text block. The highlight remains when you release the Shift key.

Deselecting Text

To *deselect* a block of text (remove the highlight), simply move the insertion point to a new location by using the mouse or keyboard. Then, if you're using the mouse, click the mouse button outside the block of text. The highlight disappears.

Using Editing Commands

Once you have selected a block of text, you can use Word commands to edit that text. Figure 3-6, on the following page, shows a selected block of text to be deleted. The commands in the Edit menu can move and delete blocks of text from your document. Try them now on your letter.

The first block of text you want to change is the sentence "I can't believe you did this to me, you poltroon!" which now seems a bit strong. To delete the sentence, you must first select it. Try it by using the mouse, as follows:

1. Move the pointer to the spot immediately preceding the "I" at the beginning of the sentence.

2. Drag the pointer (by holding down the mouse button) to the spot immediately preceding "Please" at the beginning of the following sentence and release the button.

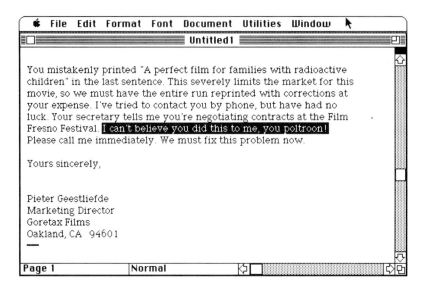

Figure 3-6. *The selected sentence is a text block to be deleted.*

When the sentence has been selected, as shown in Figure 3-6, you can cut it out of your letter. Choose the Cut command from the Edit menu. The sentence disappears from your letter, and the text following it moves to the left and upward.

Now use the Cut and Paste commands to move a word from one location to another. The phrase "Film Fresno Festival," in the last paragraph, should read "Fresno Film Festival." To move the word "Film" to a new location behind the word "Fresno," take the following steps:

1. Select the word "Film" and the space following it.

2. Choose *Cut* from the Edit menu. The word "Film" disappears from the letter.

3. Move the insertion point so it immediately precedes the letter "F" of "Festival."

4. Choose *Paste* from the Edit menu. Word inserts "Film" between "Fresno" and "Festival."

The Clipboard

When you use the Cut command, Word removes the text you selected and stores it in a part of memory called the *Clipboard*. The Copy command is similar: It instructs Word to create a copy of the selected text and place the copy on the Clipboard without removing the original text from the document. The Paste command instructs Word to insert the contents of the Clipboard into the document at the insertion-point location.

The Clipboard retains only one block of text at a time. When you use Cut or Copy on a new block of text, the old block on the Clipboard is removed from memory and disappears forever! You can use Cut, Copy, and Paste to edit small or large blocks of text, limited only by the amount of memory available to the Clipboard.

FORMATTING TEXT

After you enter and edit text, you can change its appearance to add emphasis and make the document easier to read. This is called *formatting* text. Two simple and effective types of formatting you can use are character formatting and paragraph formatting.

Character Formatting

Character formatting changes the appearance of a character or group of characters. Word offers many different types of character formatting. Most of these—such as bold, italic, and underline—are types of emphases.

Applying character formatting by using menu commands

You format characters in much the same way as you edit them: You first select a text block and then choose a formatting command to change the appearance of the selected text.

Applying emphasis: The first word you want to emphasize is the film title "Helltax!" in the middle of the letter. To format it in boldface, take the following steps:

1. Select the word "Helltax!" (including the exclamation point).
2. Choose the Bold command from the Format menu.

The word "Helltax!" now appears in boldface, which you can see when you deselect the word.

[handwritten margin notes: "Format Menu", "Control. Tab - 3", "Bold − F 10"]

Combining types of emphases

You can combine types of emphases for added effect. For example, try formatting the word "must" in boldface italic as follows:

1. Select the word "must."

2. Choose *Bold* from the Format menu.

3. Choose *Italic* from the Format menu.

The word now stands out in boldface italic.

Applying character formatting by using
the Format Character dialog box

You can open the Format Character dialog box, shown in Figure 3-7, by choosing the Character command from the Format menu.

Contrl D

    This dialog box, one of many you'll work with as you use Word, offers character-formatting options (such as Bold and Italic) that you choose to control the way Word displays your text. Many options are grouped together in a labeled section of the dialog box called an *area*. Some areas contain different

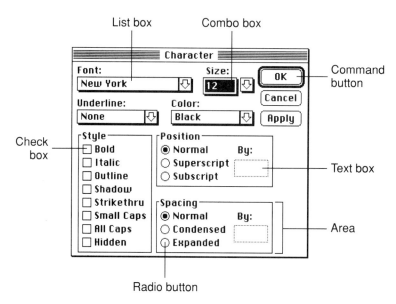

Figure 3-7. *The Format Character dialog box offers character-formatting options.*

58

types of options. Although you can use the mouse pointer to choose options from any of the areas in the dialog box, you activate each type of option in a different way, as follows:

- A *radio button* is a small, round button that precedes an option. You can turn it on and off by clicking on it. Radio-button options are grouped together in an area; you can turn on only one of the buttons in a given area at a time. For example, the Normal, Condensed, and Expanded option buttons in the Spacing area are radio buttons—you can choose only one of these options at a time. When a radio button is turned on, the button is filled with a large dot; when turned off, the button is empty.

- A *check box* is a square box that precedes an option. When the option is turned on, the check box is filled with an X; when it's turned off, the box is empty. To turn the check box on and off, click on it with the mouse pointer. Note that you can turn on more than one of the check-box options at a time. For example, you can turn on both the Bold and Italic options in the Style area.

- A *text box* is a rectangle sometimes filled with text, sometimes empty. You can change its contents or enter new text with the keyboard. To change the contents of a text box, first select it with the mouse by double-clicking on the box; this selects the entire contents of the box. When you type new characters at the keyboard, they completely replace the box's contents. In the Format Character dialog box, the By: features in the Position and Spacing areas are text boxes (which don't become active until you turn on a radio button other than Normal).

- A *list box* looks like a text box with a down arrow added to its right side. You can't type new text in a list box; instead, you choose from a list of options. To see the option list, click and hold on the list box as you would a menu name on the menu bar, and then drag the pointer downward. When you highlight an option you want, release the mouse button; the option list disappears and the option you chose appears in the list box. In the Format Character dialog box, the Font, Underline, and Color features are list boxes.

■ A *combo box* looks like a list box with a down arrow detached from the right side. It combines the functions of a list box and a text box. You can select a combo box and enter text directly into it, as you do in a list box, or you can click and hold on the down arrow and drag the pointer downward to choose from a list of options. In the Format Character dialog box, the Size feature is a combo box.

■ A *command button* is a rounded rectangle with a command displayed inside. When you select a command button, you ask Word to perform a task. Some command buttons open new dialog boxes—these contain ellipses (...) in the button; others close the current dialog box. To choose a command button, simply click on it with the pointer. If the command button is surrounded by a thick double border, you can select the button by pressing Return. In the Format Character dialog box, the OK, Cancel, and Apply buttons are command buttons. You can select the OK button by pressing Return.

Once you set the options you want in a dialog box, click on the OK button to close the dialog box and put the options into effect. If you decide not to use the options you set, click on the Cancel button or press Esc to close the dialog box. Now that you're familiar with dialog boxes, try using one to add emphasis to a word.

Applying underlining: Underline the word "radioactive" in the last paragraph by using the Format Character dialog box, as follows:

1. Select the word "radioactive."

2. Choose *Character* from the Format menu to open the Format Character dialog box.

3. Click and hold on the list box labeled *Underline*. The list opens to reveal the types of underlining available.

4. Drag the pointer down to *Single* and release the mouse button. The list closes and *Single* appears in the list box.

5. Click on the OK button (or press Return) to close the dialog box.

The word "radioactive" is now underlined with a single line.

Paragraph Formatting

Contrl·M

Paragraph formatting changes indents, line spacing, and other paragraph at-
tributes. To use paragraph-formatting commands, first select one or more
paragraphs. Paragraph-formatting commands affect complete paragraphs (remember the definition of a paragraph) whether the entire paragraph or only
part of it is selected. If you select a block of text that begins in the middle of
one paragraph, includes another full paragraph, and ends in the middle of a
third paragraph, any paragraph-formatting command changes the appearance
of all three paragraphs, including the parts of the paragraphs not selected.
This means you can select a single paragraph simply by moving the insertion
point into it.

Setting indents

The Ruler, shown in Figure 3-8, shows you the left and right indents of the
paragraph you selected. The left-indent marker is the lower half of the wedge
at the left of the Ruler. The upper half of the wedge is the first-line indent

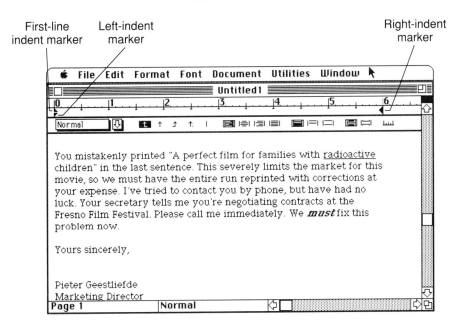

Figure 3-8. *The Ruler shows the indents of selected paragraphs.*

marker, which shows the left indent of the first line of the paragraph. (This indent can be different from the left indent of the rest of the paragraph.) The solid wedge at the right of the Ruler is the right-indent marker.

You can drag any of these markers to new locations on the Ruler to set new paragraph indents. The inch marks on the Ruler begin and end at the overall document margins. For example, if your margins are 1.25 inches from each side of an 8½-by-11-inch piece of paper, the Ruler begins (that is, aligns at 0) 1.25 inches from the left edge of the paper and ends (at the 6 mark) 1.25 inches from the right edge.

Setting the left indent: Change the left indent of the paragraph ''9/9/90'' so it starts in the middle of the page as follows:

1. Move the insertion point into the paragraph so the Ruler shows the paragraph's indent settings.

2. Drag the left-indent marker (the lower half of the wedge) from the 0 mark to the 3 mark on the Ruler. The first-line indent marker (the upper half of the wedge) moves with the left-indent marker as you drag it.

The date now appears in the middle of the screen, with its left character aligned with the new left-indent setting.

Setting left and right indents: Now try changing both left and right indents in the set-off paragraph that describes the movie. A 0.5-inch indentation from the margins on both sides sets off the paragraph from the rest of the letter as a quotation. To change the indents, take the following steps:

1. Place the insertion point anywhere in the paragraph that begins ''When IRS auditor....''

2. Drag the left-indent marker from the 0 mark to the 0.5 mark on the Ruler (halfway between the 0 and 1 marks).

3. Drag the right-indent marker from the 6 mark to the 5.5 mark on the Ruler (halfway between the 5 and 6 marks).

The paragraph is now indented from the rest of the letter by 0.5 inch on each side.

Setting alignment

While you're working on this paragraph, you can change its alignment to further set it apart from the rest of the text. Paragraphs usually appear *left aligned*; that is, the left edge of the text lines up evenly, whereas the right edge is uneven, or ragged. If you use *full justification* (called "justified" in Word), the program fits the words in each line so that both the left and right indents are aligned.

Contrl. Shift J

To set full justification for the paragraph, click on the justified-alignment icon (the seventh icon from the right side of the Ruler, showing fully justified lines of text).

Centering a paragraph

You can center each line of a paragraph. For example, the short title and subtitle paragraphs "Helltax!" and "A Horror Film for the Entire Family..." might look better if they were centered. To center them, take the following steps:

Contrl · shift · C

1. Select a text block beginning in the middle of "Helltax!" extending down to the middle of the word "Film." (Even though both paragraphs aren't fully contained in the text block, they're both fully selected for paragraph formatting.)

2. Click on the centered-alignment icon on the Ruler (the ninth icon from the right, showing centered lines of text). The two paragraphs appear centered on the page.

That's it—you've finished formatting your letter! It should now look like the document in Figure 3-1, at the beginning of the chapter.

SAVING A DOCUMENT

Once the document is in its final form, with editing and formatting completed, it's wise to save it on disk before you print it. It's even wiser to save a document every 15 minutes as you work on it. If you lose power and your document disappears from the screen, you can always restart Word and open the latest saved version of the document. Saving every 15 minutes ensures that you won't lose more than 15 minutes' worth of work.

Using the Save Command

File Menu

Contrl · Tab – 1

The letter has yet to be saved. You can tell by looking at the title bar of the Word window: The document is untitled because you haven't saved it. To save it, you must give the document a name.

A document name can be no longer than 31 characters. You can use any characters except the colon (:) in the name. Try to choose a name that reminds you of the contents of your document.

To save your sample letter, take the following steps:

1. Choose the Save command from the File menu. A Save dialog box, shown in Figure 3-9, appears.

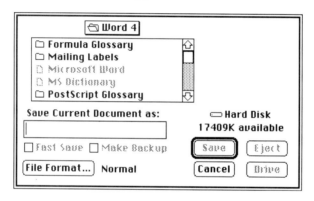

Figure 3-9. *The Save dialog box.*

2. Type *Petruchio*, a document name that reminds you of the letter's recipient, in the text box labeled *Save Current Document As*.

3. Click on the Save button or press Return.

The dialog box closes and Word saves your document to disk in the same folder in which Word is located. You'll find it under the name "Petruchio." (You'll learn to save documents to other folders in Chapter 11, "Saving, Opening, and Printing a Document.")

Using the Save As Command

Contrl · S

to

Change Filename

The Save dialog box appears only the first time you save a document using the Save command. If you revise your document and choose Save again,

Word saves the document under the same filename, erasing the last version and replacing it with the current one. To save a new version without erasing the previous one, choose *Save As* from the File menu. The Save dialog box opens, and you can then enter a new document name. Word saves your document under the new name, leaving the previous version stored intact under the old document name. The title bar shows the new name, and each time you use the Save command for this document, Word saves the revision under the new document name.

PRINTING A DOCUMENT

The last step in creating a document is printing it. Before you begin printing, take the following steps:

1. Be sure your printer is turned on.

2. Be sure your printer is *on line*, ready to accept information from your computer. (If you have an ImageWriter, a light labeled *select* will be lit if your printer is on line.)

Contrl · P

3. Be sure the paper is in the proper position for printing. If you have a LaserWriter, check the supply of paper in the paper tray. If you have an ImageWriter, check that the paper in the printer is aligned so the print head will begin printing at the very top of the page.

When your printer is ready, you can print your document. Try it now on the letter you created.

1. Choose *Print* from the File menu. The Print dialog box appears.

2. Click on the OK button to close the dialog box and begin printing.

A message box appears, indicating that your document is being printed; the bottom line of the Word window displays the page number currently being printed; and your printer begins to print. If you have a LaserWriter, the finished printout should look like Figure 3-1 (at the beginning of this chapter). If you have an ImageWriter, the printout will look similar, but the characters won't be as smooth and well formed.

BEGINNING A NEW DOCUMENT

When you have finished one document and want to begin another, use the Close and New commands to close the document you're working on and open a new one, as follows:

1. Choose *Close* from the File menu. If you've never saved the document or if you've made changes or printed since you last saved, a dialog box appears, asking whether you want to save changes.

2. To close the dialog box, click on the Yes button to save changes; select the No button to close without saving. (Click on the Cancel button if you change your mind and don't want to close the document.) When the document closes, the document window disappears from the Word window.

3. Choose *New* from the File menu to open a new document. A new, untitled document window appears.

If you want to close a document quickly without using the Close command, simply click on the close box in the upper left corner of the document window. A dialog box appears if there are any changes to save.

Opening a Previously Saved Document

To work on a previously saved document, use the Open command, as follows:

1. Choose *Open* from the File menu. The Open dialog box, shown in Figure 3-10, appears.

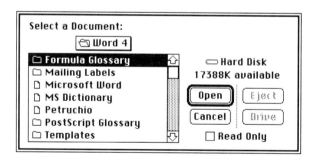

Figure 3-10. *The Open dialog box.*

2. Double-click on the name of the document in the scrolling list. The dialog box closes and the document appears in a new document window.

It's possible to have more than one open document on the screen at once; if you do, the document windows overlap each other. You'll learn how to work with multiple documents in Chapter 20, "Views, Outlines, and Document Windows."

Quitting Word

When you finish using Word, you quit by choosing *Quit* from the File menu. Word displays a message that asks whether you want to save work you haven't already saved. If you haven't changed anything since the last time you saved your document, Word quits without displaying the save query.

You've now come to the end of the first section of this book. You're an accomplished Word user and should be able to use Word to write and print your own simple documents. Congratulations! In the next section you'll begin to explore Word's features in detail so you can create more complex documents.

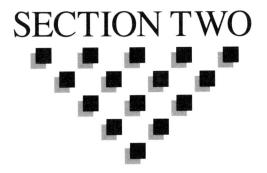

SECTION TWO

Basics

This section covers the basic features of Microsoft Word 4. You learn how to enter and format characters, insert graphics, and edit your documents. You also learn how to work with long documents, use the full power of paragraph formatting, set tabs, add page numbers to your documents, and fully control Word's printing and pagination.

Chapter 4

Entering and Formatting Characters

In Chapter 3, "The First Section," you learned to type characters, select a block of text, and change the character formatting of a selected block. This chapter teaches you how to format characters as you type—how to add character to your characters as the inspiration arises. You'll also learn how to enter special characters and invisible characters as well as how to apply different fonts, character sizes, and types of emphases to add distinction to your documents.

SETTING UP WORD

Before you begin working with the examples in this chapter, check to be sure that Microsoft Word shows full menus, as follows:

1. If you haven't done so already, turn your computer on and start Word.

2. Open the Edit menu and choose the Full Menus command to set full menus. If the Short Menus command appears instead of the Full Menus command, full menus are already set, and you can close the menu without choosing any commands.

ENTERING SPECIAL CHARACTERS

Most of the characters you enter are lowercase letters, numerals, and punctuation marks. You use the Shift key in combination with other keys to produce uppercase letters and common symbols such as the dollar sign and the percent sign. Word goes further and offers a way to produce additional characters such as foreign-language characters, special symbols, and graphical elements. You produce these special characters by using key combinations.

Using the Key Caps DA

To see the special characters available to you with the Option key or Shift-Option key combinations, you access the Key Caps DA, a desk accessory that shows the layout of the keyboard connected to your Mac. When you choose the Key Caps command from the Apple menu, the Key Caps window opens and displays the keyboard, as shown in Figure 4-1.

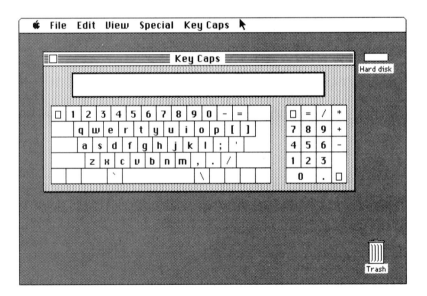

Figure 4-1. *The Key Caps DA shows the keyboard layout of your keyboard and can display the characters the keys produce when you use them in combination with Shift, Option, or Shift and Option together. (An extended keyboard is shown here.)*

The keyboard layout in the Key Caps DA normally shows the character each key produces when you press the key alone. If you hold down the Shift key, the layout shows the character each key produces when you press it in combination with Shift. If you hold down the Option key, you see the special character each key produces when pressed in combination with Option. And if you hold down Shift and Option together, you see the special character each key produces when pressed in combination with Shift and Option. By watching the layout as you try different Shift and Option combinations, you can quickly discover which key combinations produce which special characters. Then you can close the Key Caps DA window to enter the special character you want in your Word document.

Not all keys produce characters when used in combination with Option and Shift-Option. For example, pressing Shift-Option-Z produces no character in most fonts. If you press this combination, the Mac displays a hollow square on the screen to show that no character corresponds to the key combination. (Although the hollow square appears on screen, it sometimes does not appear in the printed document; instead, a blank space takes its place.

Using the Option Key and Shift Key Combinations

To produce special characters, you form key combinations with the Option key (located in the bottom row of keys on your keyboard). You hold down the Option key while pressing another key. For example, if you hold down Option and press the equal-sign key (a key combination referred to as "Option-=") you produce a not-equal sign ($\neq$) in your document. (If this combination produces a hollow box, choose another font, such as Chicago, from the Font menu before pressing the key combination. After you enter the special character, switch back to your original font.) You can hold down the Option key in combination with the Shift key to produce yet another set of special characters. If you hold down Shift and Option and press the equal-sign key (a key combination referred to as "Shift-Option-=), you enter a plus-minus sign ($\pm$) in your document.

Enter the sample memo shown in Figure 4-2, on the following page, to learn how to produce special characters. The first special character you'll enter is the trademark symbol (^{TM}) at the end of the first full paragraph of the memo. Take the following steps.

To: Copy Writers

From: Arvo Pugnace

Re: Formatting Suggestions

As we enter the season for advertising fruit, I'd like to remind each of you that by properly formatting our fruit ad copy before we send it to the printer, we can increase its impact on the reader and raise the overall level of FruitFullness™ in the ad-reading area.

I took the liberty of consulting the <u>Fruit</u> <u>Grower's</u> <u>Vade</u> <u>Mecum</u> for inspiration. I found some *great* suggestions in the section labeled A PEACHY SUGGESTION: PUT A NEW TYPEFACE ON YOUR FRUIT. You can drop by my office to read it for yourself, but I'd like to pass on a few of its suggestions:

```
"Matter-of-fact fruits such as the navel orange and the
Delicious apple look best when described in a businesslike
font such as Courier."
```

"Forceful fruits such as the pomegranate should be stamped on the page in a no-nonsense sans serif font such as Helvetica."

"Use a nicely formed serif font such as New York to describe the subtle nuance of fruits such as the persimmon, mango, and papaya."

"Always print fruit names in a large enough point size to catch the reader's eye."

"Print price increases in a small point size."

"Describe jumbo fruit in very large print!"

Figure 4-2. *This sample memo shows special characters and character formatting.*

1. Type the first three lines of text from the sample memo, pressing Return twice at the end of each line to insert a blank line between lines of text.

2. Press Tab at the beginning of the next full paragraph of text (and at the beginning of the paragraphs that follow, when you enter them) to create the indention.

3. Continue typing until you reach the trademark symbol.

4. Press Option–keypad 2 to enter the trademark symbol.

5. Type the rest of the sentence, including the period, and then stop before you press Return.

Word treats special characters as it treats standard characters. You can select, format, and edit special characters exactly as you would standard characters.

FONTS AND SPECIAL CHARACTERS

Not all fonts produce the same special characters; each font has its own character set and might have a completely different set of special characters.

To see the special characters available in different fonts, choose a new font name from the Key Caps menu that appears when you run Key Caps. Key Caps then shows you the characters that belong to that font. When you press Option or Shift-Option, the font's special characters appear.

Diacritical Marks

Many foreign languages use diacritical marks, such as accents (á) and tildes (~), over some letters. The following option-key combinations create these marks:

■ Option-' creates a grave accent (`)

■ Option-E creates an acute accent (´)

■ Option-I creates a circumflex (^)

■ Option-U creates an umlaut (¨)

■ Option-N creates a tilde (~)

To add a diacritical mark to a letter, you press the Option key combination for the mark, release all the keys (nothing happens), and then press the letter you want marked. The letter then appears with the mark over it. For example, to add an umlaut over an *o* in a German word such as *können*, press Option-U, release the combination, and then press *o*. The umlauted *o* appears.

If you press a key combination for a diacritical mark and then press a key for a letter that won't work with the mark, the mark appears to the left of the letter instead of over it. You can also type the diacritical mark by itself by pressing the diacritical-mark key combination twice in a row; the mark appears alone, without a letter beneath it.

Invisible Characters

Invisible characters are those characters that you enter normally with the keyboard but that don't appear in the text window. The most common invisible character is the space. Each time you press the space bar, the insertion point on the screen moves to the right and leaves a blank space to its left. Although nothing appears on the screen, Word treats that space as a character.

The tab space is another invisible character. Each time you press Tab, the insertion point jumps to the right or, if it's at the end of a line, to the next line. Although nothing appears on the screen, Word treats that tab as a character.

The paragraph mark is also an invisible character. When you press Return at the end of a paragraph, Word places a paragraph mark (¶) at the insertion point's location and then moves the insertion point down to the beginning of a new line. Although the paragraph mark isn't visible, you can select and edit it as you can the other invisible characters.

It's much easier to select and edit invisible characters if you can see them. To view the invisible characters in the text you typed, Choose *Show ¶* from the Edit menu. Previously invisible characters now appear with symbols in their places, as shown in Figure 4-3.

A space in the text appears as a dot between other characters, a tab appear as a right-pointing arrow, and a paragraph mark appears as a traditional proofreader's paragraph mark. Notice that a paragraph mark follows the end of the last sentence of the memo you entered, even though you didn't press Return there. Word always begins a new document with a single paragraph mark that remains at the very end of anything you enter. A paragraph mark must appear at the end of each document; you can't delete this mark.

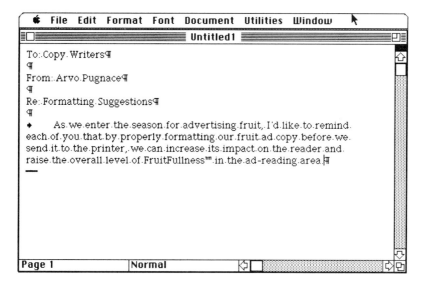

Figure 4-3. *The text you entered earlier now shows all the invisible characters.*

If you no longer want to see the invisible characters, choose *Hide ¶* from the Edit menu.

CHARACTER FORMATTING

You already know how to apply some character formatting to text—you applied italics, boldface, and underlining in Chapter 3, ''The First Session.'' These formats belong to a type of character formatting called *type style*. Word offers three ways to format characters, as follows:

- Changing fonts (the typeface used to display and print text)

- Setting character size (the height and width of the characters)

- Applying type styles (formats such as underlining and boldface)

Applying Character Formatting

In the previous chapter you entered text, selected a block of text, and then applied character formatting to the selected text. It's often more convenient to apply character formatting as you enter text. To do so, first choose a format, type some text using that format, and then turn the format off. As long as a particular formatting option is turned on, everything you type appears in that format. For example, to type the sentence "There were <u>two</u> of them!" you would type the text to the word "two" and then turn the underline format on. When you type "two," it appears with an underline. Before you continue typing, turn the underline format off.

Whether you apply formatting as you type or later on selected text, you can use any one of the following three application methods:

- Choosing character-formatting options directly from the Format or Font menu

- Choosing character-formatting options from the Format Character dialog box

- Setting character formatting by using keyboard shortcuts

The Format and Font menus

The Format menu offers a choice of type styles, such as Bold and Italic, that you can turn on or off by choosing them. The Font menu offers a choice of character sizes at the top of the menu and a choice of fonts at the bottom of the menu. Your menus should look similar to those shown in Figure 4-4.

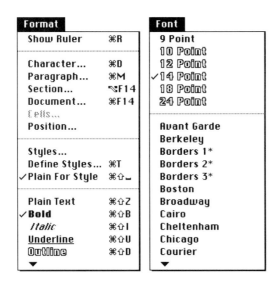

Figure 4-4. *The Format and Font menus.*

The Format Character dialog box

When you choose the Character command from the Format menu, the Format Character dialog box, shown in Figure 4-5, opens. You choose the options in the box to control character formatting: Use the Font list box to change fonts, the Size combo box to set character size, the Underline list box to apply types of underlining, and the Color list box to change the color of characters displayed on a color monitor or printed with a color printer. The eight check boxes in the Style area turn different type styles on and off. The radio buttons in the Position area turn text into superscript or subscript and use the distance set in the By text box to position the characters above or below normal text. The Spacing area's radio buttons control the amount of space between characters, adding or subtracting the amount of space set in the By text box.

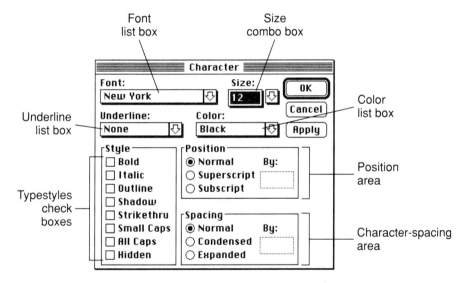

Figure 4-5. *The Format Character dialog box.*

Keyboard shortcuts

Keyboard shortcuts offer most of the formatting power of the other two methods but allow you to change formats quickly without removing your hands from the keyboard. Character-formatting keyboard shortcuts usually require a combination of Shift, Command, and a letter key. Each command's shortcut key combination appears to the right of the command in the menu list. When you press the key combination, you turn a type of character formatting on or off.

Applying Type Styles

Type styles are the simplest kinds of character formatting to apply and are often the most effective. The memo you began earlier contains a paragraph, shown in Figure 4-6, that demonstrates several types of emphases available in Microsoft Word.

I took the liberty of consulting the Fruit Grower's Vade Mecum for inspiration. I found some *great* suggestions in the section labeled A PEACHY SUGGESTION: PUT A NEW TYPEFACE ON YOUR FRUIT. You can drop by my office to read it for yourself, but I'd like to pass on a few of its suggestions:

Figure 4-6. *This paragraph of the sample memo includes three different type styles—underlining, small caps, and italics—that emphasize words and phrases.*

Continue entering the text of the memo to try your hand at applying type styles in the sample paragraph. You'll use all three methods of character formatting. Take the following steps:

1. Press Return twice, ending the last text paragraph you typed and inserting a blank line before the new text paragraph.

2. Press Tab to indent, and then type to the beginning of the word "Fruit."

3. Press Shift-Command-] (close bracket) to turn word underlining on, a type of underlining that underscores words but not the spaces between them.

4. Type *Fruit Grower's Vade Mecum.* The words appear with an underline.

5. Press Shift-Command-] (close bracket) a second time to turn word underlining off.

6. Type the second sentence to the beginning of the word "great."

7. Choose *Italic* from the Format menu to turn italic formatting on.

8. Type the word "great." It appears in italic.

9. Choose *Italic* a second time from the Format menu to turn italic formatting off.

10. Continue typing the second sentence to the beginning of the phrase ''A PEACHY SUGGESTION.''

11. Choose *Character* from the Format menu to open the Format Character dialog box.

12. Click on the Small Caps check box in the Style area, and then click on the OK button to close the dialog box and turn on small caps, a type style that uses small uppercase characters in place of lowercase characters.

13. Type *A Peachy Suggestion: Put a New Typeface on Your Fruit.* (Be sure to use uppercase and lowercase characters as you type.) The words appear in small caps.

14. Choose *Character* from the Format menu again to open the Format Characters dialog box, click on the Small Caps option to turn the check box off, and then click on the OK button to close the dialog box and turn off small caps.

15. Finish typing the rest of the paragraph, pressing Return twice at the end of the paragraph to prepare for entering the next text paragraph.

Each of the three methods you used to apply type styles offers its own advantages: Keyboard shortcuts are fast and simple; formatting from the Format and Font menus doesn't require you to memorize key combinations; and the Format Character dialog box offers more types of character formatting than do the other two methods. Table 4-1, on the following page, shows all the type styles available in Microsoft Word and how to apply them by using any of the three application methods.

Note that you probably won't find all the type styles listed in this table in the normal Format menu even if you have long menus turned on. To add the missing type styles to the Format menu, you must customize your menus as described in Chapter 22, ''Customizing Word.'' Because these type styles are less often used than the others that are normally found in the menu, you might find that keyboard shortcuts and the Format Character dialog box provide all the access you need to them.

Type style	Keyboard Shortcut	Format Menu Command	Format Character Dialog Box Option	Explanation
Boldface	Shift-Command-B	Bold	Bold check box	Thickens and emphasizes each character
Italic	Shift-Command-I	Italic	Italic check box	Slants each character to the right
Underline	Shift-Command-U	Underline	*Single* in the Underline list box	Places a single line under every character you type, including spaces
Word Underline	Shift-Command-]	Word Underline	*Word* in the Underline list box	Underlines words you type, but not blank spaces
Double Underline	Shift-Command-[	Double Underline	*Double* in the Underline list box	Places a double underline under every character you type, including spaces
Dotted Underline	Shift-Command-\	Dotted Underline	*Dotted* in the Underline list box	Places a dotted underline under every character you type, including spaces
Strikethru	Shift-Command-/	Strikethru	Strikethru check box	Strikes a dash through the middle of each character
Outline	Shift-Command-D	Outline	Outline check box	Creates a hollow outline of each character
Shadow	Shift-Command-W	Shadow	Shadow check box	Creates a drop shadow beneath an outline of each character
SMALL CAPS	Shift-Command-H	Small Caps	Small Caps check box	Turns lowercase letters into small, uppercase letters
ALL CAPS	Shift-Command-K	All Caps	All Caps check box	Turns lowercase letters into uppercase letters
Hidden Text	Shift-Command-V	Hidden Text	Hidden check box	Hides selected characters
Colors	No keyboard shortcut available	The name of the color you want	The name of the color you want from the Color list box	Displays the characters in the color you choose (if you have a color monitor or printer)

Table 4-1. *Microsoft Word offers these type styles.*

Color text

Color text prints only with color printers and appear only on color monitors. Text displayed on monochrome monitors appears black regardless of the color setting. To set a color, you can choose any one of eight colors—black, blue, cyan, green, red, magenta, yellow, and white—from the Color list box in the Format Character dialog box or from the Format menu if the Format menu has been customized to include them. Note that if you choose white, you won't be able to see any characters you enter against the white background of the monitor. White is normally used only for printing on nonwhite paper.

Hidden text

The Hidden Text type style hides selected characters. Even though characters formatted as hidden text are stored in your document, they don't appear on the monitor screen or in printed documents unless you specifically ask Word to show or print hidden text.

To see hidden text on the screen, choose *Preferences* from the Edit menu, and then turn on the Show Hidden Text check box in the Preferences dialog box. (You'll learn more about using this dialog box in Chapter 22, ''Customizing Word.'') Word shows hidden text as characters underlined with a dotted line. If you set Word to hide hidden text, the text around the hidden text closes up. If you type with the Hidden Text type style turned on and the Show Hidden Text option turned off, you'll see the cursor remain in one place as you type—you're entering characters that Word stores in your document but doesn't display on the screen.

When you print a document that contains hidden text, you can print it with or without the hidden text. This feature makes hidden text a useful tool for adding confidential information, such as salaries or financial projections, to a document. You can print one version of the document for general release, hidden text not showing, and another version for private distribution that displays the hidden text.

Changing Fonts

A font as defined in the Macintosh world is a family of characters that have the same design. You can see in this book that the characters in the main body of the text belong to the same font (technically called a *typeface*). Although you see many different characters and sections of text that are italic or bold-face, a stylistic unity ties together all the characters in one family.

To change fonts, you select a new font by its name. In the sample memo, a new font begins at the beginning of the third paragraph. The font you've used thus far is New York, the font Word uses when you start a new document. To try a new font, choose a font name from the bottom section of the Font menu and then begin entering the paragraph as follows:

1. Choose *Courier* from the Font menu to choose the Courier font.

2. Press Tab for an indent, enter the paragraph that begins "Matter-of-fact fruits..." and then end by pressing Return twice, adding a blank line before the next paragraph. The text you type appears in the Courier font.

You can use a keyboard shortcut to change fonts if you know the name of the font you want. The key combination Shift-Command-E prompts you for the font name in the page-number area at the bottom of the document window. Simply type the name of the font you want and press Return. Take the following steps to change the font to Helvetica:

1. Press Shift-Command-E. The page-number area turns black and prompts you with the word "Font."

2. Type *Helvetica* and press return.

3. Press Tab to indent the first line, and then enter the paragraph that begins "Forceful fruits...", ending by pressing Return twice to add a blank line before the next paragraph. The text you type appears in the Helvetica font.

4. Choose *New York* from the Fonts menu to change back to the New York font for the rest of the memo.

5. Press Tab to indent the first line, and then enter the paragraph that begins "Use a nicely formed...", ending by pressing Return twice to add a blank line before the next paragraph. The text you type appears in the New York font.

You've changed fonts by choosing a name from the Font menu and by using a keyboard shortcut; you can also change a font in the Format Character dialog box if you so choose—you'll find the same list of fonts in the Font list box that you find in the Font menu.

Choosing a Point Size

Changing the point size changes the size of the characters you enter. Character size is measured in *points*, traditional typesetting units of measurement equal to approximately ¹⁄₇₂ of an inch. The point size of a character refers to its height from the bottom of a descender to the top of a capital letter. For example, a 14-point character is taller (and correspondingly wider) than a 10-point character.

Changing the point size is like changing fonts; you can choose a size from the Font menu, you can use a keyboard shortcut, or you can choose a size from the Format Character dialog box. The keyboard shortcut Shift-Command-> (greater-than symbol) increases the point size, and Shift-Command-< (less-than symbol) decreases the point size. Each time you press one of these key combinations, you increase or decrease the point size, and the page-number area tells you the new point size you have set.

When you choose a point size from the Font menu, the menu might show some of the point sizes in outline characters and some in regular characters. The sizes listed in outline characters are those that your Mac stores in its System file for the currently set font. These sizes will appear clear on screen and on a printed page. The sizes listed in regular characters aren't stored in the System file and will look ragged on the screen and on an ImageWriter printer. (Nonsystem point sizes might appear clear on a LaserWriter printer if the font is a laser font; you can read more about these fonts and point sizes in Chapter 19, ''Printing Variations and Document Export,'' which includes a discussion of laser printing.)

If you open the list of sizes in the Size combo box of the Format Character dialog box, it shows only the point sizes available in the system for the currently set font. If you want to set a nonsystem point size, you must enter it directly into the Size box.

Try setting different point sizes in the last paragraph of the memo:

1. Press Shift-Command-> (greater-than symbol) twice to increase the point size to 18 points. The page-number area displays *14 Point* at the first press and *18 Point* at the second.

2. Press Tab for an indent, and then type the sentence that begins ''Always print fruit names....'' The sentence appears in 18-point characters.

3. At the end of the sentence, choose *10 Point* from the Font menu to reduce the character size to 10 points.

4. Type the sentence that begins "Print price increases...." It appears in 10-point text.

5. Choose *Character* from the Format menu to open the Format Character dialog box. The Size combo box shows the currently selected point size highlighted in black.

6. Type *36*, and then press Return. The Size box displays *36*, and then the dialog box closes.

7. Type the sentence that begins "Describe jumbo fruit...." It appears in 36-point text.

Notice as you type text in large point sizes that Word changes the line spacing to accommodate the larger characters. When you type different point sizes in one line, Word moves the line down far enough from the previous line (or from the top of the document) to make room for the largest characters in the line.

The 36-point sentence you typed most likely appeared on the screen in ragged-looking characters. Most Macs don't include 36-point New York in the System file, so the Mac's system software estimated what that point size would look like, blowing up a smaller-point-size version of New York to 36 points. The sample memo at the beginning of this chapter was printed on a LaserWriter printer that can print 36-point characters, so these same characters that look ragged on the screen look smooth in the printout.

Combining Fonts, Sizes, and Type Styles

You can use almost any combination of font, point size, and type style to get exactly the effect that you want in text. Although you're limited to one font and one size at a time, you can combine type styles. For example, you can use a 24-point Helvetica font with bold, italic, and underlining turned on at the same time.

Some type styles, however, can't be combined. You can use only one underline emphasis at a time; choosing any underline emphasis turns off any other underline emphasis. Likewise, you can't use superscript and subscript simultaneously. Choosing one turns off the other.

Inserting Characters in Formatted Text

After you type text, you can move the insertion point back to the middle of the text and insert more text. When you do, Word applies the formatting (font, size, and type style) of the character immediately to the left of the inscrtion point. This can save you work as you insert and delete text. For example, move the insertion point to anywhere in the small-capped phrase "A PEACHY SUGGESTION" and type some text. The new text you type will appear in small caps. Move the insertion point to the middle of the underlined word "Vade" and type some text. This text will be underlined to match the text surrounding it.

You've now learned many ways to enter characters in a Word document. You've learned how to enter special characters and set typestyles, fonts, and point sizes. In the next chapter you'll learn how to add a bit of flair to your documents by inserting graphics.

Chapter 5

Adding Graphics

Effective graphics add focus to a document. Graphics can illustrate text and vividly impress on your readers a concept you're trying to convey. In this chapter you'll learn how easy it is to add pictures, charts, graphs, or any types of graphics to a Word 4 document. You'll begin by creating your own graphics in SuperPaint, the graphics program that comes with Microsoft Word. You'll then learn how to insert the graphics in a Word document and to change the size of the graphics to suit the layout. You'll also learn how to trim a graphical image, how to add a border around an image for emphasis, and how to position a graphical element in your document.

SETTING UP WORD

Before you begin working with the examples in this chapter, be sure that Microsoft Word shows full menus, that the Scrapbook DA is installed in your System file (you'll use it to transport pictures), that SuperPaint is accessible on your hard-disk drive (if you have one) or on the Utilities 2 floppy disk that comes with Word 4, and that Word is set to display graphics. Take the following steps:

1. If you haven't done so already, turn your computer on and start Word.

2. Open the Edit menu, and if the Full Menus command appears, choose it to set full menus. If the Short Menus command appears instead of the Full Menus command, full menus are already set, and you can close the menu without choosing any commands.

3. Open the Apple menu to see the list of available DAs, and check that *Scrapbook* appears in the DA list. If it doesn't, you need to install the Scrapbook DA by using the Font/DA Mover utility. You'll find the Font/DA Mover and the Scrapbook DA on the floppy disks that come with your Macintosh and directions for their use in the manual set that comes with your Mac.

4. If you have a hard-disk drive, check whether SuperPaint has been installed. If it hasn't, copy SuperPaint to the drive from the Utilities 2 floppy disk that comes with Word 4. If you don't have a hard-disk drive, keep the Utilities 2 floppy disk close at hand so you can run SuperPaint from the disk.

5. Choose *Preferences* from the Edit menu to open the Preferences dialog box, and then check whether the Use Picture Placeholders option (located near the top of the box) is turned on or off. If it's turned on (an X appears in its check box), turn it off by clicking on the check box and then click on the OK button to close the dialog box. If the Use Picture Placeholders option is already turned off, click on the Cancel button to close the dialog box.

If the Use Picture Placeholders option is turned on, Word shows only gray rectangles in place of graphics, which speeds up scrolling through the document. If you want to see the graphics you insert, the option must be turned off.

The sample document for this chapter, shown in Figure 5-1, is a report that includes two graphical elements: the fancy letter "M" at the beginning of the report and the pie chart in the middle of the report. You create both graphics in SuperPaint, transfer them to the report in Word, and then size and position them and add borders where necessary.

A GRAPHICS PRIMER

To add a graphical element to a Microsoft Word document, you must create the graphic, transport it to Word, and then position the graphic where you want it. You'll add a graphic to a document later in this chapter, but before you do, a few simple facts about graphics and the process of bringing them into Word will help you understand what you're doing as you re-create the sample document.

Mama LaGuido's does it again! Through mushroom melees, sallies of sausage, and anchovy ambushes, Mama reigns supreme, the Big Cheese of pizza purveyors. The pie chart below shows our slice of the market in round figures:

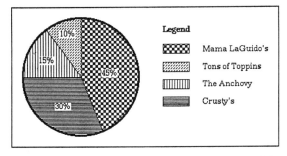

Principal profits posted are the product of the public and pundits' panning of pies in parlors past their prime. Rave reviews of our renovated restaurants resulted in regal revenues recently revealed. Your bonus checks are in the mail.

Figure 5-1. *This report includes graphical elements that enhance the text.*

Creating a Graphic

You can create a graphic on the Macintosh by using any of a large variety of programs and hardware. The three most common tools for creating or reproducing a graphic are as follows:

■ *Paint programs,* in which the screen of the Macintosh simulates a canvas. You use the program's tools to draw figures in *pixels,* the small dots that make up pictures on the screen. Once you draw a shape on the screen, you can't alter any part of it without changing the image around it. When you save a graphic created with a paint program, the graphic is stored exactly the way you see it on the screen—as a large pattern of pixels. This pattern of pixels is called a *bitmap.* When you open a saved bitmap, the program simply displays its pixel pattern directly on the screen.

■ *Draw programs,* in which the screen simulates a drafting table. You use the program's tools to draw figures as you would in a paint program, but you have one major advantage over using a paint program: The draw program remembers each pictorial component you create, so you can alter each component later without affecting any other parts of the drawing. When you save a graphic created with a draw program, the program doesn't save the file as a simple bitmap; it saves mathematical descriptions of each component of the drawing. When you open a saved drawing, the program uses these descriptions to redraw the entire graphic.

■ *Scanners,* machines with software that reproduces an already printed image as a bitmap you can see on your Macintosh screen or print on a printer. This process is called *digitizing.* Most scanners offer you several different *resolutions* (measured in dots per inch, *dpi* for short) in which to digitize a picture. Each resolution uses a different pixel size, which controls the coarseness or fineness of the image—large pixels produce a grainy image and small pixels produce a more detailed, finer image. When you save a digitized image, it's saved as a bitmap, the same way a paint image is stored.

Note: Your ideal resolution depends on your particular printer and Mac screen. If you digitize a graphical image for use in Word, use the resolution that matches the resolution of your Mac's screen.

SuperPaint—the graphics program included in the Word 4 package—is both a paint and a draw program; you can choose either mode to create a graphical element. You'll find that some types of graphics are easier to create as a painted bitmap, others as a drawn image. Whenever possible, use drawn images for importing to a Word document; drawn images are much easier to resize once you transfer them to the document, and they look much smoother if you print your document with a laser printer. You'll see the advantages and disadvantages of both painted and drawn graphical images in the examples later in this chapter.

Transporting a Graphic into Word

To transport a graphic into Word, you first display the image using any graphics program capable of displaying it. You then select the graphic or whatever part of the graphic you want and choose *Copy* from the program's Edit menu to copy the graphic onto the Mac's Clipboard. (Choosing *Copy*, *Cut*, or *Paste* from the Edit menu accesses the Clipboard, the Mac's temporary holding space for graphics and text.) You can then return directly to Word to paste the graphic from the Clipboard directly into a document.

Transporting Multiple Graphics into Word

If you're transporting more than one graphic into Word, keep in mind that the Clipboard can store only one graphic at a time. You can, of course, run a graphics program, copy an image, move to Word, paste an image, return to the graphics program, copy another image, move back to Word, paste an image, and so on, until you have all the graphics you want, but why work that hard when the Scrapbook can simplify your work?

The Scrapbook is a desk accessory that comes with your Macintosh. Because it's a desk accessory, you can run it at any time—while you're running a graphics program or while you're running Word. Its purpose is to store up to 256 graphics and chunks of text. You can paste the contents of the Clipboard into the Scrapbook at any time. You can open the Scrapbook again later, look through its contents, and copy every graphic or chunk of text onto the Clipboard (one at a time) to paste into whatever program you're using. You'll learn how to use the Scrapbook later in this chapter.

Inserting a Graphic in a Word Document

To insert a graphic stored on the Clipboard in a Word document, you put the insertion point where you want the graphic to appear and then choose *Paste* from Word's Edit menu. The graphic appears in the document, and Word treats the graphic as a single character. Like any single character, you can insert the graphic between characters in a line of text. You can select the graphic as you would a character and delete, copy, or cut it as you see fit. You can even format it (to a limited extent) as you would format any other character. For example, you can format a picture as hidden text so it won't print or appear unless you specifically ask for it.

CREATING THE SAMPLE GRAPHICS

To create the graphics in the sample memo for this chapter, you'll use Super-Paint. You create the letter "M" at the beginning of the report by using SuperPaint as a draw program, and you create the pie chart in the middle of the report by using SuperPaint as a paint program. You then transfer both images to the Scrapbook so you can insert them in your pizza report as needed.

Learning to use SuperPaint is a topic for a book in its own right, so we won't go into great detail here. After all, your purpose is simply to supply two graphics to use in Word. The steps that follow describe how to create the graphics. If you're unfamiliar with SuperPaint, you might want to read the SuperPaint manual before you try the following examples.

Running SuperPaint

To run SuperPaint, you first need to leave Word. If you're running Multi-Finder and have enough RAM in your Mac to run both programs simultaneously, simply choose *Finder* from the Apple menu to return to the desktop. Word will remain open in the background. If you're running Finder instead of MultiFinder or if you have limited memory, quit Word by choosing *Quit* from the File menu.

Start SuperPaint by double-clicking on its icon. (If you don't have Super-Paint on a hard disk, insert Word's Utilities 2 disk, double-click on its icon to open its window, and then double-click on the SuperPaint icon there.) SuperPaint appears on the screen.

Creating the Letter "M"

Your first task is to create a letter "M." You first set SuperPaint to act as a draw program and then use the polygon tool to create the "M." Figure 5-2 labels the parts of SuperPaint you use.

1. Click on the layer selector in the upper left corner of the screen so the compass is uppermost instead of the paintbrush. This selects the draw layer of SuperPaint so you can use it as a drawing program.

2. Click on the polygon tool icon in the tool palette.

3. Click on the cross-weave pattern at the bottom of the screen to choose it as the fill pattern. The right side of the line/fill selector (located to the left of the fill patterns) should now show the cross-weave pattern.

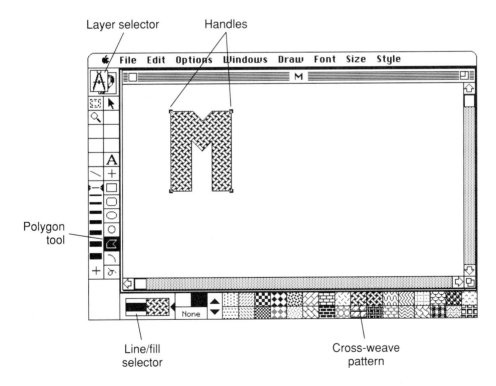

Figure 5-2. *Use the labeled parts of the SuperPaint screen display to draw the letter "M."*

4. Move the pointer into the drawing window and click once to begin drawing the ''M.'' Move the pointer and continue clicking until you finish all 12 sides of the ''M.'' When you connect the last side to your starting point, double-click to stop drawing. SuperPaint stops drawing and fills the ''M'' with the selected fill pattern. If you want to change the shape or size of your ''M,'' choose *Reshape Polygon* from the Draw menu. When handles appear on each corner of the ''M,'' drag each to a new position to reshape the ''M.''

5. Save the ''M'' so that a chance mishap doesn't erase it before you transport it to Microsoft Word: Choose *Save* from the File menu, type the filename *M*, and click on the Save button.

Creating the Pie Chart

To create the pie chart, you set SuperPaint to act as a paint program. You then use the paint tools to draw the pie chart. Figure 5-3 labels the parts of the SuperPaint screen display you use.

1. Choose *New* from the File menu to open a new window.

2. Click on the layer selector in the upper left corner of the screen so the paintbrush is uppermost instead of the compass. This selects the paint layer of SuperPaint so you can use it as a paint program.

3. Click on the circle tool icon in the tool palette.

4. Select the second line thickness in the tool palette. (It's labeled ''Thicker line'' in Figure 5-3.)

5. Click on the None fill box to set the circle tool to create an unfilled circle.

6. Move the pointer to the upper left corner of the window, and then drag down and to the right to create a circle.

7. Click on the line tool icon and then click on the first line thickness (labeled ''Thinner line'' in Figure 5-3) so you can draw straight, thin lines.

8. Draw straight lines from the center of the circle to the outer radius, dividing the circle into the wedges shown in Figure 5-3.

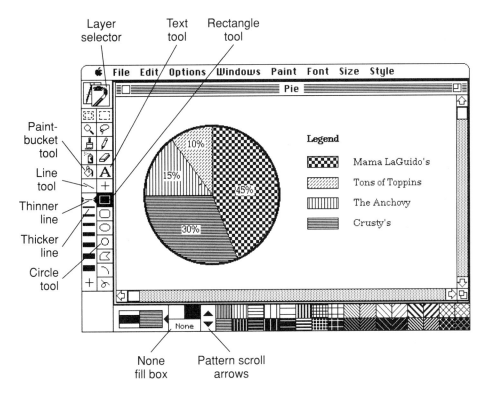

Figure 5-3. *Use the labeled tools to paint the pie chart.*

9. Click on the paint-bucket tool icon, choose the checkerboard fill pattern, and then use the tool to fill the largest wedge with checks. Repeat with the appropriate fill patterns for the other wedges. (If you don't see the patterns you need, use the pattern scroll arrows to show more fill patterns.)

10. Click on the text tool.

11. Move the cursor to the uppermost wedge of the pie chart, click to position the insertion point, and type *10%*. Repeat to enter *15%*, *30%*, and *45%* in the appropriate wedges.

12. Select *Bold* from the Style menu, position the insertion point in the upper center of the window, and type *Legend*.

13. Select *Bold* again from the Style menu to turn off boldface, and then move the insertion point to type *Mama LaGuido's*, *Tons of Toppins*, *The Anchovy*, and *Crusty's* in the appropriate locations in the window.

14. Select the rectangle tool, and then select the checkerboard fill pattern to match Mama LaGuido's slice of pie.

15. Draw a filled rectangle in front of the "Mama LaGuido's" label. Repeat with the appropriate fill pattern for each of the remaining three rectangles.

16. Save the picture (perhaps as "Pie") so you won't accidentally lose it before you transport it to Word.

Adding Graphics to the Scrapbook

Now that you've created the graphics, you can add them to the Scrapbook so you can transfer them to your Word document. Take the following steps:

1. Click on the selection tool (the single-dotted-line rectangle below the layer selector).

2. Hold down the Command key, move the pointer to the upper left corner of the window, drag it down to the lower right corner of the window, and then release the mouse button and the Command key. A selection rectangle appears around the pie chart. (Holding down the Command key makes the rectangle shrink to the smallest possible size capable of containing the pie chart.)

3. Choose *Copy* from the Edit menu to copy the contents of the selection rectangle into the Clipboard.

4. Choose *Scrapbook* from the Apple menu to open the Scrapbook.

5. Choose *Paste* from the Edit menu to paste the pie chart from the Clipboard into the Scrapbook. The pie chart appears in the Scrapbook window, as shown in Figure 5-4.

6. Close the Scrapbook by clicking on its close box.

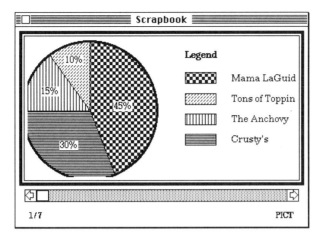

Figure 5-4. *The Scrapbook window shows one of the graphics it stores. Use the scroll bar at the bottom to browse through the contents of the Scrapbook.*

7. Close the pie chart window by clicking on its close box. If Super-Paint asks whether you want to save changes, click on the No button because you've already saved it (unless of course, you made changes—in which case you should click on the Yes button). The ''M'' window that was underneath the pie chart window should appear.

8. Click on the ''M'' with the selection arrow. The handles appear, showing that the ''M'' is selected.

9. Choose *Copy* from the Edit menu to copy the ''M'' onto the Clipboard.

10. Choose *Scrapbook* from the Apple menu to open the Scrapbook, choose *Paste* from the Edit menu to paste the ''M'' from the Clipboard into the Scrapbook (it appears in the Scrapbook's window), and then click on the Scrapbook's close box to close the Scrapbook.

11. Choose *Quit* from SuperPaint's File menu to quit SuperPaint. If SuperPaint displays a message that asks you whether you want to save changes, click on the No button because you've already saved the letter ''M.''

PASTING GRAPHICS
INTO THE SAMPLE DOCUMENT

Now that you've created the letter ''M'' and the pie-chart graphics and stored them in the Scrapbook, you can paste them into your pizza report.

First you must return to Word. If you left Word running under Multi-Finder, simply click on the Word icon in the right end of the menu bar to reactivate Word. If you quit Word to run SuperPaint, double-click on the Word icon to restart the program. When Word appears with a new, blank document, you can begin creating your document by inserting the ''M'' and then continue by adding text and the pie-chart graphic. Take the following steps:

1. Choose *Scrapbook* from the Apple menu to open the Scrapbook.

2. If the ''M'' doesn't appear in the Scrapbook's window, click on the right scroll bar arrow to scroll through the other scrapbook entries until the ''M'' appears. When the ''M'' appears, choose *Copy* from the Edit menu to copy the ''M'' into the Clipboard.

3. Click on the Scrapbook's close box to close the Scrapbook.

4. Choose *Paste* from the Edit menu to transfer the ''M'' from the Clipboard into the new document. The insertion point is already at the very beginning of the document, so you don't need to move the cursor to indicate where you want to place the graphic. The ''M'' appears there, where you want it. The insertion point stretches out to the same height as the ''M'' because Word treats the graphic as a single character and allows enough space between lines to accommodate the height of the graphic.

5. Press the space bar to insert a space after the ''M,'' and then begin typing the text of the report: *ama LaGuido's does it again!* and continue, entering *slice of the market in round figures:* at the end of the paragraph. Press Return once to end the paragraph.

6. Open the Scrapbook again, scroll through the entries to find the pie chart, choose *Copy* to copy the pie chart onto the Clipboard, and then close the Scrapbook.

7. Choose *Paste* from the Edit menu to paste the pie chart from the Clipboard into the document at the insertion point. Press Return once.

8. Type the last paragraph of the report, ending with *Your bonus checks are in the mail.*

Notice that you've created a one-character paragraph in the middle of the report—the pie-chart graphic is the single character. It's followed by a paragraph mark, setting it off as a single-character paragraph.

A note about the Scrapbook: Whenever you choose *Copy* to copy a Scrapbook entry onto the Clipboard, the entry remains in the Scrapbook so you can use it again later. If you want to remove the entry to free up space on your system disk, display the entry in the Scrapbook window and then choose *Cut* from the Edit menu.

FORMATTING THE SAMPLE GRAPHICS

You can use Word's graphics-editing features to trim unwanted sections of a graphic, called *cropping,* or to resize a graphic, called *scaling.* You can also use graphics-editing features to add a border and to position a graphic where you want it in relation to the text around it.

Selecting a Graphic

You can select a graphic in a document by simply clicking on it, or you can click and hold the mouse button and drag across the graphic with the pointer to select it as part of a text block. Try selecting the pie chart in the middle of the report by moving the pointer to the middle of the pie chart and clicking the mouse button.

When the graphic is selected, three small squares, called *sizing handles,* frame its right, bottom, and lower right edges, as shown in Figure 5-5, on the following page. You can drag the sizing handles to scale and crop the graphic. The handle on the right edge scales the graphic horizontally, the handle on the bottom edge scales the graphic vertically, and the handle in the lower right corner scales the graphic both vertically and horizontally.

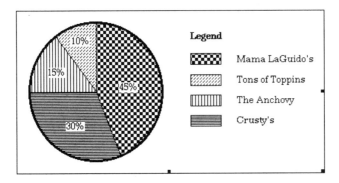

Figure 5-5. *When a graphic is selected, sizing handles appear on its right, bottom, and lower right edges.*

Scaling a Graphic

When you scale a graphic, you stretch or shrink the image to make it wider, skinnier, taller, shorter, larger, or smaller. To scale a graphic, hold down the Shift key as you drag one of the graphic's sizing handles. The right handle scales the width of the image, the bottom handle scales its height, and the corner handle scales width and height equally to increase or decrease the image's overall size. Try shortening the height of the ''M'' so it doesn't stand out quite as much:

1. Click on the ''M'' to select it.

2. Hold down the Shift key and drag the bottom sizing handle upward. As you drag, the height of the ''M'' is reduced and the page-number area at the bottom of the window displays the height of the graphic in inches. When the height reaches the measure you want (perhaps 1 inch), release the mouse button and the Shift key.

If you scale an image out of proportion and want to return it to its original size, simply double-click on the image.

When you scaled the ''M,'' the fill pattern remained intact, without any distortion. This is because the ''M'' is a drawn image whose file contains records of each of its individual components. Now try scaling the pie chart to see the effects of scaling on a bitmap image as follows:

1. Click on the pie chart to select it.

2. Hold down the Shift key and drag the corner sizing handle upward and to the left to shrink the overall size of the pie chart. The page-number area displays the size as a percentage of its original size. Release the mouse button and Shift key when the image is reduced to 80 percent of its original size. Notice that the text and fill patterns in the picture appear distorted, as shown in Figure 5-6.

3. Double-click on the pie chart to return it to its original size.

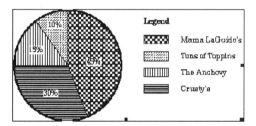

Figure 5-6. *When the pie chart, a bitmap image created by a paint program, is scaled, the fill patterns and text appear severely distorted.*

When Word scales a bitmapped image, it doesn't know much about the form of the bitmap. Although you see a circle, lines, characters, and fill patterns, it sees a collection of black and white pixels. When it resizes the bitmap it decides, by performing logical operations, which pixels will be black and which pixels will be white. Given these limitations, distortion is inevitable.

Word has a record of each component of a drawn image—circles, lines, or characters—and it knows exactly how to redraw them most clearly in a new size. Some distortion can creep in, but it's usually minimal. For example, Figure 5-7, on the following page, shows the same pie chart created in the draw layer of SuperPaint instead of the paint layer. It too is scaled down to 80 percent of its original size. Notice that it appears clearer than the painted image. It's always best to use a drawn image if you think you'll resize it later.

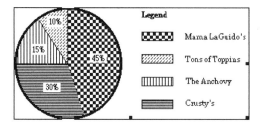

Figure 5-7. *A drawn image appears clearer after scaling than a painted image does.*

Cropping a Graphic

Cropping a graphic doesn't change its size, but it does control how much of the graphic appears and how much blank space appears around the edge of the graphic. To crop a graphic, drag the sizing handles (without holding down the Shift key as you do for scaling). Dragging a handle inward removes some of the graphic; moving it outward adds blank space around the graphic. It's important to note that you can trim parts from only the right and bottom sides of a graphical image. However, if you drag a handle outward to add blank space to a graphic, Word centers the graphic in the blank space, so the effect is the same as adding blank space to both sides or to the top and bottom.

Try cropping the pie chart, first to remove part of the image and then to add space above and below the image so it stands out from the surrounding text, as follows:

1. Drag the corner handle of the pie chart inward toward the middle of the chart. As you drag, the page-number area displays the percentage of the original image that remains. When the graphic is reduced to 80 percent, release the mouse button. The graphic is now cropped as shown in Figure 5-8, hiding the bottom of the pie chart and some of the pizza-parlor names.

2. Double-click on the graphic to remove the cropping and return it to its original size.

3. Drag the bottom handle of the pie chart downward. As you drag, you can see the border as a dotted line moving into the text below the chart. When you've dragged it downward, past two lines of

text, release the mouse button. Word adds approximately two lines of space to the graphic, one line at the top and one at the bottom, setting the chart apart from the surrounding text.

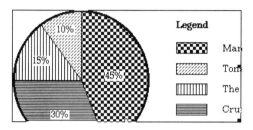

Figure 5-8. *This pie chart has been cropped to 80 percent of its original size, hiding its right and bottom edges.*

Adding a Border to a Graphic

Sometimes you need a border around a graphic to keep it from looking lost on the page. To add a simple border, first select the graphic, and then choose *Outline* from the Format menu. A border appears around the graphic. To add extra space between the graphic and its border, use the cropping handles to add extra space around the edge of the graphic.

Try adding a border to the pie chart, and then use the cropping handles to add some blank space to the left and right sides of the chart, as follows:

1. Choose *Outline* from the Format menu. A border frames the pie chart. The space you added earlier above and below the chart keeps the border some distance above the top and below the bottom of the chart, but the border crowds the left and right sides of the chart.

2. Drag the right-side sizing handle about ½ inch to the right and release the handle. One-quarter inch of white space appears on each side of the pie chart, moving the border farther away from the graphical image.

Positioning a Graphic

Once a graphic is in place within a document, you might want to position it relative to the surrounding text. To add space above or below the graphic (outside its boundaries), simply position the insertion point before or after the graphic and press Return to enter blank lines. To move the graphic to the left or right on the page, reposition the paragraph that contains the graphic by changing its indents or its alignment.

The paragraph containing the pie chart is currently aligned flush left so that the image also aligns with the left indent. Try changing its position by changing paragraph indents. When you change the first-line indent, you change the horizontal location of the graphic, as follows:

1. If the Ruler isn't visible in the document window, choose *Show Ruler* from the Format menu.

2. Move the first-line indent to the 2-inch mark. (The first-line indent controls the graphic's location because the paragraph contains only one line.) The graphic moves so that its left border aligns 2 inches from the left margin of the document.

3. Reset the first-line indent to 0 to return the graphic to its original position.

Setting the first-line indent when the graphic is aligned flush left is a convenient way to position the graphic in the precise horizontal location you want. To center the graphic, you can simply choose center alignment by clicking on the center icon in the Ruler. The graphic moves to the horizontal center of the document.

Here's one more touch to make the pie chart look even better—add a blank line above it and below it so its borders don't cramp the text. Take the following steps:

1. Position the insertion point to the left of the pie chart by pressing the left-arrow cursor key once, and then press Return to add a blank line above the chart.

2. Position the insertion point to the right of the pie chart and press Return to add a blank line below the chart.

You've now re-created the sample report complete with graphics, and you've seen how Word handles pictures within a document. In the next chapter you'll learn to use some simple editing tools to change text in a document.

Chapter 6

Editing Text

It's a rare document that springs forth from its writer's fingers and leaps directly onto the printed page. Most are subject to second thoughts, third thoughts, misgivings, and tinkering around with before they finally emerge from the printer's maw. When you sit down to polish your documents, the last thing you want to add to your editorial turmoil is the distraction of having to wrestle with your Macintosh to make your changes. They should appear without effort or pause.

In this chapter you'll learn how to edit documents quickly, without stopping to choose commands from a menu. You'll learn some convenient keyboard shortcuts that move the cursor from character to character, from word to word, from line to line, and almost anywhere you want. You'll also learn to shuffle blocks of text around in a document without using the Cut, Copy, or Paste command. The last part of the chapter introduces you to the Find and Change commands, which can ease the task of finding and changing text scattered throughout a long document.

SETTING UP WORD

Before you attempt to re-create the examples in this chapter, be sure that Microsoft Word shows full menus, as follows:

1. If you haven't done so already, turn your computer on and start Microsoft Word.

2. Open the Edit menu, and if the Full Menus command appears, choose it to set full menus. If the Short Menus command

appears instead of the Full Menus command, full menus are already set, and you can close the menu without choosing any commands.

The examples in this chapter require a long document that you can scroll through and edit. With some help from the Copy and Paste commands, you can duplicate the paragraph in Figure 6-1 (a fine example of technobabble) to create a long document with minimal typing. Take the following steps:

1. Type the paragraph shown in Figure 6-1. Use the underline type style to emphasize the expression "counterclockwise." The invisible characters (visible here) show you where to press Tab and Return. Be sure to press Return twice at the end of the paragraph to create a blank line following the paragraph.

2. Select the block of text that extends from the first character of the paragraph through the end of the blank line following it.

3. Choose *Copy* from the Edit menu to transfer a copy of the text block to the Clipboard.

4. Move the insertion point to the end of the document.

5. Choose *Paste* from the Edit menu 13 times to insert 13 copies of the paragraph into the document (or press Command-V as a shortcut for the Paste command). Each paragraph should be separated from the next by a blank line.

6. Save the document under the name "Instructions."

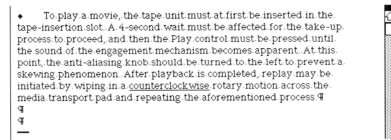

Figure 6-1. *Enter this sample paragraph.*

You now have a three-page document filled with unclear technical instructions, eminently suitable for altering with editing examples.

MOVING THE INSERTION POINT

In previous chapters, you learned how to move the insertion point by pointing and clicking with the mouse. You also learned how to move it a character or a line at a time by pressing the cursor keys or the 2, 4, 6, and 8 keys on the numeric keypad. You can also use keyboard combinations to move the insertion point through larger sections of text—a word, sentence, paragraph, screen of text, or even the entire document—all without taking your hands from the keyboard.

Table 6-1 shows the keys and key combinations that move the insertion point. Try using them to move through your sample document:

Insertion-Point Movement	Key or Key Combination
Single character forward	Right-arrow cursor key or keypad 6
Single character backward	Left-arrow cursor key or keypad 4
Single line up	Up-arrow cursor key or keypad 8
Single line down	Down-arrow cursor key or keypad 2
Beginning of the current line	Keypad 7
End of the current line	Keypad 1
Beginning of the current, then previous, word	Command–right-arrow cursor key or Command–keypad 4
Beginning of the next word	Command–left-arrow cursor key or Command–keypad 6
Beginning of the current, then previous, sentence	Command–keypad 7
Beginning of the next sentence	Command–keypad 1
Beginning of the current, then previous, paragraph	Command–keypad 8 or Option-Command-Y
Beginning of the next paragraph	Command–keypad 2 or Option-Command-B
Top of the window	Home key (only on an extended keyboard) or Command–keypad 5
Bottom of the window	End key (only on an extended keyboard)
Up one screen	Page Up key (only on an extended keyboard)
Down one screen	Page Down key (only on an extended keyboard)

(continued)

Table 6-1. *Keyboard shortcuts for moving the insertion point.*

Table 6-1. *continued*

Insertion-Point Movement	Key or Key Combination
Beginning of the document	Command-Home (only on an extended keyboard) or Command–keypad 9
End of the document	Command-End (only on an extended keyboard) or Command–keypad 3

Use these keys and key combinations to move the insertion point to a new location. For example, if you type a sentence and notice that you forgot to capitalize the first letter of the paragraph, you can press Command–keypad 8 to jump back to the beginning of the paragraph, where you can correct your mistake. Or if you need to change something at the beginning of the document, you can press Command–keypad 9.

Returning to a Previous Location

As you edit, you might need to jump to a distant point in the document, work on that section, and then return to your previous location. Word remembers your last three insertion-point locations. To go back, choose *Go Back* from the Utilities menu, or press either keypad 0 or Option-Command-Z. Each time you use the Go Back command, the insertion point jumps back one location. After it returns to three previous locations, the cursor returns to your original location.

A good rule of thumb for using the Go Back command is to press keypad 0 until you find the previous location you want or until you return to the same spot. If you don't find the location you want after cycling through the previous spots, you'll need to scroll to find the location.

Jumping to a Specific Page

In particularly long documents, you might want to jump to a specific page. To do so, watch the page-number area at the bottom of the window as you drag the scroll box downward or upward; the page-number area changes to show you the page numbers of the pages you're scrolling through. When you see the number of the page you want, release the scroll box; Word displays the portion of that page appearing at the location you scrolled to.

A more precise way to jump to a specific page is to choose *Go To* from the Utilities menu and enter your page selection in the Go To dialog box, shown in Figure 6-2. Type the page number you want in the Page Number text box, and then click on the OK button. Word scrolls the text window to the top of that page and places the insertion point there.

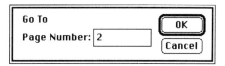

Figure 6-2. *Use the Go To dialog box to jump to a set page number.*

An Example

Because the sample document you created has so many identical paragraphs, you can identify them by numbering each paragraph. That way, you'll know where you are as you scroll through your document. When you finish, you can try your hand at jumping through your document to look at your handi-work. Take the following steps:

1. Press Command–keypad 9 to jump to the beginning of the document if the insertion point isn't already located there.

2. Type *1.* to number this paragraph as the first paragraph.

3. Press Command–keypad 2 twice to jump down to the beginning of the next paragraph of text. (The second press moves the cursor past the blank-line paragraph separating the two text paragraphs.)

4. Type *2.* to number this paragraph as the second paragraph.

5. Use the same procedure to move to the beginning of each follow-ing paragraph, numbering the paragraphs consecutively up to 14.

6. Press keypad 0 to jump to your previous editing location. Word jumps the insertion point to the beginning of paragraph 13, where you typed *13.*

7. Choose *Go To* from the Utilities menu to open the Go To dialog box, type *2.*, and then press Return to jump to the beginning of page 2 of your document.

8. Press Command–keypad 9 to move back to the beginning of your document.

SELECTING TEXT

You learned in Chapter 3, "The First Session," how to select text by clicking and holding the mouse button while dragging the pointer across text or by holding down Shift as you move the insertion point by using the cursor or keypad keys. If you want to select text even faster, Word offers some special selection techniques that use both the mouse and the keyboard.

Selecting Text with the Mouse

Word allows you to select parts of your document with the mouse. Using any of several techniques, you can select a single letter, a word, a sentence, a line, a paragraph, or the entire document. The different techniques involve single-clicking and double-clicking on text elements, methods with which you're already familiar, and working with an area of the text window called the *selection bar*. The selection bar is the thin, vertical, blank area of the document window immediately to the left of the text. When you move the insertion point to the selection bar, the I-beam becomes a right-pointing arrow. Figure 6-3 shows the pointer resting in the selection bar.

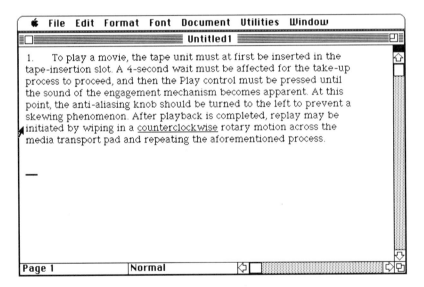

Figure 6-3. *The I-beam pointer becomes a right-pointing arrow when it is in the selection bar.*

To select a specific block of text, you can use one of the following techniques:

- To select a word: Place the insertion point in the word and double-click the mouse button.

- To select a sentence: Place the insertion point in the sentence, hold down Command, and click the mouse button.

- To select a line: Place the pointer in the selection bar immediately to the left of the line and click the mouse button.

- To select a paragraph: Place the pointer in the selection bar immediately to the left of the paragraph and double-click the mouse button.

- To select the entire document: Place the pointer anywhere in the selection bar, hold down Command, and click the mouse button.

Selecting Text with the Keyboard

To select text using keyboard shortcuts, simply hold down the Shift key as you use the shortcuts from Table 6-1, on page 109, to move the insertion point. For example, you can select a word you just typed by pressing Shift–Command–left-arrow cursor key. Or you can press Command–keypad 9 to move the insertion point to the beginning of the document and then press Shift–Command–keypad 3 to move the insertion point to the end of the document, selecting the entire document. An even easier way to select the entire document is to use the keyboard shortcut Option-Command-M.

An Example

Try the following mouse and keyboard selection techniques on the first paragraph of the document:

1. Move the pointer to the middle of the word "tape" in the first line and double-click the mouse button. Word selects the entire word and the space following it.

2. Move the pointer into the selection bar immediately to the left of the number "1," and click the mouse button. Word selects the entire first line of the paragraph.

3. With the pointer remaining in the selection bar, double-click the mouse button. Word selects the entire paragraph.

4. With the pointer remaining in the selection bar, press Command and click the mouse button. Word selects the entire document.

5. Move the pointer to the middle of the word "tape." Press Shift–Command–keypad 6 to select the entire word. (Command–keypad 6 moves the insertion point by one word. Shift–keypad 6 extends the selection character by character.)

6. Press Shift–Command–keypad 6 again to add the following word to the selected text block. To continue adding words to the text block, continue pressing keypad 6 while holding down Shift-Command .

7. Press Command–keypad 9 to move the cursor back to the top of the document and deselect the text block.

KEYBOARD EDITING COMMANDS

As you know, Word offers keyboard shortcuts for common editing commands. Word also offers some special keyboard commands (not available in the menus) that let you move blocks of text without using the Clipboard and delete a word of text with a single stroke.

Using Cut, Copy, and Paste

Cut, Copy, and Paste are the three most commonly used commands in Word's Edit menu. Each one has a convenient keyboard shortcut, so you can "choose" a command without using the mouse: Cut by pressing Command-X, copy by pressing Command-C, and paste by pressing Command-V. If you have an extended keyboard, you can cut by pressing F2, copy by pressing F3, and paste by pressing F4.

Moving Text Without Using the Clipboard

Each time you use the Cut or Copy command to move a block of text, the text is inserted onto the Clipboard, and the previous contents of the Clipboard are erased. If you're storing in the Clipboard a graphic or a block of text that you don't want to lose, you can use two special keyboard commands—Move Text and Copy Text—to move text in a document without changing the contents of the Clipboard.

To use either command, you must first select a text block. To move the text block, press Option-Command-X. The page-number display area shows the message *Move to*, and the text remains selected. Now move the insertion point to the desired location of the text block. The insertion point appears as a dotted line, showing that Move To is in effect. When you have positioned it where you want it, press Return. Word moves the selected text block to the new location without changing the contents of the Clipboard.

To copy the selected text block to a new location, press the key combination Option-Command-C. The page-number display area displays the message *Copy to*, and the text remains selected. Move the dotted insertion point to the desired location of the selected text, and then press Return. Word inserts a copy of the text at that location without changing the contents of the Clipboard.

An Example

Try using the Move To command to move the first paragraph of the document to below the second paragraph. Take the following steps:

1. Double-click on the word "tape" to select it, and then press Command-C to copy it to the Clipboard. (This isn't a necessary step for using the Move To command, but it does put "tape" in the Clipboard so you can see that Move To doesn't touch the contents of the Clipboard.)

2. Select the entire first paragraph and the blank-line paragraph following it.

3. Press Option-Command-X. The page-number display area shows the message *Move to*.

4. Move the pointer to the spot that precedes the *3* at the beginning of the third paragraph of text, and click to position the insertion point there. The insertion point appears as a dotted line, indicating that Move To is in effect.

5. Press Return. Paragraph number 1 disappears from the beginning of the document and appears between paragraphs 2 and 3.

6. Choose *Show Clipboard* from the Window menu to open the Clipboard window. It shows *tape*, its original contents before you used the Move To command. Close the Clipboard window.

Deleting Text One Word at a Time

As you enter text in a document, you can fix most typing errors by pressing the Delete key and deleting one character at a time until you eliminate the error. Some errors, however, stretch out across the screen and take a long time to delete in this way. An easier way to delete long stretches of text is to use the key combination Option-Command-Delete. Each time you press the combination, Word deletes an entire word and the following space, working from the insertion point back to the text to the left of the cursor. You can delete words following the insertion point by pressing Option-Command-G.

FINDING TEXT

To find specific text in a document, you can search through the document yourself, scrolling page by page with an observant eye. If your document is long, however, it's much easier to use the Find command.

Choosing the Find command opens the Find dialog box shown in Figure 6-4, in which you can enter the first word or words of the text you want to find. Clicking on the Start Search button prompts Word to pore diligently over the characters in the document until it finds that text. Word then selects the text it found and scrolls the view of the document window to show its location.

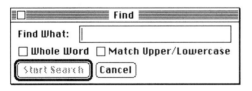

Figure 6-4. *The Find dialog box asks you for the text you want to find.*

To find text, choose *Find* from the Utilities menu to open the Find dialog box. In the text box labeled Find What, type the text you want to find. If you fill the text box, Word scrolls your string to the left so that you can continue typing characters. You can enter a maximum of 255 characters as search text. If you want to enter more than 255 characters or if you want Word to find a graphic, you can select a text block that contains the text or graphic you want and then use Copy and Paste to paste it into the Find What text box.

After you enter your search characters, click on the Start Search button. Word searches from the insertion point to the end of the document. If it finds an occurrence of your search text, it selects it and changes the view to show the text's location. The Start Search button then changes to Find Next; click on it if you want to continue the search. If Word doesn't find the text, it opens a dialog box asking whether you want to continue searching from the beginning of the document. If you click on the Yes button, Word continues searching until it either finds your search text or reaches the end of the document again. If you click on the No button, Word ends the search.

When you search for text with the Find command, the Find dialog box remains open on the screen so you can continue searching. If you want to search for text without having the open dialog box displayed on screen, you can choose the Find Again command in the Utilities menu to ask Word to search for whatever text and options were last entered in the Find dialog box. Word then conducts its search without reopening the dialog box. To further speed the process, you can press the key combination Option-Command-A to issue the Find Again command from the keyboard.

An Example

Try searching for the word ''play'' in your document as follows:

1. Move the insertion point to the beginning of the document to begin the search there.

2. Choose *Find* from the Utilities menu to open the Find dialog box.

3. Type *play* in the Find What text box.

4. Click on the Start Search button to begin the search. When Word encounters the first instance of ''play,'' it selects the word in the documents, and the Start Search button becomes the Find Next button, as shown in Figure 6-5, on the following page.

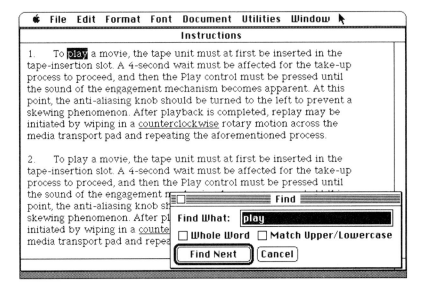

Figure 6-5. *When Word finds search text, it selects the text in the document, and the Start Search button becomes the Find Next button.*

5. Click on the Find Next button, which appears in place of the Start Search button, to continue searching. Word searches from the location of the selected word and selects ''Play'' in the middle of the second sentence.

6. Close the Find dialog box.

7. Choose *Find Again* from the Utilities menu. Word selects the next occurrence of the word ''play,'' which is the first half of the word ''playback.'' It doesn't open the Find dialog box to conduct its search.

8. Press Option-Command-A. Word moves on to select ''play'' in the second part of the word ''replay.''

Searching for Whole Words

In the preceding example, Word selected ''play'' even though it was part of another word. The Find command doesn't normally distinguish between whole words and parts of words. To look for a whole word only (that is, a string of characters with a space or punctuation at each end), turn the Whole Word option on in the Find dialog box as follows:

1. Choose *Find* once more to reopen the Find dialog box. It appears with "play" still entered in the Find What text box.

2. Click on the Whole Word option's check box. (The check box contains an X when the option is on.)

3. Choose *Start Search* to begin the search. Word finds "play" at the beginning of the next paragraph and selects it.

4. Click on the Find Next button to continue the search. Word finds "Play" in the middle of the next sentence and selects it.

5. Click on the Find Next button again to continue searching. Word skips over "playback" and "replay" to select "play" at the beginning of the next paragraph.

Matching Case

Word now searches for whole-word occurrences of "play," but it doesn't distinguish between "play" and "Play." To tell it to match the case of the characters in the Find What text box, turn the Match Upper/Lowercase option on as follows:

1. Click on the Match Upper/Lowercase option to insert an X in its check box.

2. Click on the Find Next button to continue searching. Word skips over "Play," "playback," and "replay" to select "play" at the beginning of the next paragraph. It is now looking for "play" only as a whole word in lowercase characters.

3. Continue clicking on the Find Next button (or pressing Return) until you reach the end of the document. Word continues to select "play" as it finds it. When you reach the end, a new dialog box opens, asking whether you want to continue from the beginning of the document. Click on the No button.

4. Close the Find dialog box and return the insertion point to the beginning of the document.

Searching for Unspecified Characters

To search for a string of text without specifying all the characters, use *wild-card* characters in the Find What text box. A wildcard holds a place in a string but doesn't specify any particular character. Type a question mark in the Search For text box to specify an indeterminate character. For example, to find all four-letter words that begin with "fl", you would type *fl??* in the Find What text box. Word would then look for "f" and "l" followed by any two characters and select all four characters if it found them. Typing *fl??* would find and select "flag," "flit," and "flop," but not "foot" (because it doesn't start with "fl"), "floor" (because it has too many letters), or "fly" (because it has too few letters).

Using wildcard characters works best when the Whole Word option is turned on. If the option isn't on, Word finds your search string in words of any length, even if the string appears as part of another word.

Searching for Special Characters

To search for special characters such as tabs and paragraph marks, you need to type a code before entering them in the Find What text box. The code is a caret (^) followed by a single letter. The following codes are used to search for special characters you learned to use in previous chapters:

- ■ ^w—a blank space

- ■ ^t—a tab

- ■ ^p—a paragraph mark

For example, if you enter *^tThree*, Word searches for a tab followed by the word "Three."

Because Word interprets question marks and carets as wildcard characters or code starters, you use special codes to search for literal occurrences of them, as follows:

- ■ ^?—a question mark

- ■ ^^—a caret

Codes for other special characters (section marks and soft hyphens, for example) appear in the Finding and Changing section of *Reference to Microsoft Word*. You'll learn to use some of these special characters in later chapters.

CHANGING TEXT

The purpose of most searches is to locate a piece of text and replace it with different text. Choose the Change command from the Utilities menu to open the Change dialog box, shown in Figure 6-6, and tell Word what to search for and what to use as a replacement. The Change dialog box offers all the features of the Find dialog box but adds a Change To text box and two buttons: Change and Change All.

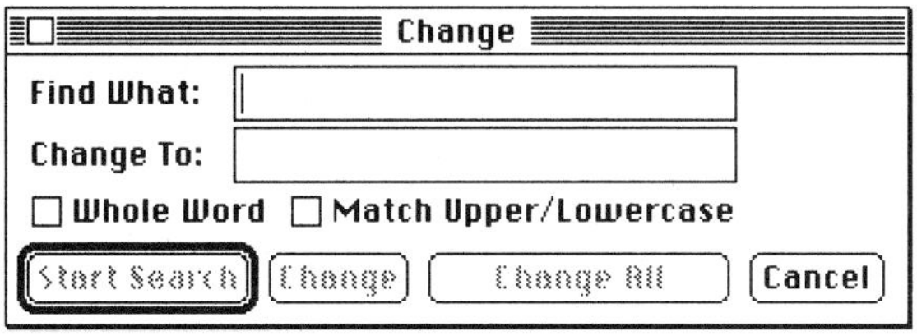

```
▤□▤▤▤▤▤▤▤▤▤ Change ▤▤▤▤▤▤▤
Find What:  [|                              ]
Change To:  [                               ]
□ Whole Word  □ Match Upper/Lowercase
[ Start Search ] [ Change ] [ Change All ] [ Cancel ]
```

Figure 6-6. *Use the Change dialog box to type a string of text to be replaced with another string.*

The Find What text box and the Whole Word and Match Upper/Lowercase options function as they do in the Find dialog box; you enter the text you want to find in the Find What text box and turn on the search options you want Word to use. You use the Change To text box to enter a string of replacement text for the text in the Find What text box.

When you choose the Change command, you can ask Word to search through the entire document or only a part of the document. To search through a single part of the document, select that part as a text block; if no text block is selected, Word searches through the entire document.

If you have a text block selected when you first open the Change dialog box, Word displays a Change Selection button. If no text block is selected, a Change All button appears in its place. If you click on the Change All button, Word finds all occurrences of the search text in the entire document and replaces each occurrence with the replacement text. If you click on the Change Selection button, Word finds and changes only the text selection you highlighted before opening the Change dialog box, leaving the rest of the document intact. In both cases, Word performs all the changes at once; you don't see each change as it happens. Instead, the page-number area at the bottom of the window displays how many changes Word made.

Reviewing Changes

One problem with a blanket find-and-change operation is that you can end up making some changes you didn't want. For example, if you replace every occurrence of the word "mark" in a document with the word "check," you might find that the name Mark Smith has now been changed to Check Smith. Worse yet, you have no idea that the name has been changed, because you didn't see it happen.

To avoid problems like this, it is best to review each change Word makes. To do so, click on the Start Search button. Word finds the first occurrence of your search text, selects it, and then turns the Start Search button into a No Change button. You now have the choice of clicking on the No Change button or pressing Return, in which case Word leaves the selected text alone and looks for the next occurrence of the search text, or clicking on the Change button, in which case Word replaces the selected text and then moves on to the next occurrence of the text. You can proceed through the entire document in this way, reviewing each proposed change before it is made, approving only the changes you want by clicking on the Change button.

Note: Word follows whatever initial and full capitalization is present when it changes words unless the Match Upper/Lowercase option is turned on. For example, if you're changing the word "cat" to "dog" throughout a document, Word replaces "cat" with "dog," "Cat" with "Dog," and "CAT" with "DOG." If the Match Upper/Lowercase option is turned on, Word uses only the capitalization in the Find What and Change To text boxes for its searches and changes.

An Example

Try replacing the word "play" in your document with the word "view" as follows:

1. Choose *Change* from the Utilities menu to open the Change dialog box.

2. Enter *play* in the Find What text box and *view* in the Change To text box, and then check that both the Whole Word and the Match Upper/Lowercase options are turned off.

3. Choose *Start Search* to begin the search. Word shows you each proposed change. It selects "play" in the first sentence.

4. Click on the Change button. Word changes "play" to "view" in the document and then continues, selecting "Play" in the second sentence.

5. Click on the Change button again. Word changes "Play" to "View" and then continues, selecting "play" in "playback."

6. Click on the No Change button to reject this change. Word continues, selecting "play" from "replay."

7. Click on the No Change button to reject this change, and then close the Change dialog box.

8. Select the second text paragraph in the document, and then reopen the *Change* dialog box by choosing *Change* from the Utilities menu (or by pressing Command-H). The dialog box appears, offering a Change Selection button.

9. Turn on the Whole Word option so that Word won't change "playback" and "replay" to "viewback" and "review."

10. Click on the Change Selection button. Word replaces every occurrence of "play" in the paragraph with "view" and reports *4 changes* in the page-number area.

11. Close the Change dialog box and deselect the paragraph by moving the insertion point to the beginning of the document.

12. Open the Change dialog box once more and click on the Change All button to replace every "play" in the document with "view." Word changes the text and reports the number of changes in the page-number area at the bottom of the document window.

13. Close the Change dialog box and scroll through the document to view Word's changes.

You've now learned some quick and easy ways to edit your text. In the next chapter you'll learn how to format paragraphs to make your edited text look even better.

Chapter 7

Paragraph Formatting

Paragraph formatting, more than any other type of formatting, controls your document's overall appearance. In this chapter you'll learn to shape paragraphs by setting indents, changing alignments, controlling line spacing, and adding borders. You'll learn how to cut, copy, paste, and enter paragraph marks, the invisible characters that store formats and mold paragraphs. You'll also learn how to prevent paragraphs from being split apart during pagination.

SETTING UP WORD

Before you begin working with the examples in this chapter, check to be sure that Word shows full menus, as follows:

1. If you haven't done so already, turn your computer on and start Word.

2. Open the Edit menu, and if the Full Menus command appears, choose it to set full menus. If the Short Menus command appears instead of the Full Menus command, full menus are already set, and you can close the menu without choosing any commands.

The sample document for this chapter, shown in Figure 7-1 on the following page, is a simple collection of paragraphs that use different paragraph formats. You'll re-create these paragraphs as you work through the examples.

This paragraph is left aligned and has a 0.5-inch first-line indention. The text is single spaced, and the paragraph is open, meaning a blank line separates it from the next paragraph. Notice that text at the left margin aligns, whereas text at the right margin appears ragged—characteristics of a left-aligned paragraph.

This paragraph is also left aligned, but it has no first-line indention. The left and right indents are both set in by 0.5 inch, so the paragraph has a shorter width than that of the paragraph above. The text is single spaced.

> This paragraph is center aligned. The text block appears ragged on both sides because each line of text is centered on the 3-inch mark on the measure. There is no first-line indention, and both indents are set in by 0.5 inch. The border around this paragraph shows the locations of the indents. The text is single spaced.

This paragraph is justified; the text aligns at both the left

and right indents. Word pads each line of text with extra

blank space to push the last word of the line all the way

to the right indent. The text is double spaced.

Figure 7-1. *This sample document uses a variety of paragraph formats.*

PARAGRAPH MARKS

You learned in Chapter 3, "The First Session," that Word enters a paragraph mark (an invisible character) in a document each time you press Return. The paragraph mark does more than mark the end of a paragraph, however. It also stores the paragraph's formatting specifications—its indents, alignment, line spacing, border type, and other information.

Think of each paragraph mark as a text "mold" for the paragraph. Any text you type to the left of a paragraph mark conforms to the mark's formatting. For example, if you enter text to the left of a paragraph mark that is set to be left aligned and double spaced, Word aligns each new line with the left margin and inserts a blank line between every two lines of text.

At the beginning of every new document, Word inserts a paragraph mark that is set for default formatting, and any text you type follows the paragraph mark's default formatting. When you press Return at the end of the first paragraph, Word duplicates the paragraph mark at the end of the paragraph and keeps the original mark at the end of the document. You can't delete the original paragraph mark, but you can change its formatting.

CHANGING PARAGRAPH FORMATS

To apply a new paragraph format, you first select the paragraph or paragraphs to be changed. You learned in Chapter 3, "The First Session," to select a single paragraph for formatting by placing the insertion point anywhere in the paragraph (which means that a paragraph is always selected for formatting as you type it). You also learned that when you select a text block for paragraph formatting, Word formats all the paragraphs that are part of that text block, even if only portions of some paragraphs are selected.

Paragraph Formatting Methods

Once you select a paragraph, you can change formats with any of the following tools:

- The Ruler

- The Format Paragraph command

- Keyboard shortcuts

The following sections describe each tool and how to use it.

The Ruler

The Ruler, shown in Figure 7-2, lets you use the mouse to change paragraph formatting. Each time you open a new document window in Word, Word displays the window without the Ruler. To display the Ruler, choose *Show Ruler* from the Format menu. To remove the Ruler, choose *Hide Ruler* from the Format menu.

As shown in Figure 7-2, the Ruler's four center icons set paragraph alignment. The three icons to the right of the center four set line spacing, and the two icons to the right of those close or open a line space before each paragraph. You move the wedges at the left and right ends of the measure, located above the icons, to set paragraph indents.

You'll learn about the other parts of the Ruler, such as the style-selection box and the icons for setting tab stops, in following chapters.

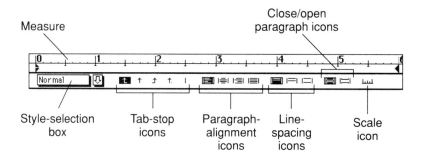

Figure 7-2. *The parts of the Ruler.*

The Format Paragraph command

Choosing the Paragraph command in the Format menu opens the Paragraph dialog box, shown in Figure 7-3, and displays the Ruler if it isn't already visible.

You can use the Paragraph dialog box to control the appearance of a selected paragraph or paragraphs. The three Indents text boxes in the upper left corner set paragraph indents, and the Spacing text boxes control line spacing. The four option boxes below the text boxes include three options that control the way page breaks split paragraphs and one option that turns line numbering on.

You use the three buttons at the bottom of the dialog box to open three dialog boxes: Clicking on the Tabs button opens a dialog box in which you can set tab stops within a paragraph or paragraphs; clicking on the Borders button opens a dialog box in which you can add borders to a paragraph or paragraphs; and clicking on the Position button opens a dialog box in which you can position a paragraph or paragraphs in a fixed location on a page.

You'll learn to use many of these features in later chapters.

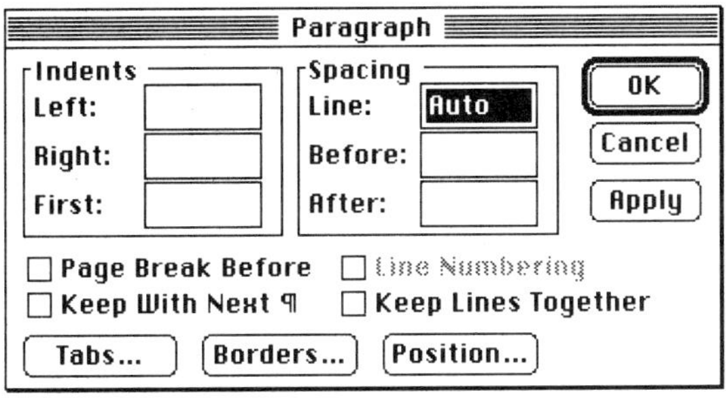

Figure 7-3. *The Paragraph dialog box offers settings that shape paragraphs within a document.*

Keyboard shortcuts

Keyboard shortcuts include some of the paragraph formats you can set with the Ruler and in the Paragraph dialog box. The shortcuts, listed throughout this chapter, require that you press a combination of Option-Command plus a letter key.

SETTING PARAGRAPH INDENTS

You can set any of three kinds of indents for a paragraph: left, right, and first-line. Word measures each indent from the left and right margins of the document. The left and right margins' default placement is 1.25 inches from the left and right edges of the page. The top and bottom margins' default placement is 1 inch from the top and bottom edges of the page. In the discussion that follows, we'll assume the default margin settings. (You'll learn how to change margin settings in Chapter 17, "Document Formatting.")

A paragraph's left indent controls the left edge of all lines except the first. The indent is measured from the left margin. If the left indent is set to 0, text aligns exactly on the left margin—1.25 inches from the left edge of the paper. If the left indent is set to 1 inch, text aligns 1 inch to the right of the left margin—2.25 inches from the left edge of the page.

A paragraph's right indent controls the right edge of all lines in the paragraph. The way you measure the indent depends on whether you use the Ruler or the Paragraph dialog box. On the Ruler, the right indent is measured in terms of the left margin. When the right indent is set to 6 inches, it rests 6 inches to the right of the left margin—7.25 inches from the left edge of the page (or 1.25 inches from the right edge of the page). In the Paragraph dialog box, the right indent is measured from the right margin. If the right indent is set to 0, text aligns on the right margin—1.25 inches from the right edge of the page. If the right indent is set to 0.75 inch, text aligns 0.75 inch to the left of the right margin—2 inches from the right edge of the page.

The first-line indent determines the left edge of the paragraph's first line. Like the left indent, the first-line indent is measured from the left margin. By setting the value of the first-line indent to be greater than 0 in the Paragraph dialog box or to the right of the left indent on the Ruler, you indent the first line to the right of the following lines' edge. Setting its value to less than 0 in the Paragraph dialog box or to the left of the left indent on the Ruler moves the first line to the left of the following lines' edge, creating a "hanging indent."

Setting Indents by Using the Ruler

To set indents by using the Ruler, you use the mouse to drag the appropriate indent marker to the position you want on the measure and then release the mouse button. Figure 7-4 labels the three indent markers. As you drag any one of the indent markers, the page-number area at the bottom of the document window displays the marker's location (in inch designation).

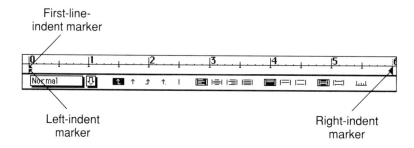

Figure 7-4. *Use the Ruler's three indent markers to control a paragraph's indents.*

Note that when you move the left-indent marker, the first-line-indent marker moves with it, keeping the first-line indent set relative to the left indent. You can move the first-line-indent marker by itself to change the first line's indention, but to move the left-indent marker by itself, you need to hold the Shift key down as you drag it.

Setting Indents by Using the Paragraph Dialog Box

To set indents by using the Paragraph dialog box, first choose *Paragraph* from the Format menu. When the dialog box appears, click on the appropriate Indents text box: *Left* for the left indent, *Right* for the right indent, and *First* for the first-line indent. Enter the indent setting you want, and then press Return to close the dialog box and apply the indent.

Setting Indents by Using Keyboard Shortcuts

Four keyboard shortcuts let you change indents:

■ Shift-Command-N moves the left and first-line indents to the right 0.5 inch (a process called *nesting*).

■ Shift-Command-M moves the left indent to the left 0.5 inch and moves the first-line indent so it is even with the left indent.

■ Shift-Command-F moves the first-line indent 0.5 inch to the right of the left indent.

■ Shift-Command-T creates a hanging indent by moving the left indent to the right 0.5 inch.

An Indention Example

Try setting indents as you re-create the sample document shown in Figure 7-1, on page 126. Take the following steps:

1. Before you type the first paragraph, set the first-line indent to 0.5 inch by dragging the first-line-indent marker to the 0.5-inch position on the measure, creating a first-line indention.

2. Type the first paragraph, and press Return after you finish.

3. Type the second paragraph, stopping before you press Return. Notice that the indention you created in the first paragraph is duplicated in this paragraph.

4. Choose *Paragraph* from the Format menu to open the Paragraph dialog box.

5. Type *.5* in the Left text box, *.5* in the Right text box, and *0* in the First text box.

6. Press Return to close the dialog box and apply the new margins. The text moves in 0.5 inch on both sides, and the first-line indention disappears.

7. Press Return to end the paragraph.

SETTING PARAGRAPH ALIGNMENT

Word can align paragraphs in the following four styles:

- *Left alignment,* in which all text aligns with the left indent, leaving a ragged right edge.

- *Right alignment,* in which all text aligns with the right indent, leaving a ragged left edge.

- *Centered alignment,* in which all text centers exactly between the left and right indents, leaving ragged edges on both edges.

- *Justified alignment,* in which all text aligns with both the left and right indents (except the last line, which might be shorter than the other lines and would therefore align only with the left indent) to create smooth edges. Word adjusts the blank space between words to create full justification.

You can apply each type of alignment by using either the Ruler or keyboard shortcuts.

Setting Alignment by Using the Ruler

To align a paragraph by using the Ruler, simply click on the appropriate alignment icon. All the text in the selected paragraphs conforms to the alignment you choose.

Setting Alignment by Using Keyboard Shortcuts

The following keyboard shortcuts align selected paragraphs:

- Shift-Command-L applies left alignment.

- Shift-Command-R applies right alignment.

- Shift-Command-C applies centered alignment.

- Shift-Command-J applies justified alignment.

An Alignment Example

Try the different methods of setting paragraph alignment as follows:

1. Type the third paragraph of the document, stopping before you press Return.

2. To center each line of text in this paragraph, click on the Ruler's center-alignment icon.

3. Press Return to begin a new paragraph, and then type the fourth paragraph, again stopping before you press Return.

4. Press Shift-Command-J to apply justified alignment. The text in the paragraph aligns with both the left and right indents.

SETTING LINE SPACING

Line space is the amount of space between lines of text in a paragraph. Word measures this space in points, the same unit of measurement it uses to measure the height of fonts. It measures from the bottom of one line of text to the bottom of the line below it. The bottom of a text line is determined by the lowest point of the font's *descenders*, as shown in Figure 7-5. Descenders are "tails" on characters such as j and p.

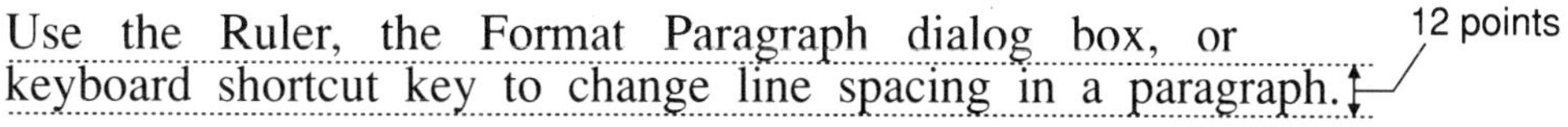

Use the Ruler, the Format Paragraph dialog box, or   12 points
keyboard shortcut key to change line spacing in a paragraph.

Figure 7-5. *Word measures line space from the bottom of one line to the bottom of the following line.*

Word sets the default line spacing to one line, a unit of measurement that Word interprets as 12 points. Line spacing is flexible, however, so if you use characters larger than 12 points in size, Word adjusts the line space to accommodate the point size of the largest character in the line. If you set line spacing to 18 points and then enter 24-point text, Word sets the line spacing for that line to approximately 30 points so that the top of the tallest character doesn't run into the descenders in the line above it. However, if you set line spacing to 18 points and then use a 10-point font size, Word doesn't decrease the space to match the small font. Line spacing remains at 18 points; therefore, more space appears between text lines. You can use the Ruler, the Paragraph dialog box, or keyboard shortcuts to increase the line spacing in a paragraph and add more space between lines of text. The following sections describe each method.

Setting Line Spacing by Using the Ruler

The Ruler displays three icons you can use to set line spacing:

- Single-spacing icon—instructs Word to set 12 points between lines

- One-and-one-half-spacing icon—instructs Word to set 18 points between lines

- Double-spacing icon—instructs Word to set 24 points between lines

Because these settings have fixed point sizes, they work best with 12-point or smaller type sizes. If you use a larger type size, such as 24-point, these line-spacing settings have no effect.

To set line spacing, click on the appropriate line-spacing icon on the Ruler. Figure 7-6 labels the icons.

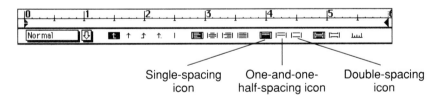

Figure 7-6. *The line-spacing icons on the Ruler set line spacing in selected paragraphs.*

Setting Line Spacing by Using the Paragraph Dialog Box

To set line spacing by using the Paragraph dialog box, choose *Paragraph* from the Format menu to open the box. Enter the line-spacing value in point increments in the Line text box in the Spacing section. For example, entering *24 pt* specifies line spacing of 24 points. You can also enter the distance between lines in line increments. Type *li* following the number so that Word knows you're specifying a line measure. (Remember that one line equals 12 points regardless of the size of the characters in the line.) If you don't specify *li* or *pt*, Word assumes points. If you want Word to set line spacing automatically, enter *auto* or *0*; Word then increases or decreases line spacing to match the largest type size in each line.

Setting Line Spacing by Using Keyboard Shortcuts

Word offers one keyboard shortcut for setting line spacing: Shift-Command-Y, which sets double spacing (24-point line spacing).

Inserting Space Before and After Each Paragraph

In addition to controlling the amount of space between lines, Word controls the amount of space between paragraphs. Two icons on the Ruler, shown in Figure 7-7, let you add space or not add space before a paragraph. Clicking on the open-line icon adds 12 points of space before each selected paragraph, and clicking on the close-line icon formats the paragraph without an extra 12 points before each selected paragraph.

Entering a line or point measurement in the Before text box in the Paragraph dialog box instructs Word to add that much space *before* each selected paragraph. Entering a measurement in the After text box instructs Word to add that much space *after* each selected paragraph.

Figure 7-7. *The paragraph-spacing icons on the Ruler set paragraph spacing for selected paragraphs.*

Word offers one keyboard shortcut for setting paragraph spacing: Shift-Command-O, which adds 12 points of space before each selected paragraph. Pressing Shift-Command-O has the same effect as clicking on the open-line icon in the Ruler.

A Line-Spacing Example

Change the spacing of the last paragraph you typed, as follows:

1. Select the fourth paragraph of the sample document.

2. Open the Paragraph dialog box by choosing *Paragraph* from the Format menu.

3. Type *36 pt* in the Line text box, and press Return to apply the spacing. All the lines in the paragraph are separated by 36 points from line bottom to line bottom.

4. Click on the double-spacing icon on the Ruler. The line spacing reduces to 24 points (two lines).

Now try adding a single line before each paragraph in your document as follows:

1. Select the entire document by pressing Option-Command-M.

2. Click on the open-line icon on the Ruler. An extra 12 points of space precedes each paragraph in the document.

ADDING PARAGRAPH BORDERS

Word can add borders around any paragraph or paragraphs in your document. The border can be as simple as an underline under the last line of a paragraph or as fancy as a shadow box framing a paragraph. To add borders, first select as a text block the paragraph or paragraphs you want bordered. Choose *Paragraph* from the Format menu to open the Paragraph dialog box, and then click on the Borders button to open the Paragraph Borders dialog box, shown in Figure 7-8.

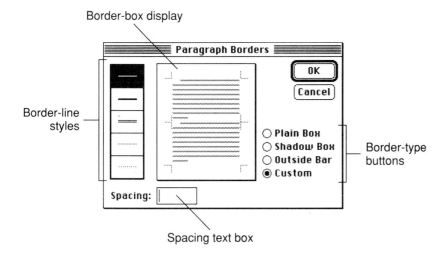

Figure 7-8. *Use the Paragraph Borders dialog box to set a border around selected paragraphs.*

Border Options

The Paragraph Borders dialog box offers four groups of controls that set the type of border you add to selected paragraphs:

- The border-line styles, a choice of line widths and styles for the border

- The border-box display, an area where you can create custom boxes for paragraphs

- The border-type buttons, a choice of four border styles to add to a paragraph

- The spacing text box, a text box in which you can specify (in points) the amount of space between the paragraph text and the border

Setting a Border Type and Line Style

Word offers four border types, as shown in Figure 7-9 on the following page. To set a border type, click on one of the border-type buttons; the border box in the center of the dialog box displays the border you select. The four border types are described at the top of page 139.

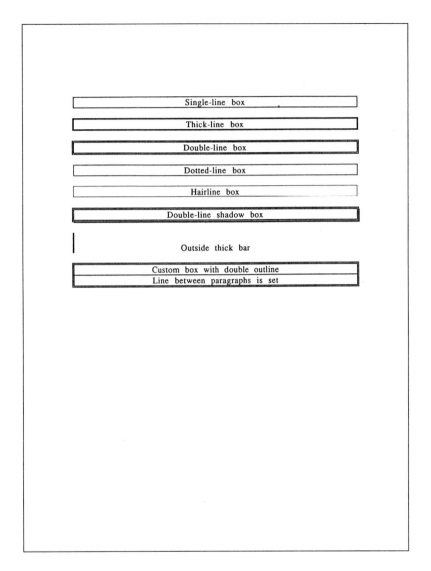

Figure 7-9. *This document shows the variety of paragraph borders.*

■ *Plain Box,* which encloses selected paragraphs in a simple, four-sided box.

■ *Shadow Box,* which creates a box with a shadow on its bottom and right sides.

■ *Outside Bar,* which adds a vertical bar to the left or right edge of the paragraph. (When you learn to create left and right pages in following chapters, you'll find that Word adds the vertical bar on the left edge of left pages and the right edge of right pages so that it's always on the outer edge of the paragraph.)

■ *Custom,* which lets you create your own border by using the border-box display.

After you click on one of the first three border styles, Word displays the border, using the selected line style. The selected border appears in the border-box display. To change the line style, simply click on a different style, and Word changes the lines in the border-box display to match. The available line styles are (from top to bottom) single line, thick line, double line, dotted line, hairline, and combinations with the shadow box, the outside bar, and the custom box.

The document in Figure 7-9 shows all the line styles. Notice that the hairline border is a very thin border, a line as thin as the printer can print. Although it appears as a one-pixel-wide line on the screen, it appears as a much thinner line in a LaserWriter printout.

Creating a Custom Border

When you click on the Custom button, Word clears the border-box display so you can create your own borders, adding lines where you want them. To add a line to the display, move the pointer in the display area and click the mouse button; Word uses the currently selected line style to add a line. To remove a line, move the pointer onto the line and click. As you add and delete lines, try using different line styles to create borders that mix line styles.

The border-box display shows representations of two paragraphs (two groups of gray horizontal lines) and a set of border guides, the small brackets at the paragraph corners. The border guides set four sides—top, bottom, left, and right—and one line that you can place between paragraphs. If you're placing a border around a single paragraph, adding the line between paragraphs in the display area has no effect unless you later split the paragraph into two or more paragraphs. If you're placing a border around more than one paragraph, adding the line between paragraphs will add a line between all paragraphs in your selection.

Adding Space Between Borders and Text

If the Spacing text box at the bottom of the Paragraph Borders dialog box is empty, Word adds 2 points of space between the edges of the paragraph (set by its indents and its line spacing) and the border. If you want to add more space, enter a point value in the Spacing text box. Word adds that amount of space to the existing 2-point spacing. For example, entering *10* in the Spacing text box moves the border away from the paragraph on all sides by a total of 12 points—the 10 you entered and the 2 already added by default.

When you've finished setting all the border options you want, click on the OK button to close the Paragraph Borders dialog box, and then click on the OK button to close the Paragraph dialog box. Word adds the border to the selected paragraphs.

A Border Example

Try adding a border to the third paragraph of the sample document as follows:

1. Move the insertion point into the third paragraph.

2. Choose *Paragraph* from the Format menu to open the Paragraph dialog box.

3. Click on the Borders button to open the Paragraph Borders dialog box.

4. Click on the double-line style to set a double line.

5. Click on the Plain Box button to create a plain box. A double-line box appears in the border box display.

6. Click on the OK button to close the Paragraph Borders dialog box, and then click on the OK button to close the Paragraph dialog box. Word adds a double-line box around the third paragraph.

SPLITTING AND COMBINING PARAGRAPHS

As you cut, copy, paste, and insert blocks of text, you might highlight paragraph marks along with the rest of the text in your selection. Including a paragraph mark in a selection means that the paragraph's formatting information is also selected and will move with the paragraph. Simple explanations of two basic paragraph operations—splitting a paragraph and combining two paragraphs—will show you the effect editing has on paragraphs.

Splitting a Paragraph

The simplest way to split a paragraph is to move the insertion point to the location where you want the split and then press Return. The paragraph mark you insert splits the paragraph into two new paragraphs. Both have the same paragraph formatting because Word copies the formatting from the paragraph mark at the end of the original paragraph into the inserted paragraph mark.

If you cut or copy a text block that contains a paragraph mark and then paste the block into another paragraph (the target paragraph), the target paragraph splits into two paragraphs that might have different formats. If the pasted paragraph mark contains paragraph formatting different from that of the target paragraph mark, the pasted paragraph mark formats the first of the split paragraphs, and the second of the split paragraphs retains its original formatting.

Take the following steps to see how this works:

1. Select a block in the sample document extending from the beginning of the word "border" in the third paragraph to the end of the word "justified" in the fourth. This block contains the paragraph mark (located at the end of the third paragraph) that contains centered and bordered paragraph formatting.

2. Select *Copy* from the Edit menu (or press Command-C) to copy the text block onto the Clipboard.

3. Move the insertion point to the middle of the first paragraph, and choose *Paste* from the Edit menu (or press Command-V) to paste the text block into the middle of the first paragraph.

The first paragraph splits into two paragraphs. The first of the split paragraphs is centered and bordered because it ends with the paragraph mark copied from a centered and bordered paragraph. The second of the split paragraphs retains its original paragraph formatting because it ends with the original paragraph mark.

Combining Paragraphs

To combine two paragraphs, delete the paragraph mark at the end of the first paragraph. Word runs in all the text from the first paragraph with the text in the second paragraph. If the two paragraphs have different paragraph formatting, the formatting of the first paragraph will be lost (along with its paragraph mark). To prevent this from happening accidentally, Word won't let you use the Delete key when the cursor is positioned between two paragraphs with different formatting.

If you do want to remove a paragraph mark from between two differently formatted paragraphs, select the paragraph mark and choose *Cut* or press the Delete key to remove the mark. (You might need to make it visible first by choosing *Show ¶* from Edit menu.) Try combining the third and fourth paragraphs of the sample document as follows.

1. Place the insertion point at the end of the third paragraph and double-click. Word selects the paragraph mark at the end of the paragraph.

2. Press Delete.

The two paragraphs combine, and the formatting of the third paragraph changes to match that of the fourth: justified and double spaced.

PARAGRAPHS AND PAGINATION

When Word prints a document, it breaks the document into pages. If Word reaches the end of a page in the middle of a paragraph, it splits the paragraph with a page break. You can prevent a paragraph's being split by turning the options in the Paragraph dialog box on.

Turning the Keep Lines Together option on prevents Word's splitting any selected paragraphs with a page break. If a protected paragraph is too long to fit at the end of a page, Word moves the entire paragraph to the beginning of the next page.

The Keep With Next ¶ option binds two paragraphs together so that Word won't split them apart with a page break. When you turn this option on, Word binds the selected paragraph to the paragraph immediately following it. If both paragraphs won't fit at the end of a page, Word moves them to the beginning of the next page.

The Page Break Before option inserts a page break before the selected paragraph. Page Break Before guarantees that the selected paragraph will appear at the top of a page.

You've now learned how to format paragraphs to control the appearance of text in a document. In the next chapter you'll learn about an aspect of paragraph formatting not covered in this chapter: setting tabs.

Chapter 8

Tabs

Tab stops have traditionally helped typists line up columns of text by setting position markers across the width of a page. A press of the Tab key moved the typewriter carriage to the next tab stop, where typing would resume. Word 4 offers more advanced tabbing capability. With the Word 4 tabs, you can not only set position markers across a page, but you can also align text by its right or left edge, center text, and align numbers by their decimal point. You can also fill in the spaces between columns with dotted-line, dashed-line, or solid-line leaders. Once columns of text are in place, changing the tab stops moves the columns to their new tab positions on the page.

In this chapter you'll learn how to set tab stops, use the Tab key, and change existing tab stops. You'll learn about tab styles, tab alignment, and tab leaders and use what you learn to create a sample restaurant menu filled with columns, leaders, and other challenging elements.

SETTING UP WORD

Before you begin working with the examples in this chapter, check to be sure that Word shows full menus and the Ruler is displayed, as follows:

1. If you haven't done so already, turn your computer on and start Word.

2. Open the Edit menu and if the Full Menus command appears, choose it to set full menus. If the Short Menus command appears instead of the Full Menus command, full menus are already set, and you can close the menu without choosing any commands.

3. If the Ruler is not visible, choose the *Show Ruler* command from the Format menu.

The sample document for this chapter, shown in Figure 8-1, is a menu for Señor Fujiyama's Japanese-Mexican restaurant. The examples in this chapter re-create the menu by using tabs to align the columns of items and prices, to create the leaders that connect the items and prices, and to align the parts of the menu heading.

October 7, 1990 **Señor Fujiyama's** Today's Menu

For the finest in Japanese-Mexican cuisine!

Entrees

All entrees come with a side of refried beans, miso menudo, and pickled ginger.

Yakitori chorizo..................7.95	Tripe tempura..................10.50
Hamachi en chile burrito 5.95	Quail eggs rancheros........7.50
Puerco sashimi plate..... 13.95	

Side Dishes

Tripe roll..............................2.50	Sushi de pollo......................3.25
Sushi de sesos.....................4.50	Ahi refritos...........................1.75

Drinks

Casa Tofu beer....................1.95	Shiso margarita..................3.50
Ginger cooler........................1.50	Agua mizu.............................4.95

We accept MasterCharge, Federal Express, and petrodollars.

Figure 8-1. *This restaurant menu uses tabs to align columns and to position information within lines.*

TAB STOPS

As you learned in previous chapters, pressing the Tab key moves the insertion point to the right. The stopping point is called a *tab stop*. Tab stops are position markers; when you press Tab, the insertion point moves to the right along the current line to the next tab stop. If no tab stop remains on the line, the insertion point moves to the next line and stops at the first tab stop on that line.

Each tab stop performs three functions:

- It marks a location where the insertion point stops after you press Tab.

- It controls the alignment of the text you type after you press Tab.

- It can add a dotted-line, dashed-line, or solid-line leader in the space between tabbed columns.

Because setting tab stops is a type of paragraph formatting, each paragraph has its own set of tab stops. Any tab stops you set are stored in the paragraph mark and duplicated in the next paragraph when you press Return.

In previous chapters you used the Tab key to jump to Word's *default tab stops*. If you don't set tab stops, Word sets default tab stops every half inch along the Ruler's measure. Tab stops are marked with small horizontal lines, as shown in Figure 8-2.

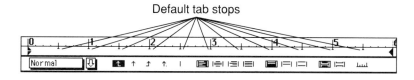

Figure 8-2. *Default tab stops appear every half inch along the Ruler's measure.*

Setting a tab stop is a simple matter of inserting a tab-stop marker on the measure. Word offers five types of tab stops: left-align, center-align, right-align, decimal-align, and bar. Figure 8-3, on the following page, shows the Ruler icon for each type of tab stop.

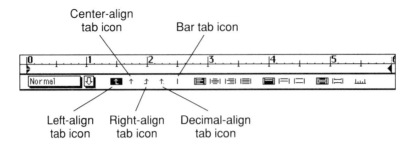

Figure 8-3. *The five tab-stop icons of the Ruler.*

All types of tab stops except one control the alignment of the text you type after you press Tab. The exception is the bar tab, which doesn't align text but adds a vertical bar at the tab location. The bar isn't technically a tab stop, but because you set it as you set the other tab stops, Word treats it as one. Figure 8-4 shows how the four types of tab stops align text. Each tab stop is set in the middle of the page, at the 3-inch mark on the measure.

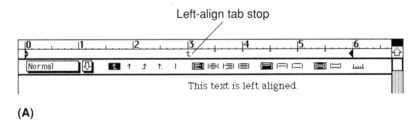

(A)

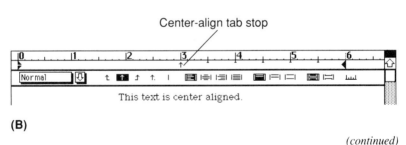

(B)

(continued)

Figure 8-4. *(A) The left-align tab stop aligns text by its left edge. (B) The center-align tab stop centers text. (C) The right-align tab stop aligns text by its right edge. (D) The decimal-align tab stop aligns numbers by their decimal point. (E) The bar tab stop adds a vertical bar at the tab-stop location.*

Figure 8-4. *continued*

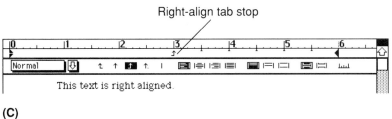

(C)

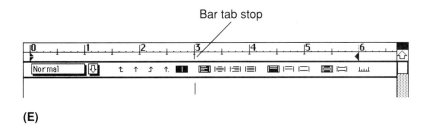

(D)

Bar tab stop

(E)

SETTING TAB STOPS

To set a tab stop, you first select a paragraph or group of paragraphs as you would for paragraph formatting. You can then position the desired tab icons on the Ruler's measure, or you can enter tab-stop locations in the Tabs dialog box, which you open by clicking on the Tabs button at the bottom of the Paragraph dialog box. When you set a tab stop, all the default tab stops to the left of the new tab stop are removed. The exception is the bar stop; when you set a bar stop, all the default tab stops remain where they are.

Setting Tab Stops by Using the Ruler

To set a tab stop by using the Ruler, click on one of the tab-stop icons. Then move the pointer to a position along the measure and click the mouse button. The selected tab stop appears in that position. If you prefer, you can also move a tab-stop icon up to the measure by dragging the icon to the desired position. Try setting a tab stop for the first paragraph of Señor Fujiyama's menu as follows:

1. Press Command-R to display the Ruler if it isn't already visible.

2. Click on the center-align tab-stop icon.

3. Move the pointer to below the 3-inch mark on the Ruler and click the mouse button. A center-align tab stop appears there.

Setting Tab Stops by Using the Tabs Dialog Box

To use the Tabs dialog box to set tab stops, first open the Paragraph dialog box by choosing *Paragraph* from the Format menu. Then click on the Tabs button to open the Tabs dialog box, shown in Figure 8-5.

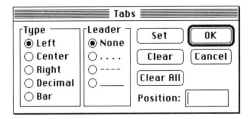

Figure 8-5. *You can enter tab-stop positions in the Tabs dialog box.*

To set a tab in the Tabs dialog box, first click on one of the tab-stop types in the Type area, and then drag the desired tab-stop marker onto the Ruler. The Position field displays the current position of the tab-stop marker. Type the desired position for the tab stop (in inches) in the Position text box. Then click on the Set button if you want to set that tab stop and keep the dialog box open to set another one. Note that you can't place tabs closer to each other than 0.0625 inch ($\frac{1}{16}$ inch) and probably wouldn't want to. When you've finished setting tab stops, click on the OK button or press Return to close the box and apply your tab stops to the selected paragraphs.

Use the Tabs dialog box to set a second tab stop for the first paragraph of the menu as follows:

1. Choose *Paragraph* from the Format menu to open the Paragraph dialog box.

2. Click on the Tabs button to open the Tabs dialog box.

3. Click on the Right button in the Type section to choose a right tab stop.

4. Click on the measure to insert a tab stop. (The position is not important here.)

5. Click on the Position text box and type the value *6* to set the tab stop at the 6-inch mark on the measure.

6. Click on the Set button to set the tab stop. A right-align tab-stop symbol appears on the right-margin marker for the paragraph.

7. Click on the OK button to close the Tabs dialog box and apply the tab stop, and then click on the OK button to close the Paragraph dialog box.

Typing Text at a Tab Stop

Now you can type text at the tab stops you set by entering the first few paragraphs of the menu. Take the following steps:

1. Type *October 7, 1990* and press Tab to jump to the center tab stop.

2. Change the font's point size to 18 and set bold text formatting.

3. Type *Señor Fujiyama's*. (To enter the ''ñ,'' press Option-N, release it, and then type *n*.) The name centers at the tab stop.

4. Press Tab to jump to the next tab stop.

5. Reduce the font's point size to 12 and turn off bold formatting.

6. Type *Today's Menu*. The phrase appears flush against the right tab stop (and the right margin). Figure 8-6, at the end of this example, shows the results.

7. To emphasize the text you entered, add a double-line border below the paragraph. Open the Paragraph Borders dialog box by clicking on the Borders button in the Paragraph dialog box. Click on the

double-line style, the Custom option, and then the bottom of the border box display to insert a line under your text. Then close the Paragraph Borders and Paragraph dialog box.

8. Press Return to begin a new paragraph. Turn off the border and change the paragraph alignment to centered. (To turn off the border, return to the Paragraph Borders dialog box and click on the bottom line in the border box display to turn off the line.)

9. Type *For the finest in Japanese-Mexican cuisine!* and press Return twice.

10. Turn on bold character formatting, type *Entrees*, and then press Return.

11. Turn off bold character formatting. Use the Paragraph dialog box to set the left paragraph indent to 1.25 inches and the right indent to 1.25 inches. Because the right margin indent is underneath the right tab stop, it is easier to move it by using the Paragraph dialog box than by clicking and dragging it on the Ruler.

12. Type *All entrees come with a side of refried beans, miso menudo, and pickled ginger.*

13. Press Return twice. Figure 8-6 shows the results. (Tab and paragraph marks are visible to indicate where to press Tab and Return.)

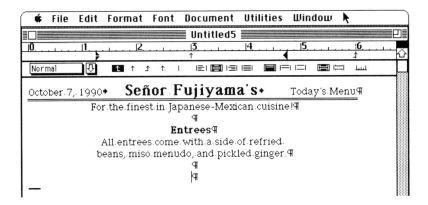

Figure 8-6. *The centered and right-aligned phrases of the first line are positioned by tab stops. Notice the tab-stop markers along the measure of the Ruler.*

Notice that the tab stops you set in the first paragraph allowed you to align text left, right, and centered, in the same paragraph.

ADDING TAB LEADERS

You can use the Tabs dialog box to add a leader to a tab stop. If you don't want to take the time to go through the Format menu and the Paragraph dialog box, you can double-click on any of the tab stops in the Ruler to open the Tabs dialog box.

The Ruler always appears with the Tabs dialog box, so you can see the tab stops for the currently selected paragraph set along the measure. Note that if you select several paragraphs that have different indents or tab stops, the bottom strip of the Ruler's measure appears gray. The tab stops and indents that appear in the gray strip are those of the first paragraph in the text block. Changing margins or tab stops in the Ruler affects *all* the selected paragraphs, not only the first paragraph.

To add a leader to a tab stop, first double-click on the tab icon on the measure. The Tabs dialog box opens and shows the type of tab stop, the leader it uses (which is probably ''None''), and its position (in inches) on the measure. To change the leader setting from None to a visible leader, click on the dotted-line, dashed-line, or solid-line button in the Leader section. You can then click on another tab stop and change its leader. Click on the OK button to close the dialog box and apply the new leader settings.

One section of the sample menu displays food prices. Set the tabs and leaders for that section as follows:

1. Reset the paragraph indents to 0 and 6 inches, set the paragraph alignment to left, and clear all tab stops from the Ruler. (To clear them, open the Tabs dialog box, click on the Clear All button, and then click on OK to close the box.)

2. Set a left tab at 0.25 inch on the Ruler.

3. Set a decimal tab at 2.5 inches.

4. Set a left tab at 3.25 inches.

5. Set a decimal tab at 5.5 inches.

6. Open the Tabs dialog box.

7. Click on the 2.5-inch tab on the Ruler and then click on the dotted-line button in the Leader section.

8. Click on the 5.5-inch tab on the Ruler and then click on the dotted-line button.

9. Click on the OK button to close the dialog box and apply the tab settings.

10. Press Tab and then type the first line of the menu, pressing Tab between each menu item and price: *Yakitori chorizo*, Tab, *7.95*, Tab, *Tripe tempura*, Tab, *10.50*. Figure 8-7 displays each tab mark.

11. Press Return to begin a new paragraph, and then enter the next two lines of the menu using the same technique. (Copy the text from Figure 8-7.) Press Return twice at the end of the "Entrees" section.

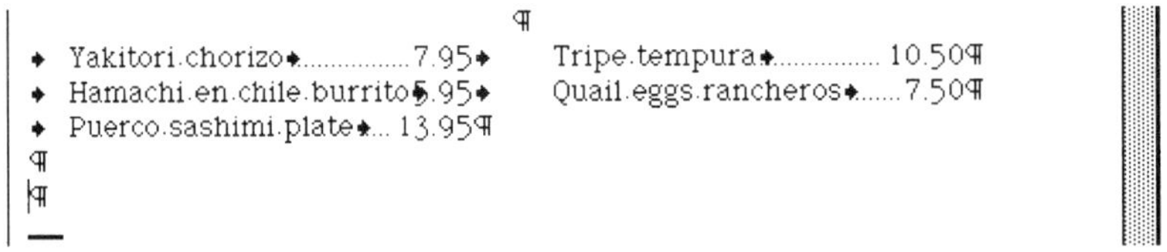

```
                                      ¶
 ◆ Yakitori.chorizo◆.............7.95◆   Tripe.tempura◆............. 10.50¶
 ◆ Hamachi.en.chile.burrito5.95◆   Quail.eggs.rancheros◆......7.50¶
 ◆ Puerco.sashimi.plate◆... 13.95¶
 ¶
 ¶
 ──
```

Figure 8-7. *Menu items and prices are connected by tab leaders.*

Notice that each time you press Tab to jump to a tab stop that has a leader, a dotted line stretches from the previous insertion point to the new location.

CHANGING TAB STOPS

You can easily change tab stops after you've inserted them. As you change tab stops, you change the position of the text aligned with them. This is a convenient tool: You can change the location of columns of text you've entered by moving tab stops to new positions. You can also change text alignment at a tab stop by changing the *type* of the tab stop, and you can change the type of leader preceding a tab stop by choosing a different leader. You can entirely remove a tab stop if necessary. Any text aligned with that tab stop would then move to the right, to the next tab stop.

Removing a Tab Stop

To remove a tab stop by using the Ruler, drag the tab-stop icon from the measure on the Ruler to any position below the measure and release the mouse button. The tab-stop icon disappears. To remove a tab stop by using the Tabs dialog box, click on a tab-stop icon on the Ruler and then click on the Clear button in the dialog box. To remove all the tab stops from the Ruler, click on the Clear All button in the Tabs dialog box.

Changing a Tab-Stop Position

To change a tab-stop position by using the Ruler, simply drag a tab-stop icon from one position on the measure to another; any text aligned with that tab stop moves with the tab-stop icon to its new position. To change a tab-stop position by using the Tabs dialog box, double-click on the tab-stop icon on the Ruler's measure, and then type a new value (in inches) in the Position text box in the lower right corner of the dialog box. Click on the Set button; Word moves the tab stop to the position you entered.

Try moving a tab stop in the last three paragraphs you entered, as follows:

1. Select the three lines of menu items beginning with ''Yakitori,'' ''Hamachi,'' and ''Puerco.''

2. Move the left tab stop at the 0.25 mark on the Ruler to the 0.5 mark. All the text in the first column moves with the mark.

3. Return the tab stop to the 0.25 position. All the text moves back to its original position.

Notice that changing the tab stops moved columns of text only in the paragraphs you selected.

Changing Tab-Stop Alignment

To change the text alignment of a tab stop by using the Ruler, first remove the tab-stop icon from the measure and then replace it with a different type of tab-stop icon. To change text alignment by using the Tabs dialog box, double-click on the desired tab-stop marker on the measure, click on a different button in the Type section of the Tabs dialog box, and then click on the

Set button. As soon as you change the alignment, all the text aligned at that tab stop changes its alignment to match the selected tab-stop type.

Changing a Tab-Stop Leader

To change a tab-stop leader, you must use the Tabs dialog box. Click on the desired tab-stop marker on the measure, click on a leader option in the Leader section, and then click on the Set button. If you click on the None option, you remove the leader completely. Once you change a tab-stop leader, all leaders assigned to that tab stop change to the new leader.

Completing the Sample Menu

To complete the sample menu, enter the next two sections of text as you did the first section and then finish by using a new tabbing technique. Take the following steps:

1. Turn on bold character formatting and change the paragraph alignment to centered.

2. Type *Side Dishes* and press Return twice.

3. Turn off the bold character formatting and change the paragraph alignment to left. Type the next two lines of text, pressing Tab where you see the tab marks in Figure 8-8.

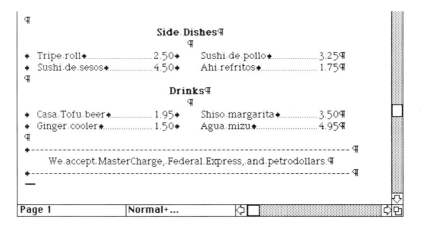

Figure 8-8. *The last section of the sample menu uses tab leaders to create two lines of dashes.*

4. Press Return twice to finish the "Side Dishes" section.

5. Enter the next section, "Drinks," as you entered the previous section. When you finish, press Return twice.

6. Clear all tab stops from the Ruler and then drag a right-align tab stop to the 6-inch mark, directly on the right margin marker.

7. Use the Tabs dialog box to turn on the dashed-line tab leader for the tab stop you inserted and then click on the OK button to close the dialog box.

8. Press Tab. A dashed line appears across the width of the page.

9. Press Return to begin a new paragraph and then set the paragraph alignment to centered.

10. Type the last sentence and press Return.

11. Press Tab to create a dashed line across the width of the page.

You finished Señor Fujiyama's menu by using a tab stop as a convenient way to add a dashed line across the width of the page. Tab leaders provide alternatives to the line patterns offered as paragraph borders.

Now that you've learned how to handle tabs, you should know most of what there is to know about paragraph formatting. In Chapter 9, "Headers and Footers," you'll learn how to add to your documents sections of text that number and identify pages.

LOVE,

Leo

Chapter 9

Headers and Footers

A document of more than one or two pages needs identification on each page to help readers navigate the document and locate particular elements. Word identifies pages with *headers* and *footers*, two features that label the top and bottom of each document page.

In this chapter you'll learn to create headers and footers that include page numbers, the date and the time, and any other text you want. You'll learn how to set header and footer positions on a page, suppress them on the first page, and create alternating headers and footers for subsequent pages. You'll also learn how to preview headers and footers before you print your document.

SETTING UP WORD

Before you begin working with the examples in this chapter, check to be sure that Word shows full menus, as follows:

1. If you haven't done so already, turn your computer on and start Word.

2. Open the Edit menu, and if the Full Menus command appears, choose it to set full menus. If the Short Menus command appears instead of the Full Menus command, full menus are already set, and you can close the menu without choosing any commands.

Because headers and footers are intended for multiple-page documents, the sample document for this chapter is a three-page report. The content of the document is not important for this discussion, so you can use the Copy and

Paste commands to duplicate a single paragraph 10 times to create the body of the document. Take the following steps:

1. Set paragraph alignment to centered and set character formatting to bold, 24-point text. Type *Reiteration Report,* and then press Return to begin a new paragraph.

2. Set paragraph formatting to insert a blank line before each paragraph.

3. Change the character size to 12-point and type *by Randall Redux.* Press Return.

4. Set paragraph alignment to left aligned and set line spacing to double spaced. Turn off bold character emphasis.

5. Type the text of the paragraph shown in Figure 9-1, and press Return at the end of the paragraph.

Reiteration Report¶

by Randall Redux¶

Researchers in rural regions relate repetitious renderings of regional revelations..."Rack and ruin!" rant reports..."Rubbish," reply rational readers..."Rout and remorse" repeat reports...Readers rejected reports; reports relinquished reliability...Repeated reporting rates reservations; recent ratings reveal retreating revenue for rumor rags... Repeating:¶

Figure 9-1. *Enter the paragraph that follows the header and duplicate it 10 times.*

6. Select the paragraph you typed, and choose *Copy* from the Edit menu.

7. Move the insertion point to the beginning of the blank line following the paragraph.

8. Press Command-V 10 times to paste 10 copies of the paragraph into the document.

The resulting document should be three pages long.

After you add headers and footers to this document, the finished document looks like the one shown in Figure 9-2.

Reiteration Report

by Randall Redux

Researchers in rural regions relate repetitious renderings of regional revelations. "Rack and ruin!" rant reports. "Rubbish," reply rational ~~renorts.~~ Readers rejected

Researchers in rural regions

revelations. "Rack and ruin!" rant reports. "Rubbish," reply rational

readers. "Rout and remorse" repeat reports. Readers rejected

reports; reports relinquished reliability. Repeated reporting rates

Redundant Research—Rights Reserved

2   Reiteration Report   11/27/90

reservations; recent ratings reveal retreating revenue for rumor rags. Repeating:

Researchers in rural regions relate repetitious renderings of regional revelations. "Rack and ruin!" rant reports. "Rubbish," reply rational ~~remorse" repeat reports.~~ Readers rejected

Researchers in rural reg-

revelations. "Rack and ruin!" rant reports. "Rubbish," reply rational

readers. "Rout and remorse" repeat reports. Readers rejected

reports; reports relinquished reliability. Repeated reporting rates

Redundant Research—Rights Reserved

(continued)

Figure 9-2. *The finished report's headers and footers identify and number its pages.*

Figure 9-2. *continued*

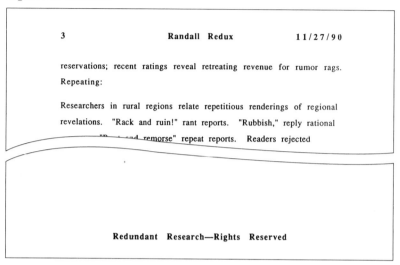

WHAT ARE HEADERS AND FOOTERS?

A *header* is a banner of text that appears at the top of each page of a printed document. A typical header includes the name of the document, the page number, and other information such as the author's name or the date on which the document was created. A header in Word can be as short or as long as you want, from a lone page number to a full page of text. You can apply character formatting and paragraph formatting to a header as you do to the main body of text. You can also add graphics.

A *footer* serves the same purpose as a header but appears at the bottom of each document page. Some documents use footers in place of headers, displaying page numbers and title information at the bottom of each page. Other documents use footers in addition to headers, displaying document information such as copyright notices or company names. A footer in Word—like a header—can be as long or as short as you want. You can apply character and paragraph formatting and add graphics to a footer. And you can insert both a footer and a header on the same page.

Footers and headers don't normally appear in the main document window on your monitor because they break up the body of your text and make editing difficult. To create and edit headers and footers, you open a special window called the *header window* (to create a header) or the *footer window* (to create a footer). Later in this chapter you'll learn how to view headers and footers with the rest of the document.

CREATING HEADERS AND FOOTERS

To open a header or footer window, choose *Open Header* or *Open Footer* from the Document menu. Choosing *Open Header* opens the header window, whose title bar displays the name of your document with the tag ''.Header.'' Choosing *Open Footer* opens the footer window, whose title bar displays the name of your document with the tag ''.Footer.'' Both windows contain the same elements, and you work with them in the same way. The only difference is that anything you enter or insert in the Header window appears as a header on the document pages, and anything you enter or insert in the Footer window appears as a footer on the document pages. Figure 9-3 shows a header window.

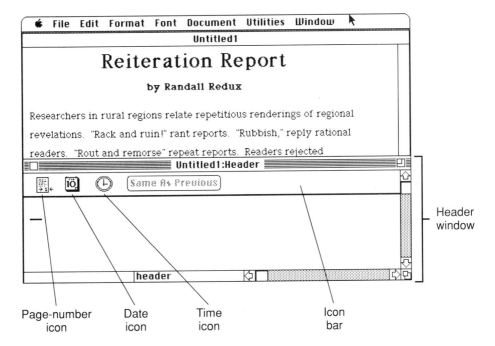

Figure 9-3. *Enter the contents of a header in the header window, which appears in the lower half of the screen.*

The bar at the top of the header window or the footer window is the *icon bar*. Clicking on one of the three icons at the left end of the icon bar instructs Word to insert the current page number, date, or time in the header. To the right of these icons is the Same As Previous button for use in documents containing more than one section.

The text area below the icon bar contains an insertion point and an end-of-document mark like those in the main document window. As you type in the text area, you enter text that becomes part of the header, not part of the body of the document.

Entering Text

You enter text in a header window or the footer window in the same way in which you enter text in the main document window. You can apply character and paragraph formatting by using the Ruler and the commands in the Format menu. Word presets two tab stops on the Ruler's measure for creating headers and footers. It sets a center-align tab stop in the middle of the measure and a right-align tab stop at the right end of the measure. Use these tab stops to center text or to right-align it at the right margin. If you prefer, you can remove these tab stops and set your own.

Entering Page Numbers, Date, and Time

Some information you enter in a header or a footer changes from page to page: the current page number, date, and time. You can click on the icons in the icon bar to insert this information. Move the insertion point to the location in the header or the footer where you want the information to appear, and then click on the appropriate icon. Word inserts the chosen information at the insertion point's location. Clicking on the three icons instructs Word to insert the following information:

- Clicking on the page-number icon inserts a number that increases by one on each subsequent page.

- Clicking on the date icon inserts the current date. Each time you open a header window or a footer window that contains an inserted date, Word reads the Macintosh's internal clock and inserts the current date in this location. Each time you print the document, Word prints the current date.

■ Clicking on the time icon inserts the current time. Each time you open a header window or a footer window containing an inserted time, Word changes the time to match that of the Macintosh's internal clock. Each time you print the document, Word inserts the time of printing.

Word treats each inserted page number, date, or time in a header or a footer as a single character. Although several characters might appear on the screen (especially in a date or a time), you can select the page number, date, or time only as a single character. You can format inserted information by selecting it and applying character formatting to it as you would to any other character.

Entering a Header

Try entering a header for your document. Take the following steps:

1. Choose *Open Header* from the Document window to open the header window.

2. Click on the page-number icon to insert a page number. The number *1* appears in boldface on the left side of the header field.

3. Press Tab to jump to the center-align tab stop in the middle of the line and then type *Reiteration Report*. The text appears centered on the line.

4. Press Tab to jump to the right-align tab stop at the end of the line and insert the date by clicking on the date icon. The current date appears right aligned at the right margin.

5. Select the entire first line of the header and apply bold character formatting.

6. Close the header window by clicking on its close box.

Entering a Footer

You create a footer in the same way that you create a header except that you enter text in the footer window instead of in the header window. Try adding a footer to your document. Take the following steps.

1. Choose *Open Footer* from the Document window to open the footer window.

2. Press Tab to move to the center-align tab stop, turn bold character formatting on, and type *Redundant Research—Rights Reserved.* (Press Shift-Option-hyphen to produce an *em dash.* The em dash is the typesetter's equivalent of two dashes.)

3. Close the footer window by clicking on its close box.

Note that when you create a header or a footer, pressing Return at the end of the last line adds a blank line below the last line of text, which increases the height of the header or footer and takes space from the main body of text.

PREVIEWING HEADERS AND FOOTERS

When you close the header window or the footer window, Word remembers the header or footer you created and adds it to the pages when you print the document. You don't normally see the header or the footer in the main text window. If you'd like to see headers and footers as they appear on the page, you can use Word's Page View feature. (You will learn how to use Page View in Chapter 20, "Views, Outlines, and Document Windows," but you can sneak a peek and use it here so you can see your header and footer handiwork.)

Using Page View

The document view you've seen up to this point is called *Galley View.* It shows all the pages of a document as one long page that you can scroll through. Pages are separated by page-break lines in Galley View. In Page View, the document window changes to show each page of the document, including the edges of each page and any headers and footers you've created. To turn Page View on, simply choose *Page View* from the Document menu. To turn it off and return to Galley View, choose *Page View* again. Try it now on your sample document:

1. Choose *Page View* from the Document menu to turn *Page View* on.

2. Drag the vertical scroll box to the top of the scroll bar. The document view moves upward so you can see the top edge of the page and the header you created earlier, as shown in Figure 9-4.

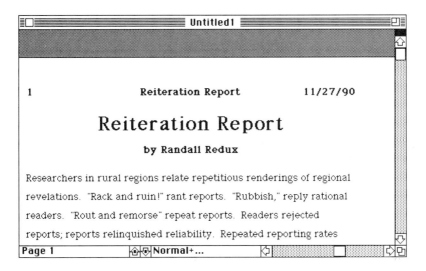

Figure 9-4. *Page View shows the top or bottom of each page, revealing any header or footer you've created.*

3. Click on the vertical scroll bar below the scroll box to move the document view downward one screen at a time until you reach the bottom of the page. You see your footer there, followed by the bottom edge of the page.

4. Click on the scroll bar below the scroll box again to move the document view downward another screen. Your view jumps to the beginning of text on the next page, skipping the header at the top of the page.

5. Click above the scroll box to move the document view to the top of the second page. You see the second-page header there. Notice that the screen displays the page number ''2.''

6. Continue scrolling through the rest of the document, viewing the headers and the footers on each page.

7. When you're finished, choose *Page View* from the Document menu to turn Page View off.

Note: Because Word operates differently when Page View is on, it's important that you return Word to Galley View to re-create the examples in this book unless they specifically ask for Page View.

HEADER AND FOOTER OPTIONS

You might want to display different headers and footers on different pages of your document. For example, the title page of the report might look better if you eliminated the header above the report title. Or you might want to display different headers on alternating pages throughout your document. Word allows you to create special treatments for headers and footers by choosing options in the Section and Document dialog boxes. The following sections explain how to do so.

Creating Headers and Footers for a Title Page

To create a special header and footer for a title page, you first open the Section dialog box, shown in Figure 9-5, by choosing *Section* from the Format menu. The Section dialog box appears. Click on the First Page Special option in the Header/Footer area (in the lower right quarter of the dialog box) to turn it on or off; it shows an X in the check box when it's turned on. When the option is set as you want it, click on the OK button to close the dialog box and apply the option.

If you turn the First Page Special option on, two new commands appear in the Document menu: Open First Header and Open First Footer. They

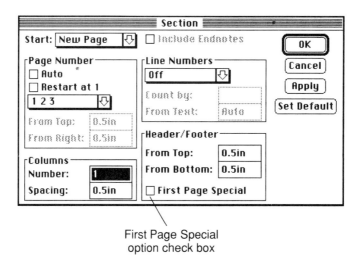

First Page Special
option check box

Figure 9-5. *Open the Section dialog box to set the First Page Special option.*

appear because your document now has two headers and two footers. The first-page header and the first-page footer contain the header and the footer that appear only on the first page of the document. The regular header and footer contain the header and the footer that appear on all subsequent pages.

To create the first-page header, choose *Open First Header* from the Document menu to open the First Header window. You enter text and fields in this window as you do when you create the regular header. Close the window when you finish. Anything you enter appears as the header on the first page only. If you enter nothing in the text area, no header appears on the first page.

You create the first-page footer by choosing *Open First Footer* from the Document menu to open the First Footer window. Any footer you create in this window appears only on the first page.

Try creating a blank header for the title page of the sample report and set the title-page footer to match the regular footer. Take the following steps:

1. Choose *Section* from the Format menu to open the Section dialog box.

2. Turn the First Page Special option on, and then click on the OK button to close the dialog box.

3. Choose *Open First Footer* from the Document menu to open the First Footer window.

4. Enter the footer used in the rest of the document: Apply bold character formatting, press Tab once to center the text, and then type *Redundant Research—Rights Reserved.*

5. Close the First Footer window.

Notice that you didn't really need to open the First Header window to create a blank header for the first page. The first-page header will be blank unless you enter text in the First Header window. You wanted the first-page header to be blank, so you didn't need to enter anything—you simply went on to the footer. The first-page footer will also be blank unless you enter text in the First Footer window, so you had to open the window and duplicate the footer used in the rest of the document. To see how your first-page header and first-page footer appear on the page, turn Page View on and scroll through the document. After you finish, turn Page View off.

Creating Headers and Footers for Facing Pages

If you create a Word document designed to print on facing pages (to be printed on both sides of the paper and then bound), you can display alternating headers and footers on even-numbered and odd-numbered pages. Displaying different headers and footers on facing pages allows you to place the page number in the outer corner of each page—in the upper right corner of odd-numbered pages and in the upper left corner of even-numbered pages. Headers and footers can also include alternating text on facing pages. You can display the document title on even-numbered pages and the section title on odd-numbered pages.

To create headers and footers for facing pages, you first open the Document dialog box, shown in Figure 9-6, by choosing *Document* from the Format menu. Click on the Even/Odd Headers option (located on the left side of the dialog box, about a third of the way from the top) to turn it on or off; it displays an X in the check box when it's turned on. When the option is set as you want it, click on the OK button to close the dialog box and apply the option.

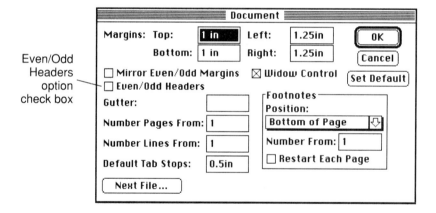

Even/Odd
Headers
option
check box

Figure 9-6. *Open the Document dialog box to set the Even/Odd Headers option.*

If you turn the Even/Odd Headers option on and then open the Document menu, you'll find that Word has replaced the Open Header and Open Footer commands with four new commands: Open Even Header, Open Even Footer, Open Odd Header, and Open Odd Footer. As you might suspect, the Open Even Header and Open Even Footer commands open windows that allow you to create headers and footers for even-numbered pages, and the Open Odd Header and Open Odd Footer commands open windows that allow you to create headers and footers for odd-numbered pages. To enter text and information for these new headers and footers, you open the header window or the footer window by choosing the appropriate command from the Document menu and then typing text or clicking on the icons in the icon bar as you do for other headers and footers.

Now try setting up the sample report's headers and footers for facing pages. Take the following steps:

1. Choose *Document* from the Format menu to open the Document dialog box.

2. Turn on the Even/Odd Headers option, and then click on the OK button to close the dialog box.

3. Choose *Open Odd Header* from the Document menu to open the odd header window.

4. Delete the text currently in the window.

5. Click on the time icon to enter the current time.

6. Press Tab to move to the center of the line and type *Randall Redux*.

7. Press Tab to move to the right end of the line, and click on the page-number icon to enter the current page number.

8. Select the entire line of text, and turn on bold character formatting to set the text in boldface.

9. Choose *Open Even Header* from the Document menu to open the Even Header window. (Note that you don't need to close the Odd Header window first; Word replaces it with the Even Header window.)

10. Delete the text currently in the window.

11. Click on the page-number icon to insert a page number to the left of the header.

12. Press Tab to jump to the center tab stop in the middle of the line and type *Reiteration Report*. It appears centered on the line.

13. Press Tab to jump to the right-align tab stop at the end of the line, and click on the date icon to enter the date. Today's date appears right aligned at the right margin.

14. Select the entire line of text and turn on bold character formatting to set the text in boldface.

15. Close the Even Header window.

16. Save this document (using the Save As command in the File menu) with the name "Redundancy." You'll use the report as a sample document in the next chapter.

Your document now has an odd-numbered page header with the time of printing in the upper left corner of the page, the author's name centered at the top of the page, and the page number in the upper right corner (the outer corner of an odd page). The even-numbered page header shows the page number in the upper left corner of the page (the outer corner of an even page), the name of the report centered at the top of the page, and the date right aligned at the right margin.

To see how your new headers and footers appear in the document, turn Page View on and scroll through the pages. The headers and the footers should look like the ones shown in Figure 9-2, at the beginning of this chapter. Turn Page View off when you finish.

CONTROLLING PAGE NUMBERS

When you insert a page number in a header or a footer, Word numbers pages using Arabic numerals, beginning with page 1. If you want to begin numbering using a number other than 1 or use letters or Roman numerals to number the pages, you can change page numbering in the Section and Document dialog boxes.

Setting the Beginning Page Number

You can set a new beginning page number for a document in the Document dialog box. Type the new beginning page number in the Number Pages From text box (located on the left side of the dialog box, halfway down from the top), and then click on the OK button to close the dialog box. Word sets the new beginning page number you entered. For example, if you entered the number 6 in the Number Pages From text box, Word numbers the first page of the document 6 and numbers the following pages 7, 8, 9, and so on. If the first page doesn't display a page number, the following pages are still numbered 7, 8, 9, and so on.

Changing the Page-Numbering Format

You can change the page-numbering format for a document in the Section dialog box. The Page Number area (located on the left side of the dialog box, close to the top) contains a list box called the number format list box, shown in Figure 9-7. It displays the page-numbering format currently in use.

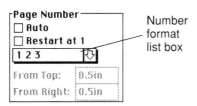

Figure 9-7. *Choose a page-numbering format in the number format list box.*

Choose the page-numbering format you want by selecting a numbering system in the list box. You click and hold on it and choose a format as you choose a command from a menu. You can choose the Arabic system (1, 2, 3), uppercase Roman numerals (I, II, III), lowercase Roman numerals (i, ii, iii), uppercase letters (A, B, C), or lowercase letters (a, b, c). When you've set the numbering format you want, click on the OK button to close the dialog box.

The two remaining options in the Page Number area offer additional page-numbering format possibilities. The Auto option, along with the From Top and From Right text boxes, lets you position a simple page number anywhere on the page without creating a header or a footer. And you can use the Restart at 1 option when you learn how to separate a document into sections in Chapter 16, "Section Formatting." You'll find more information about these features in *Reference to Microsoft Word* under the heading "Sections."

SETTING HEADER AND FOOTER LOCATIONS

Word's default header location begins 0.5 inch from the top edge of the page and extends downward as far as the text and graphics extend in the header. Word's default footer location begins 0.5 inch from the bottom of the page and extends upward as far as the text and graphics extend. You can change the locations by entering new values in the Header/Footer area of the Section dialog box, shown in Figure 9-8.

Figure 9-8. *Enter new values in the Header/Footer area to change header and footer positions.*

Enter new values in the From Top and From Bottom text boxes to set new header and footer positions. The value you enter in the From Top text box equals the distance from the top of the page to the top of the header, and the value you enter in the From Bottom text box equals the distance from the bottom of the page to the bottom of the footer. For example, if you enter *2* in the From Top text box, all headers (including the first-page header and odd and even headers) begin 2 inches from the top of the page. Entering *1.5* in the From Bottom text box positions all footers in the document 1.5 inches from the bottom of the page.

As you move headers and footers toward the middle of the page, you shrink the main text area so that Word can't fit as much of the main text body on each page. You can set the headers and the footers to appear closer to the top and the bottom of the page, which gives each page more text area, but be careful not to set a distance of less than 0.5 inch if you use a laser printer. Many laser printers can't print within 0.5 inch of the page edge and might ignore the part of the header or the footer that falls within the 0.5-inch area.

You have now learned how Word handles headers and footers and how you can use them to identify the pages of your documents. In the next chapter you'll learn how Word divides the text of a document into pages and how you can control the process to create the page breaks you want.

Chapter 10

Creating Pages

As you learned in previous chapters, Word 4 breaks long documents into pages before printing, a process called *pagination*. In this chapter you'll learn how to control Word's pagination: to set your own page breaks, to protect parts of a document from page breaks you don't want, and to choose how Word sets page breaks during pagination. You'll also learn how to preview and adjust Word's page breaks before you print.

SETTING UP WORD

Before you begin working with the examples in this chapter, check to be sure that Word shows full menus, as follows:

1. If you haven't done so already, turn your computer on and start Word.

2. Open the Edit menu, and if the Full Menus command appears, choose it to set full menus. If the Short Menus command appears instead of the Full Menus command, full menus are already set, and you can close the menu without choosing any commands.

You can use the three-page document you created and saved in the preceding chapter, "Headers and Footers," for the repagination examples in this chapter. Open the file named "Redundancy."

HOW WORD SETS PAGE BREAKS

Word treats a long document stored in the Macintosh's memory as one very long page through which you can scroll. When you instruct Word to print,

Word breaks the document into separate pages to be printed on separate sheets of paper.

To calculate where to break each page, Word first determines the amount of vertical space available on each page. It adds the measures of the top and bottom page margins—usually 1 inch each—and subtracts the total from the height of the page. It checks for headers, footers, and footnotes (which you'll learn about in Chapter 14, "Creating Footnotes"), computes their total height, and subtracts that value from the height of the page. The result equals the amount of vertical space available for text on each page.

Word then computes the maximum number of lines that can fit in the main text area of the first page, and counting from the beginning of the document, it inserts a page break after the last line that can fit. The page break appears in your document as a dotted line across the width of the text area. Word then determines the maximum number of lines that will fit in the main text area of the second page and inserts another page break there. Word continues this pagination process until it reaches the end of the document, inserting page breaks so that each page contains as much text as possible but not so much that the text overruns headers, footers, footnotes, or margins.

Automatic Page Breaks

Word's page breaks are flexible. If you edit or format the document after page breaks are in place—perhaps by inserting or cutting text in the middle of a page—you disrupt the pagination by creating too much or too little text per page. Word moves the page breaks, adjusting for any changes, and repaginates the document before printing it. These flexible page breaks are called *automatic page breaks*.

Background Repagination

Word does not normally repaginate a document until you choose the Print or Print Preview command (which you'll learn about later in this chapter) from the File menu or the Page View or Repaginate Now command from the Document menu. If you want Word to continually repaginate a document as you make changes, you can turn Word's *background repagination* feature on by choosing *Preferences* from the Edit menu and clicking on the Background Repagination option in the Preferences dialog box, shown in Figure 10-1.

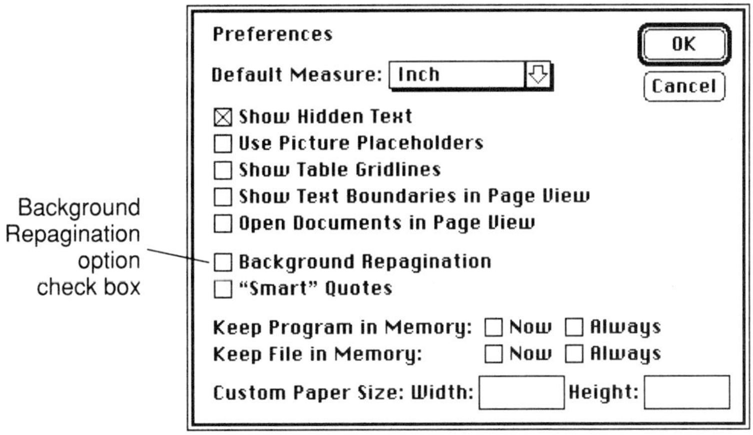

Background
Repagination
option
check box

```
┌─────────────────────────────────────────────────┐
│ Preferences                      ┌──────────┐    │
│                                  │   OK     │    │
│ Default Measure: │ Inch      │⬇│ └──────────┘    │
│                                  ┌──────────┐    │
│                                  │ Cancel   │    │
│ ⊠ Show Hidden Text               └──────────┘    │
│ ☐ Use Picture Placeholders                       │
│ ☐ Show Table Gridlines                           │
│ ☐ Show Text Boundaries in Page View              │
│ ☐ Open Documents in Page View                    │
│                                                  │
│ ☐ Background Repagination                        │
│ ☐ "Smart" Quotes                                 │
│                                                  │
│ Keep Program in Memory: ☐ Now ☐ Always           │
│ Keep File in Memory:    ☐ Now ☐ Always           │
│                                                  │
│ Custom Paper Size: Width:│    │ Height:│    │    │
└─────────────────────────────────────────────────┘
```

Figure 10-1. *Turn background repagination on and off in the Preferences dialog box.*

When background repagination is turned on, Word continually repaginates the document as you work with it. When you enter enough text to fill a page, Word inserts a page break on the screen. If you add to or subtract from the document, Word relocates the page break to adjust for your changes. If you turn background repagination off, Word stops inserting page breaks as you enter text. Any page breaks already in your document remain where they are, regardless of editing and formatting changes, until you choose the Print, Page View, Print Preview, or Repaginate Now command.

Try using background repagination while adding some text to the sample report:

1. Choose *Preferences* from the Edit menu to open the Preferences dialog box.

2. Turn the Background Repagination option on.

3. Click on the OK button to close the dialog box.

4. Scroll through the report until you find the first page break.

5. Move the insertion point to a few lines above the page break and type two or three lines of text. (Any text will do.) Word moves the page break upward several lines to accommodate the new text.

6. Choose *Preferences* from the Edit menu to reopen the Preferences dialog box.

7. Turn off the Background Repagination option, and click on the OK button to close the dialog box.

8. Enter several more lines of text.

Notice that the page break on the screen no longer changes its position as you add new lines to the page. In fact, it might disappear completely once it's been forced from its position following the last line of text.

The Repaginate Now Command

Choosing *Repaginate Now* from the Document menu instructs Word to repaginate the document. Although you don't need to use the Repaginate Now command if background repagination is turned on, you can use it to see where page breaks occur when background repagination is turned off. Try using the Repaginate Now command on the sample report by choosing *Repaginate Now* from the Document menu. The page break reappears on the screen, moving up to accommodate the new lines you previously entered. Now turn background repagination on again to complete the remaining examples in this chapter:

1. Choose *Preferences* from the Edit menu to open the Preferences dialog box.

2. Turn the Background Repagination option on, and click on the OK button to close the dialog box.

If you decide you like the background repagination feature, you can leave it turned on as you work through the remaining chapters in this book; it won't alter the results of any of the examples.

SETTING YOUR OWN PAGE BREAKS

When Word paginates a document, the page breaks might not always fall where you want them. For example, if you create a document that comprises several chapters, you might want to begin each chapter on a new page, leaving the last page of each chapter short if necessary. Because Word tries to fill each page as it paginates, the beginning of a chapter might appear in the middle of a page if the last page of the previous chapter wasn't filled. You can adjust for this by inserting your own page breaks, called *manual page breaks,* in a document. Manual page breaks don't move during repagination; they force Word to begin a new page whether or not the previous page is filled.

Inserting a Manual Page Break

To insert a manual page break, move the insertion point to the beginning of the line you want to appear at the top of a page, and choose *Insert Page Break* from the Document window or use the keyboard shortcut Shift-Enter. A manual-page-break line (a closely spaced dotted line) appears across the width of the screen above that text line. (Note that a manual page break appears as a closely spaced dotted line and an automatic page break appears as an open-spaced dotted line.)

To delete a page break, simply move the insertion point to the beginning of the text line following the page break and press Delete.

Try adding manual page breaks to the sample report:

1. Move the insertion point to the beginning of the line immediately preceding an automatic page break.

2. Press Shift-Enter. A manual page break appears above the line, and the automatic page break moves downward to a new location, one full page beyond the new manual break.

3. Move the insertion point to the beginning of the line immediately preceding the manual page break you entered, and press Shift-Enter to insert a new manual page break. A second manual page break appears.

The line between the two manual page breaks will appear alone on a page when you print the document.

Controlling Word's Automatic Page Breaks

Inserting a manual page break instructs Word to begin a new page at that location. An alternative is to select a paragraph and specify that Word insert an automatic page break before or after that paragraph when it paginates.

Placing a paragraph at the top of a page

As you learned in Chapter 7, "Paragraph Formatting," you can instruct Word to insert an automatic page break before a paragraph by choosing the Paragraph command in the Format menu and turning on the Page Break Before option in the Format Paragraph dialog box. Word inserts an automatic page break before the selected paragraph when it paginates the document. To remove the automatic page break, select the paragraph and then turn the Page Break Before option off.

Placing a paragraph on its own page

To set a paragraph so that it appears alone on a page, turn on the Page Break Before option for that paragraph and for the following paragraph.

AVOIDING UNWANTED PAGE BREAKS

A document might contain several parts that shouldn't be separated by an automatic page break. You can control where Word breaks pages within paragraphs by setting a page-break format in the Paragraph dialog box. You can also select specific parts of your document, including text blocks and graphics captions, to be "protected" from page breaks.

Widow and Orphan Control

When Word paginates a document, it checks to be sure it doesn't create *widows* and *orphans*. A widow is a single line separated from the end of a paragraph and placed alone at the top of the next page. An orphan is a single line separated from the beginning of a paragraph and left standing alone at the bottom of the preceding page.

To avoid creating widows and orphans, Word checks the lines it creates when it splits a paragraph. If an orphan exists, Word moves the page break upward by one line, moving the orphan to the beginning of the next page, where the line rejoins the paragraph. If a widow exists, Word moves the page break upward by one line, moving another line of the paragraph to join the widow on the next page. Note that Word can't protect paragraphs of two or three lines against widows and orphans. No matter how you split the paragraph, a widow, an orphan, or both can occur. You can protect short paragraphs manually, however, as the next section describes.

If you don't want Word to check for widows and orphans, you can turn this feature off by choosing *Document* from the Format menu to open the Document dialog box, shown in Figure 10-2. Turn off the Widow Control option (located in the upper center of the dialog box), and click on the OK button to close the dialog box.

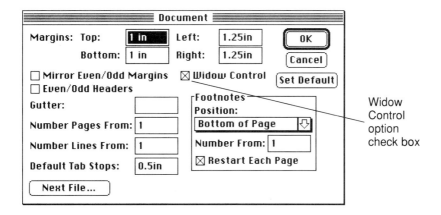

Widow
Control
option
check box

Figure 10-2. *Turn the Widow Control option on or off in the Document dialog box.*

Protecting Blocks of Text from Page Breaks

You learned in Chapter 7, "Paragraph Formatting," that the Keep Lines Together option in the Paragraph dialog box protects a paragraph from being split by a page break. You also learned that the Keep With Next ¶ option (also in the Paragraph dialog box) binds a selected paragraph to the following paragraph so that Word doesn't insert a page break between them. You can combine these options to protect blocks of text from page breaks. For example, if you select three paragraphs and turn both options on, you create a block of three paragraphs that are protected from being split or separated from each other. In addition, you bind the third paragraph to the following paragraph so that Word doesn't insert a page break between them. Using this method, it's possible to protect a block so large that it won't fit on a single page, in which case Word must split the protected block with a page break.

Protecting Graphics from Page Breaks

Word never splits a graphic with a page break because it treats the graphic as a single character. However, a page break might separate a graphic from a caption that describes it. To bind a graphic and its caption together and protect them from being separated by a page break, select the graphic and then turn on the Keep With Next ¶ option in the Paragraph dialog box. (This protection works only if the graphic and caption are two separate, adjacent paragraphs.)

USING PRINT PREVIEW

In Galley View, Word can show you where page breaks occur, but it doesn't display the page layout. You don't see headers and footers or page margins. If you choose *Page View*, you can see the page layout, but you can't see a full page at one time on most Mac monitors. To see a full-page preview of the document on the monitor before you print, you can use the Print Preview feature.

When you choose *Print Preview* from the File menu, the Print Preview window, shown in Figure 10-3, displays your document as it will appear when printed. The pages are reduced to fit in the window. Because the pages are reduced, you probably can't read the text, but you can see where the body, headers, footers, and footnotes appear on the pages. If the page layout needs adjusting, you can do so in the Print Preview window. Alternatively, you can close the Print Preview window and adjust the layout in the document window.

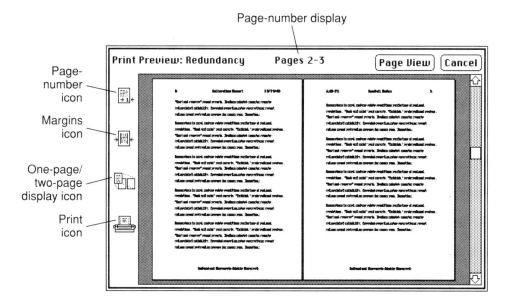

Figure 10-3. *The Print Preview window displays the full-page layout of your document pages.*

Paging Through the Document

To page through the document in the Print Preview window, use the scroll bar located on the right side of the window: Scrolling downward advances you through the pages; scrolling upward returns you back through the pages. The page-number display at the top of the window shows the current page location.

Adding a Page Number

The first icon on the left side of the Print Preview window is the *page-number icon*; use it to add page numbers to your document. When you click on the icon, the cursor turns into the number "1." You can move it onto the page in the window and click where you want to insert a page number. Word inserts a page number at that location on each page of your document. Adding a page number by clicking on this icon has the same effect as turning on the Automatic page number option—it adds a number without creating a header or a footer.

Changing Page Breaks and More

The second icon in the Print Preview window is the *margins icon*. When you click on it, Word adds dotted lines to the active page in the window, as shown in Figure 10-4. The dotted lines show the location of the page margins, the header and the footer (if they exist), the automatic page number (if there is one), page breaks, and other page elements described in the Print Preview section of the Microsoft Word manual. You can drag these elements to new locations with the pointer; when you do, the page-number area changes to show their location in inches from the upper and left edges of the page.

If you added an automatic page number to the document, the number appears as a small dotted rectangle. To change the position of an automatic page number, click on the margins icon and drag the page number to the new position. Click outside the limits of the page to update the screen image. To remove the page number completely, drag the icon off the page and then click outside the limits of the page.

A manual page break appears across the width of the page as a closely spaced dotted line. An automatic page break appears as an open-spaced dotted line, often so close to the bottom margin line that the two lines merge

Margin lines   Header box

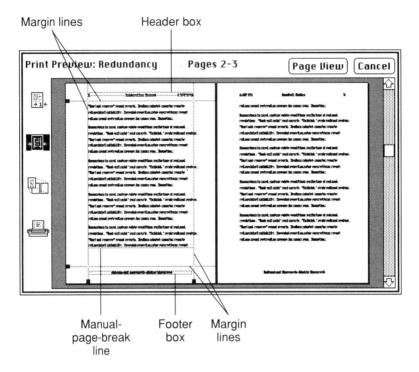

Manual-
page-break
line

Footer
box

Margin
lines

Figure 10-4. *When you click on the margins icon, the Print Preview window shows the location of page margins, the header and the footer (if they exist), the automatic page number (if one exists), page breaks, and other page elements.*

together, appearing as a dashed line. If you want to change the location of a page break, you can drag it upward or downward with the pointer to a new location. If you drag an automatic page break upward on a page, it turns into a manual page break. To remove a manual page break, drag it off the page and drop it in the gray area. Click outside the edges of the page to update the screen.

Headers and footers appear inside long, dotted rectangles at the top and the bottom of the page. To change their locations, drag them upward or downward to reposition them. You can't drag them below the top margin line or above the bottom margin line; if you could, you might cover the main text, with messy results. Click outside the edges of the page to update the screen.

The page margins appear on all four sides of the page. You can drag the margins to new positions. Chapter 17, ''Document Formatting,'' explains how margins affect your document and how to change margins in the Print Preview window.

When you're finished moving page elements, if you haven't already updated the screen image, click on the margins icon to turn it off. Word then repaginates and moves text around on the pages to match your changes.

One-Page and Two-Page Displays

The Print Preview window can show one or two pages of a document at a time. You can switch between the two display modes by clicking on the *one-page/two-page icon*, located below the margins icon. When the window displays a single page, the vertical scroll bar moves through a document one page at a time. When the window displays two pages, the vertical scroll bar moves through a document two pages at a time if the document is set for facing pages; otherwise, it scrolls one page at a time.

Printing from the Print Preview Window

The last icon in the Print Preview window is the *print icon*. If you click on it, Word opens the Print dialog box so you can print your document without leaving the Print Preview window.

Exiting from the Print Preview Window

Clicking on the two buttons in the upper right corner of the Print Preview window takes you out of the Print Preview window. Clicking on the Page View button closes the window, returns you to the document window, and turns on Page View so you can see the details of your page layout. In Page View, you can read the text on the page and make editing changes.

Clicking on the Cancel button closes the Print Preview window and returns you to your most recent view of the document in the document window.

Viewing the Sample Report

Use the print preview feature now to view your sample report:

1. Choose *Print Preview* from the File menu. Page 1 appears in the text window.

2. Click on the down arrow of the scroll bar. Page 2 of your document appears in the window.

3. Click on the one-page/two-page display icon to turn the two-page display on. Two pages of the report appear at the same time in the window.

4. Click on the margins icon. Page-margin lines, header and footer boxes, and page-break lines appear on page 3 of your document.

5. Click on page 2 (the left-side page of the two pages displayed). The page now shows margin lines.

6. Move the pointer to the combined bottom-margin/automatic-page-break line at the bottom of the page (it should appear as a dashed line instead of as a dotted line), and use the pointer to drag it up the page. As you drag, Word moves only the page-break line, not the margin line, and turns it into a manual-page-break line. The page-number display area shows the exact location of the page break in inches from the top of the page.

7. Drag the page break to a new location, higher on the page. Word repaginates the entire document to show you the new page break and clears all the text from below the new page break.

8. Drag the manual-page-break line off the page and drop it into the gray area. Word repaginates the entire document.

9. Click on the Cancel button to close the Print Preview window.

You've now learned how to control Word's page breaks in order to create the page layout you want. In the next chapter you'll learn some techniques for saving, opening, and printing finished documents.

Chapter 11

Saving, Opening, and Printing a Document

There comes a time in the life of every Word 4 document when you decide whether to print it, store it away for another day, or dismiss it forever in a flash of fleeting electrons so you can begin again. You'll learn how in this chapter.

This chapter discusses activities important to completing a Word document: saving and retrieving your work and printing your document. You'll learn how to store your documents in folders and on disks, how to save your documents so that you can use them with other programs, and how to delete document files already stored on disk.

The last section of this chapter discusses printing options. You'll learn how to choose a printer, how to print a limited number of pages of a document, and how to print several copies of a document.

SETTING UP WORD

Before you begin working with the examples in this chapter, check to be sure that Word shows full menus and that Page View is turned off, as follows:

1. If you haven't done so already, turn your computer on and start Word.

2. Open the Edit menu. If the Full Menus command appears, choose it to set full menus. If the Short Menus command appears instead of the

Full Menus command, full menus are already set, and you can close the menu without choosing any commands.

3. Open the Document menu, and if a check mark appears before the Page View command, choose it to turn Page View off.

To work with the examples in this chapter, you need a multiple-page document. Open the three-page report that you created in Chapter 9, "Headers and Footers," and saved as "Redundancy."

SAVING A DOCUMENT

As you learned in Chapter 3, "The First Session," saving a document is an important safeguard. It ensures that all your work won't disappear in an instant of interrupted electrical power. For effective protection, you should save frequently both as you work and before you turn your computer off. You can open your saved document later to continue your work, or you can recall previously completed documents to reuse them in a slightly altered form (a boon to teachers who use the same multiple-choice tests year after year).

Using the Save and Save As Commands

Both the Save and the Save As commands instruct Word to save documents. The first time you choose *Save* while working on a document, the Save As dialog box appears. Once you name the document and save it, choosing *Save* again saves the document on disk without opening the dialog box—Word replaces with the new version the disk file you last saved. Choosing *Save As*, on the other hand, opens the Save As dialog box every time you choose the command so that you can rename your document or set an option in the dialog box.

Entering a Document Name in the Save As Dialog Box

Choose the Save As command to open the Save As dialog box. It appears as shown in Figure 11-1.

In this case, Word proposes the name "Redundancy" in the Save Current Document As text box because you previously saved the document with that name. The text box would be blank if the document had never been saved.

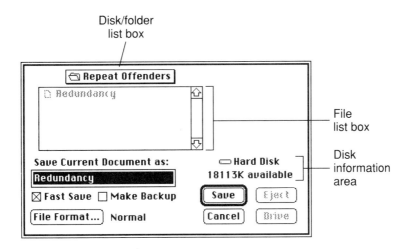

Figure 11-1. *Use the Save As dialog box to name a document and to save it in any folder on any disk.*

Type a new document name in the Save Current Document As text box. Then click on the Save button to close the dialog box and instruct Word to save the document, assigning it the new filename. Before it saves, Word checks to see whether another file in the current folder already has the new name, and if it finds one, it displays a dialog box asking whether you want to replace that file with the recently saved document. If you click on the Yes button, Word erases the old file and replaces it with the new one.

If you save a document once and then rename the document in the Save As dialog box and save it again, you'll have two copies of the document, one saved under the new name and one saved under the original name.

Changing Folders

When you click on the Save button in the Save As dialog box, Word saves the document in the folder and on the disk currently selected in the dialog box, usually the folder and the disk from which you started Word. The disk information at the right side of the dialog box displays the name of the currently selected disk, and the disk/folder list box shows the name of the folder currently selected. If no folder is selected, the disk/folder list box shows the name of the disk.

If you don't know where the current folder is located on a disk (folders can be contained within folders within folders), you can move the pointer to the disk/folder list box and hold down the mouse button; the list drops and shows the hierarchical order of folders at that location. You read the list from top to bottom, from your current folder to the folders that contain it, and finally to the disk that contains all the folders. Figure 11-2 shows an open disk/folder list box. The top name—*Circulation Reports*—is the current folder, and the name below it—*Market Research*—is the name of the folder that contains the folder Circulation Reports. The name listed below Market Research is *Enquire*, the name of the disk that contains all the folders.

The file list box below the disk/folder list box displays all the document files and folders contained in the current folder. Document filenames are marked with document-file icons that appear gray. You can't open document files from the Save As dialog box; they appear only for reference. Folder names are marked with file-folder icons and appear black. You can double-click on a folder icon to move into that folder. The disk/folder list box then displays the name of the folder you are currently in, and the file list box displays the names of all files and folders contained in that folder.

To move back to a previous folder or out of all folders to the disk, choose a name from the disk/folder list box. The disk/folder list box displays the name of the folder you moved to, and the file list box displays the names of all files and folders contained in that folder.

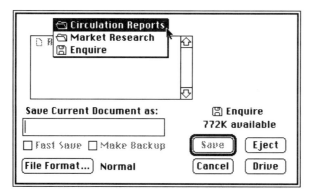

Figure 11-2. *Open the disk/folder list box, and read it from top to bottom to see the currently selected folder, the folders in which the selected folder is located, and the disk on which the selected folder resides.*

Changing Disks

You might not want to save a document on the currently selected disk. For example, after looking at the disk information at the right side of the dialog box, which lists the amount of free disk space in kilobytes, you might notice that the remaining space is not sufficient to store your document. If so, you can move to another disk.

If you have more than one disk drive connected to your Macintosh—for example, one hard-disk drive and two floppy-disk drives—you can move from one drive to another by clicking on the Drive button. With each click, Word moves from one drive to the next until it returns to the original drive. Each time it moves to a new drive, the disk/folder list box and the file list box display the contents of the disk in that drive. The disk-information display shows the name of the disk and the amount of free space available for storing documents.

If you switch to a floppy-disk drive and decide you don't want to use the floppy disk that's currently inserted in the drive, you can eject the disk by clicking on the Eject button. Word ejects the disk, and you can insert another disk. Once the disk is inserted, the dialog box displays the disk's name and its contents.

Note that if you insert an unformatted disk, the Mac displays a dialog box that asks whether you want to initialize the disk. Answer yes by clicking on either the One-Sided button or the Two-Sided button to indicate the type of disk you've inserted. Another dialog box appears, stating that this process will erase everything on the disk; click on the Erase button. Yet another dialog box appears, prompting you to name the disk. After you type a name and click on the OK button, the Mac initializes the disk, and the Save As dialog box soon displays the new disk's name in the disk-information area.

Using Save Options

The Save As dialog box offers three save options—Fast Save, Make Backup, and File Format. Setting these options lets you control the way Word saves your document.

Fast Save

When you first save a document, Word stores all the characters and formatting in a disk file. If you then add text to the document or otherwise revise it,

Word uses a feature called *Fast Save* the next time you choose *Save*. Fast Save saves only additions or changes to the original document, appending them to the document's disk file. Fast save is much faster than *Full Save*, which saves the entire contents of the document.

Word uses Fast Save when you choose *Save* more than once in a document. It continues to use Fast Save until the accumulated changes become too much for it to handle. Word then uses Full Save to incorporate all the changes and resave the entire document.

To instruct Word to use Fast Save, turn the Fast Save option on in the Save As dialog box; to instruct Word to use Full Save, turn the Fast Save option off. Although Full Save is slower, you'll find that it compacts the size of your document file, thereby allowing Word to work more quickly with the document.

Make Backup

Turning the Make Backup option on instructs Word to create two saved versions of your document—the most recently saved version and the previously saved version. When you first save a document, you name it and save it in a folder. The second time you save the document (after revising it or adding to it), choose *Save As* to open the Save As dialog box, turn the Make Backup option on, and press Return to save the document again. Word asks whether you want to replace the original file; click on the Yes button. Word then saves your updated document under the original document name and renames the old document file "Backup of" plus your document name. For example, the document named "Automobile" will be renamed "Backup of Automobile" when the "Automobile" file is updated. The new, updated file will be named "Automobile."

Make Backup remains turned on so that anytime you choose the Save command while working on that document, Word continues to turn the most recently saved version of your document into a backup file. You can turn the Make Backup option off by choosing the Save As command to open the Save As dialog box, clicking on the Make Backup option box, and then clicking on the Save button.

The Make Backup feature ensures that you always have two versions of your document: the most recently saved version and the previously saved version. A backup is useful if you make extensive changes to a document, save it, and then realize you don't want those changes. You can always open the backup file to retrieve the version of your document that doesn't include the changes.

Note: Because Word saves the full file when making a backup, you cannot use Fast Save when Make Backup is turned on.

File Format

Clicking on the File Format button, in the lower left corner of the Save dialog box, opens a second dialog box where you can choose different formats in which to save your document. In Word's usual format, labeled *Normal*, Word saves all characters and formatting in a form that it can read quickly and easily when you open the document again. Because not all programs can read this format, if you save a Word document in this format and then open the file in another text program, the program is likely to display the file as gibberish if it can translate it at all. You can make your document compatible with other programs by saving it in a compatible format. The following are Word's format options:

- *Text Only* saves a document as characters only, without any formatting. It inserts a single paragraph mark at the end of each paragraph. Almost all programs can read a text-only file, so use this format if you're transferring a document to a program you think might not be compatible with other file formats.

- *Text Only with Line Breaks* saves a document as characters only, without any formatting. It inserts a single paragraph mark at the end of each line of text in the document instead of only at the end of each paragraph. Many telecommunications programs require a document in this format so that they don't transmit each paragraph as a single long line that runs off the edge of the screen.

- *Microsoft Word 1.0/Microsoft Works* saves a document in a file format that Word version 1.0 and the word processor in Microsoft Works can read. Because these word processors aren't capable of as much formatting as Word 4, some formatting in Word 4 documents might be lost in the transfer to this format.

- *Microsoft Word 3.0/Microsoft Write* saves a document in a file format that Word versions 3.0 and 4 and Microsoft Write can read.

Although both programs are capable of more formatting than Word 1.0, some formatting in Word 4 documents might be lost in the transfer to this format.

- *Microsoft Word MS-DOS* saves a document in a file format that Microsoft Word for MS-DOS (Word 4's sister program on IBM and compatible computers) can read. Again, some Word 4 formatting might be lost in the transfer. If you use a telecommunications program to transfer a document in this format from your Mac to an IBM computer, be sure you use a transfer protocol such as XMODEM or Kermit to send the document. If you transfer it as a straight text file, extra or missing characters might make the file unreadable when you try to open it in Word for MS-DOS.

- *MacWrite* saves a document in a file format that MacWrite and MacWrite II can read. Not all Word 4 formatting makes it through the transfer, but because most programs can read MacWrite files, this format might be the most successful for transferring formatted Word 4 documents to other programs, especially older versions of programs.

- *Interchange format (also called RTF, for Rich Text Format)* saves a document in a format that other Microsoft applications can read.

The documentation for the program to which you're transferring a document lists the file formats the program can read. Click on the File Format button to open the File Format dialog box, and click on a compatible file-format option. Then click on the OK button to close the dialog box. The area to the right of the File Format button in the Save dialog box shows the currently set file format.

Once you save a document in a file format other than Normal, it remains in that format until you choose the Save command again. Choosing *Save* saves the document to the same filename but in Normal format, overwriting the alternate file format you instructed Word to use earlier. If you want to set the document so that Save always saves it using an alternate file format, reopen the File Format dialog box, click on the file-format option you want, turn the Default Format For File option on at the bottom of the box, and then click on the OK button to close the dialog box. Once the option is turned on,

Word uses the alternate file format to save the document each time you choose the Save command.

OPENING A DOCUMENT

Once you save and close a document, you use the Open command as your tool for retrieving it from the disk and folder where you saved it. You can also use the Open command to open documents created with different word processors and to open graphics files.

Finding a Document in the Open Dialog Box

To open a document, choose *Open* from the Edit menu. The Open dialog box appears as shown in Figure 11-3.

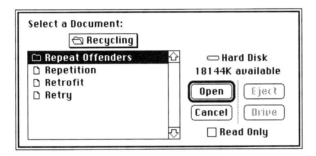

Figure 11-3. *Open the Open dialog box to choose a document to be opened.*

Most of the features in the Open dialog box are the same as those you used in the Save dialog box. You choose names in the disk/folder list box and the file list box to move from folder to folder, and you click on the Drive and Eject buttons to change disks. The file list box in the Open dialog box shows both files and folders, so you can choose either type. To open a document, either double-click on its name in the file list box or click once on its name to select it and then click on the Open button.

When Word opens your document, it positions the document window in the same place and at the same size as when you last saved the document. It places the insertion point at the beginning of the document, but it also remembers the location of the insertion point when you last saved the document; to return to that location, choose *Go Back* from the Utilities menu (or press keypad 0).

Using the Read Only Option

You might want to open a document for reading only and not take the chance of accidentally making changes. If so, you can turn the Read Only option on in the Open dialog box before you open a document. When it's turned on, Word opens the document and lets you make changes but won't let you save those changes to the original file. You can save them under a new filename instead, or you can close the document without saving any changes. This option is very handy if you're using a document as a base for creating another document and don't want to alter your original document.

Opening Documents from Other Programs

When you open the Open dialog box by choosing the Open command, the file list box displays only the names of files that Word can open as documents. These include documents saved in all the file formats in which Word can save as well as graphics saved in the MacPaint file format. When Word opens a document stored in a format other than its Normal format, it might present a message on the screen informing you that it's translating the document, or it might display the document on the screen and show its file format in the page-number area. If Word opens a MacPaint file, it creates a new document that includes only the graphic, which it positions at the top of the page.

When you choose *Save* or *Save As* to save a document that uses an alternate file format, Word saves the document in Normal format unless you specifically choose another file format in the File Format dialog box.

DELETING A DOCUMENT

You probably won't need to keep all the documents you create. If you're working on a document that you've never saved, you can delete it simply by clicking on its close box or by choosing *Close* from the File menu and then clicking on the No button when the dialog box appears, asking whether you want to save changes. If you want to delete a document that you've already saved on disk, you have two choices: You can return to the desktop, where you can drag the document into the Trashcan and then choose *Empty Trash* from the Special menu; or you can choose *Delete* from the File menu.

When you choose *Delete*, Word opens the Delete dialog box, shown in Figure 11-4. It looks almost exactly like the Open dialog box except that it contains a Delete button instead of an Open button, and it has a file-size display area at the bottom of the box that shows the size, in kilobytes, of any file you select in the file list box.

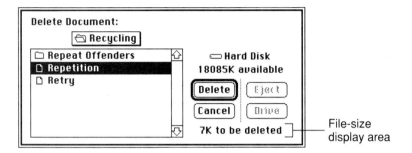

Figure 11-4. *Open the Delete dialog box to choose a document to be deleted.*

The file list box in the Delete dialog box displays *all* files in the current folder (with the fortunate exception of any currently open files or their backups), so you can delete from the file list box any files that you normally would drag into the Trashcan on the Mac desktop. To delete a file, simply double-click on the filename, or click once on the filename to select it and then click on the Delete button. Word displays a dialog box asking whether you want to delete the file you selected. If you click on the Yes button, Word deletes the file and returns you to the Delete dialog box so you can delete another file. If you click on the No button, Word leaves the file alone and returns you to the Delete dialog box. If you click on the Cancel button, Word leaves the file alone and closes the Delete dialog box completely.

Be very careful when you use Delete—it's possible to delete many important files from a disk, and once they're gone, you can't get them back unless you've saved copies of them on another disk.

PRINTING A DOCUMENT

After creating and saving a document, the big payoff is turning your printer on and printing the document on paper. In Chapter 3, "The First Session," printing was a simple matter of choosing the Print command, clicking on the OK button in the Print dialog box, and waiting for your printer to print the document. This section presents some useful alternatives that make printing more flexible and convenient.

Using the Chooser

If you have more than one printer connected to your Macintosh, you can choose any of those printers to print your document by using the Chooser desk accessory. You learned to use the Chooser in Chapter 1, "Setting Up Word 4," to set up your printer. The Chooser is especially useful if your Mac is part of a network of computers and printers. If one printer is busy, you can choose another for printing and then close the window and print.

You can open the Chooser window, shown in Figure 11-5, at any time by choosing *Chooser* from the Apple menu. The printer icons in the printer-icon list box show the types of printers that are connected via AppleTalk or the ports on the back of your Mac. Click on any one of the icons to select the type of printer you want. If more than one printer of that type is available, the printer-name list box at the right side of the Chooser window shows the names of those printers. Click on the name of the printer you want.

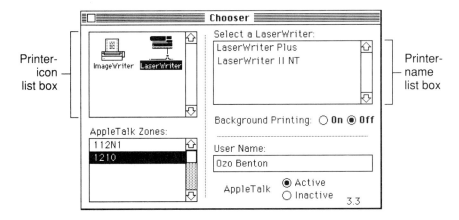

Figure 11-5. *The Chooser window shows all printers available to your Macintosh.*

Once you've set a new printer, close the Chooser window. Any printing you do now is sent to the selected printer.

Using the ImageWriter Print Dialog Box

If you choose *Print* from the File menu when the Chooser is set to print with an ImageWriter printer, Word opens the ImageWriter Print dialog box, shown in Figure 11-6, which offers printing options for an ImageWriter. Set the options you want here, and then click on the OK button to close the box and begin printing. The sections that follow describe the available printing options.

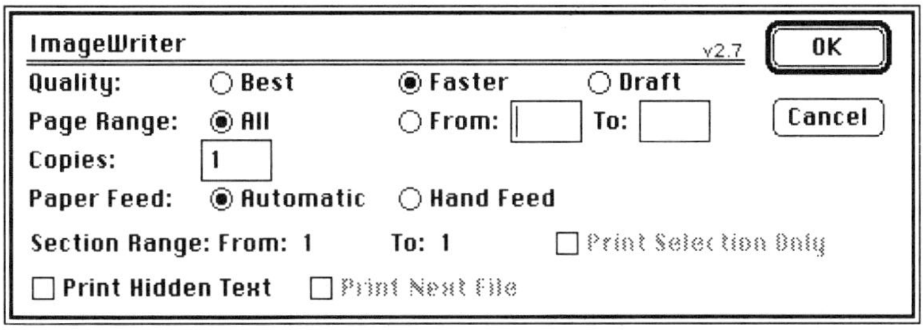

Figure 11-6. *The ImageWriter Print dialog box offers printing options for the ImageWriter printer.*

Using the LaserWriter Print Dialog Box

If you choose *Print* from the File menu when the Chooser is set to print with a LaserWriter printer, Word opens the LaserWriter Print dialog box, shown in Figure 11-7. Although this dialog box contains many of the options available in the ImageWriter Print dialog box, it also offers some special options that work only with LaserWriters.

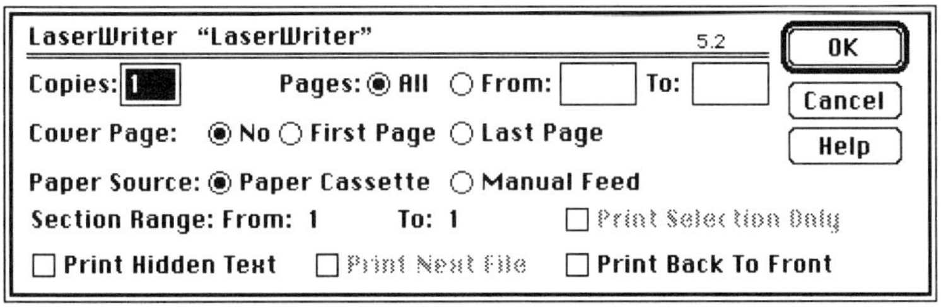

Figure 11-7. *The LaserWriter Print dialog box offers printing options for the LaserWriter printer.*

Printing Several Copies

To print more than one copy of a document, enter the number of copies you want in the Copies text box in either the ImageWriter or the LaserWriter dialog box.

Printing a Range of Pages

The Page Range section in the ImageWriter dialog box and the Pages section in the LaserWriter dialog box control the range of pages that Word prints. Clicking on the default option All instructs Word to print all the pages. To print a limited range of pages, click on the From To option, and then enter the beginning page number in the From text box and the ending page number in the To text box. To print a single page, enter the same page number in both the From and To text boxes. To print from any page in the document to the end of the document when you don't know the final page number, leave the To box empty; Word will print to the end of the document and stop.

To print a section of a document that doesn't begin or end neatly at a page break, first select as a text block the section you want to print, and then turn on the Print Selection Only option before you print. Word prints only the section you selected and repaginates the printout so that the beginning of the selected section starts at the top of the first page.

Printing Section Ranges

When you learn to divide a document into sections in Chapter 16, ''Section Formatting,'' you can use the Section Range option to print a range of pages that extends over more than one section. The sections in a document are numbered beginning with the number 1, and the page numbers within each section can be independent of page numbers in other sections. To print a range of pages that extends across sections, type the beginning section number in the Section Range: From text box and the beginning page number (within that section) in the Page Range: From text box. Then enter the ending section number in the Section Range: To text box and the ending page number (within that section) in the Page Range: To text box.

Printing a Linked Document

In Chapter 17, "Document Formatting," you'll learn to link one document with another so that Word prints the second linked document when it finishes printing the first linked document. When you open the Print dialog box to instruct Word to print a document that has been linked to a following document, the Print Next File option will be turned on. If you instruct Word to print when the option is turned on, Word begins printing the next linked document when it finishes printing the current document. Turn the Print Next File option off if you want to print only the current document.

Printing Hidden Text

When you learned to format characters in Chapter 4, "Entering and Formatting Characters," you learned to apply the Hidden Text type style to text that you didn't want to appear in a document. Word doesn't normally print hidden text, but it will print it if you turn the Print Hidden Text option on.

Setting Paper Feed

The Apple ImageWriter and LaserWriter printers have different paper-feeding capabilities. The ImageWriter printer can accept a single hand-fed sheet of paper (useful for letterhead or other special paper) or can print continuously on sheets of fanfold paper fed through the rollers by the printer's tractors. The LaserWriter printer can also print on hand-fed sheets of paper or on single sheets that feed into its rollers from a paper cassette.

Word offers two Paper Feed options in the ImageWriter dialog box: Automatic and Hand Feed. Choose *Automatic* if you're printing on fanfold paper or *Hand Feed* if you're feeding the printer one sheet at a time. Word offers two similar options in the LaserWriter dialog box: Paper Cassette and Manual Feed. Choose *Paper Cassette* if you're printing on paper from the printer's paper cassette or *Manual Feed* if you're feeding the printer one sheet at a time.

If you choose *Hand Feed* or *Manual Feed,* Word stops before printing each page and displays a dialog box that asks whether you want to print the page. You can then insert a sheet of paper by hand and click on the OK button to print the page. You repeat this procedure until you finish printing the document or until you click on the Cancel button in the dialog box.

Setting ImageWriter Print Quality

The ImageWriter dialog box offers three different qualities of printing in the Quality line at the top of the box. Choose the one that best suits your purposes:

- *Draft* offers a very fast printing speed, but pages printed in draft quality don't include graphics, show only rudimentary type styles, and display only one character size. Draft-quality printing is only a crude approximation of what you see on the Mac screen because it uses the printer's built-in character set instead of actual fonts. Use draft quality when you want to proofread text and don't require exact formatting.

- *Faster* prints slower than Draft and faster than Best. It shows all the graphics and formatting you've added to your document and uses the fonts you see on the Mac screen. The faster setting is perhaps the most useful print-quality setting for everyday printing.

- *Best* prints substantially slower than Faster but improves the quality of the printed characters by printing them in a higher resolution. Although Best doesn't show any more formatting or graphics than Faster does, its printout is darker and the characters are better formed. Use Best when you print a document for copying or when you really want to impress the reader.

Note one quirk of Best-quality printing: Some fonts won't print in exactly the same way in Best as they appear on the Mac screen, which changes character spacing and can throw off right-margin alignment. If you find that's the case when you print your document, you might benefit from installing a new ribbon on your printer (for better print quality) and using Faster-quality printing. Faster isn't subject to the same character-spacing problems.

Setting LaserWriter Cover Page and Page-Printing Order

The LaserWriter dialog box offers two unique options: Cover Page and Print Back to Front. The Cover Page option offers a cover page that prints before or after your document prints. The cover page lists the document title, your name, and other information that identifies your document—a very useful feature if you share your printer with other users.

If you set the Cover Page option to No, Word prints no cover page with your document. If you set it to First Page, Word prints the cover page before it prints your document. And if you set it to Last Page, Word prints the cover page after it finishes printing your document.

Word normally prints a document beginning with the first page and working toward the last page. If your LaserWriter is set up to deposit one printed page on top of another with the printed side up, then you'll find your document is arranged in a pile that reads from the last page through the first. To print in the opposite order, turn the Print Back To Front option on; Word then prints in the reverse order so your pile of printed pages reads from the first page through the last.

Printing

To begin printing after you set the printing options you want, simply click on the OK button. Word displays a message telling you that it's printing, and the page-number area at the bottom of the document window displays the number of the page currently being printed. If you want to stop printing at any time, press Command-. (period). Word stops printing and returns you to the document window.

Try printing two copies of two pages of the document "Redundancy":

1. Choose *Print* from the File menu to open the Print dialog box for your printer.

2. Type *2* in the Copies text box.

3. In the Pages line (LaserWriter) or the Page Range line (Image-Writer), turn the From To option on.

4. Type *2* in the From text box and *3* in the To text box.

5. Click on the OK button to begin printing.

Word prints two copies of pages 2 and 3 and displays the page number in the page-number area as it prints.

You now know how to handle finished documents—saving, opening, and printing them using many different printing options. You've reached the end of this section, which means you should now be an experienced Word user. Congratulations! In the next section you'll go beyond basics to learn about Word's more advanced features.

SECTION THREE

Beyond Basics

In this section you'll learn Word 4 features that go beyond document basics. These features make your work easier: They help you find the best word to use, check your spelling, sort lists, calculate numbers, and let you apply many formats with one simple command. They also help you create complex documents with footnotes, columnar text, and advanced page layout. Mastering the features described in this section puts you firmly and comfortably in control of Word.

Chapter 12

Writing Tools

Writing is a process with momentum. A quick stop to fumble for the right word or to calculate a number can quickly become a long stop as you try to recapture your thoughts and continue the flow of writing. Word 4 offers several tools that can keep you writing without interruption: The Word Finder DA provides an online thesaurus at the tips of your fingers; the Calculate command instructs Word to perform calculations on numbers in a text block so that you don't need to stop writing to use a calculator; and the glossary feature lets you create a collection of frequently used phrases, paragraphs, headings, graphics, and other document elements that you can insert with a minimum of typing. In this chapter you'll learn to use these tools to your advantage.

SETTING UP WORD

Before you begin working with the examples in this chapter, check to be sure that Word shows full menus, that Page View is turned off, and that Word Finder is installed on your system disk:

1. If you haven't done so already, turn your computer on and start Word.

2. Open the Edit menu, and if the Full Menus command appears, choose it to set full menus. If the Short Menus command appears instead of the Full Menus command, full menus are already set, and you can close the menu without choosing any commands.

3. Open the Document menu. If a check mark appears to the left of the Page View command, choose the Page View command to turn Page View off.

4. Open the Apple menu and check to be sure that the Word Finder command is listed. If it doesn't appear, the Word Finder desk accessory hasn't been installed on your system disk. Follow the instructions in Chapter 1, ''Setting Up Word 4,'' to install it.

Figure 12-1 shows the memo you will re-create as you follow the examples in this chapter. As you take on the role of conductor of the Beautiful Music Symphonette of Glamour Valley, you'll find that this memo not only motivates your employees to increase their productivity but also gives you the opportunity to use Word's writing tools.

USING WORD FINDER

Word Finder is a thesaurus desk accessory that you run from the Apple menu. If you're an old hand with a thesaurus in book form, you'll find that Word Finder's online thesaurus minimizes interruptions while you write—you won't need to stop writing in order to open a book, look up a word in the index, and turn to the word's location.

If you've never used a thesaurus, using Word Finder is an easy way to learn the value of a thesaurus for finding synonyms or for finding a word when you know the meaning but not the word. It's a simple matter of selecting a word in your document, running Word Finder, and then choosing from the synonyms it offers.

Starting Word Finder

To start Word Finder, you choose *Word Finder*® from the Apple menu. If you run your Mac using Finder rather than MultiFinder, the Word Finder window opens on your screen, and a new menu labeled ''WF'' appears in the menu bar to the right of Word's menus. Click on the Cancel button to close the window. Word Finder is now running, and you can use it by choosing one of the commands in the WF menu.

If you run your Macintosh using MultiFinder, when you choose *Word Finder*® from the Apple menu to start Word Finder, Word Finder's own menu bar appears at the top of the screen, and the program icon at the right end of

Beautiful Music Symphonette
of Glamour Valley

Music That Won't Surprise You

To: All Employees
From: Maestro Edouard Amadeus Thompson
Re: Monthly productivity awards

I want to take this opportunity as conductor and commander of the Beautiful Music Symphonette of Glamour Valley to tell you the results of this month's productivity survey. The string division has topped the other divisions by playing the most notes per player this concert month, followed by the woodwinds, brasses, and (ahem!) percussion. The table below shows our most productive players with their weekly note tallies:

Week	Bo Longo	Raoul Romero	Tanya Pitchov
One	62,709	55,465	64,012
Two	54,809	49,441	75,545
Three	57,669	58,710	81,003
Four	62,466	60,989	1,079
Totals:	237,653	224,605	221,639

Violist Bo wins a recording of the complete set of the waltzes of Johann Strauss, Jr., as transcribed for flute and harp by Emil Waldteufel—a full 32-compact-disk set donated by the Beautiful Music Symphonette of Glamour Valley Docent Society. Harpist Raoul, a grizzled veteran of the Sugarplum Variations, wins the fully annotated scores of Leroy Anderson's Christmas works—the famous "Winter Wonder" and "Sleighride of Joy" masses—donated by the Beautiful Music Symphonette of Glamour Valley Junior Auxiliary. Flutist Tanya is, alas, in the hospital recuperating from cruelly chapped lips after her solo performance of *Satyagraha* for the Beautiful Music Symphonette of Glamour Valley Musician's Relief Fund. We know she'll be back in the running soon.

Good health, Tanya, and thank you one and all for a productive month!

Maestro Edouard Amadeus Thompson

P.S. The brass division might have a better notes-per-player-per-week rating if the trombone section stopped reading automobile magazines during long rests.

Figure 12-1. *You will use the Word Finder desk accessory, the glossary feature, and the Calculate command to create this document.*

the menu bar shows a suitcase with an Apple on it—the symbol that indicates a desk accessory is the currently running program. Click on the icon to return to Word. (The Word symbol will appear in place of the desk-accessory symbol at the right end of the menu bar.) You'll find that Word now has added a new menu—WF—to its menus. You can now use Word Finder by choosing one of the commands in the WF menu.

Looking Up a Word

You can use Word Finder to find synonyms for a word you've typed or to look for the most appropriate word before you type. To find synonyms for a word you've already typed, select the word in your Word document and then choose *Lookup* from the WF menu (or press Command–keypad 1). Word Finder's window, shown in Figure 12-2, opens on the screen, displaying your selected word in the Find text box.

To find a word before you type it, choose *Lookup* from the WF menu without selecting a word in your document. When the Word Finder window appears, type the word in the Find box and then click on the Lookup button.

If Word Finder can't find your word in its more than 220,000-word thesaurus, it informs you that it can't find the word and displays a list of 24 words in the thesaurus that are alphabetically close to the word you selected or typed. You can then select a word from that list by clicking on the word and then clicking on the Lookup button; or you can type a new word in the Find text box and then click on the Lookup button.

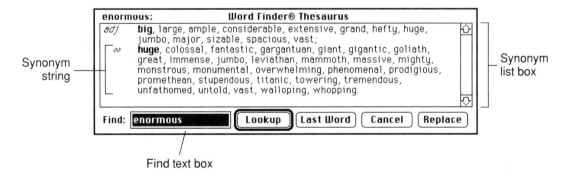

Figure 12-2. *The Word Finder window shows synonyms for the word displayed in the Find text box.*

Reading Word Finder's Synonym List

When Word Finder finds a word in its thesaurus, it displays synonyms for the word in the synonym list box in the middle of the window. The synonyms are divided into large groups labeled by parts of speech—noun, adjective, adverb, and so on—and each large group is divided into smaller groups that have different shades of meaning. These smaller groupings are called *synonym strings*. Each synonym string is marked at the beginning with a ∞ symbol. Figure 12-3 shows the synonym list for the word *shout*. The first two synonym strings are nouns, and the last three are verbs.

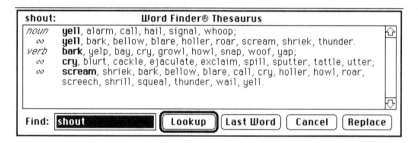

Figure 12-3. *The synonym list for the word* shout *includes synonym strings with five distinct shades of meaning.*

Inserting a Synonym in Your Document

If you see a word in the synonym list that you want to insert in your document, select it and then click on the Replace button, or simply double-click on it. The Word Finder window closes, and Word inserts the synonym in your document at the insertion-point location, replacing the word you selected if you selected one. If you decide that you don't like the replacement, you can choose *Undo* from Word's Edit menu to delete the synonym and restore any text that Word Finder might have replaced.

Customizing Word Finder's Settings

You can customize two of Word Finder's settings: The keyboard shortcut you use to open its window and the location where the window appears. To change the keyboard shortcut, choose *Change Command Key* from the WF menu to open the command-key window, shown in Figure 12-4, on the following page.

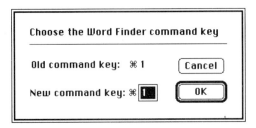

Figure 12-4. *Open Word Finder's command-key window to change the keyboard shortcut that opens Word Finder's window.*

Word Finder's keyboard shortcut is always a combination of the command key and another key on the keyboard. To set the second key to a key other than *1*, type the key's character in the New Command Key text box and then click on the OK button. Be careful not to duplicate one of Word's own keyboard shortcuts—for example, the shortcut Command-O, which opens a document. Word Finder's original shortcut, Command–keypad 1, doesn't conflict with any Word keyboard shortcuts, so you might want to consider leaving it in effect.

Word Finder offers three window-placement options, as follows:

■ *Window Automatic*, in which Word Finder places its window in the upper half of the screen if your selected word appears in the lower half of the screen, or in the lower half of the screen if your selected word appears in the upper half of the screen. This is Word Finder's default setting; it ensures that you can always see your selected word in the document.

■ *Window Above*, in which Word Finder always places its window in the upper half of the screen.

■ *Window Below*, in which Word Finder always places its window in the lower half of the screen.

To change the window placement, select the option you want from the WF menu. A check mark appears to the left of the option, indicating that it's in effect.

Closing Word Finder

When you're finished using Word Finder and want to close its window without inserting a synonym in your document, click on the Cancel button. Word Finder remains running in the background, waiting for the next time you want to look for a word. While it runs, it takes up some of your Mac's memory. If you find that your Mac is short of memory when you try to open documents or perform other Word activities, you can shut down Word Finder by choosing *Close* from the WF menu. Word Finder shuts down and removes its WF menu from the menu bar. You can always recall Word Finder later by opening it from the Apple menu.

A Word Finder Example

The first part of the sample memo, shown in Figure 12-5, on the following page, as you'll first enter it, provides a good place to try out Word Finder. As you write the memo, you want to describe your authority as conductor in no uncertain terms. For some reason, though, the phrase ''conductor and dictator'' seems too harsh. Word Finder offers some alternatives.

1. Choose *New* from the File menu to open a new document, and begin typing the memo.

2. If you are set up to print on a LaserWriter, set the right margin to 6.25 inches so the entire letter will print on a single page. (Chapter 19, ''Printing Variations and Document Export,'' explains why LaserWriters offer less text per line than ImageWriters do.)

3. Set paragraph formatting to centered alignment and character formatting to 18-point bold.

4. Type the first two lines of the memo, pressing Return at the end of each line.

5. Reduce the character size to 12 points, and then press Return to create a blank line.

6. Type *Music That Won't Surprise You* and press Return twice.

7. Change paragraph alignment to left, and turn the bold character formatting off.

Figure 12-5. *Type the first part of the sample memo as shown here.*

8. Type the next three lines of the memo, and press Return twice at the end of the third line.

9. Begin typing the first paragraph of the body of the memo as it appears in Figure 12-5. Stop typing at the end of "dictator."

10. Select the word "dictator."

11. Choose *Word Finder*® from the Apple menu. If you're running your Mac with Finder, the Word Finder window opens, showing a list of synonyms for "dictator." If you're running your Mac with Multi-Finder, the menu bar changes to show Word Finder's menu bar. Click on the icon at the right end of the menu bar to return to Word, and then choose *Lookup* from the WF menu to open the Word Finder window. The window opens, showing a list of synonyms for "dictator."

12. You see three synonym strings, as shown in Figure 12-6. The first two, with meanings close to "authoritarian" and "tyrant," seem harsh, so you decide to choose a word whose meaning is closer to that of "leader." Double-click on the word "commander." The Word Finder window disappears, and the word "dictator" is replaced with the word "commander."

13. Finish typing the paragraph and then press Return twice.

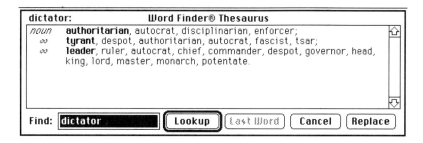

Figure 12-6. *Word Finder shows three synonym strings for the word "dictator."*

USING THE CALCULATE COMMAND

Some documents contain lists of numbers that need to be added, numeric expressions that need to be resolved, or require other mathematical operations that can force you to stop writing to pull out a calculator (or use a calculator DA) and determine the result before you can go back to writing. The Calculate command in the Utilities menu can save you the trouble of reentering all those numbers. You simply select a block of text and choose *Calculate*. Word performs any simple mathematical operations contained in the text block and places the result on the Clipboard.

Selecting Text for Calculation

You can select a block of text for calculation using normal selection techniques, which select text in rows. There are instances, however, especially with numbers, when you want to select a column of text for addition (such as the columns of note tallies in the sample memo). If you use normal selection techniques, you can't separate one column from the next because Word selects an entire row before it moves down to select another row. To select a column by itself without selecting text to either side, you use a special selection technique called *column selection*.

To use column selection, hold down the Option key and drag the pointer from one corner of the column to its opposite corner. The selection rectangle stretches only as wide as your pointer moves so that you don't select parts of rows that extend outside the column. Release the mouse button when you have selected the column.

You can also use extended selection in column selection: Move the pointer to one corner of the column, and click the mouse button to place the insertion point there. Move the pointer to the opposite corner of the column, hold down Shift-Option, and click the mouse button. Word selects the entire column.

Calculating

Choose *Calculate* from the Utilities menu to begin calculating within a text block. The order in which Word encounters numbers and mathematical operators in the text determines the result.

Mathematical operators

A mathematical operator is a symbol that tells Word to perform a particular mathematical operation. Word recognizes five types of operators that add, subtract, multiply, divide, and set percentages:

- + (or no symbol) for addition

- − (or enclosing parentheses) for subtraction

- * for multiplication

- / for division

- % for percent (the same as dividing the percentage number by 100)

Place operators, except the percent sign, directly to the left of a number. Place a percent sign directly to the right of a number. If you use parentheses instead of a subtraction sign, enclose the number you wish to subtract. A few examples: *45* means to divide by 45, *34%* means to multiply by 34 percent, *(72)* means to subtract 72, and *4* by itself means to add 4.

Order of calculation

Word calculates by reading the selected text block from left to right, top to bottom (as you read a page) and by performing operations in the order in which it encounters them. It ignores any text between numbers and operators. For example, if you select a text block that reads ''34 shoulder pads at *$5.00 each multiplied by *15%,'' Word calculates *34 * 5.00 * 15%*, which is 34 multiplied by 5.00 multiplied by 15 percent, which equals 25.50.

Decimal places

After Word calculates, it returns a result that contains a number of decimal places equal to the maximum number of decimal places in the text block. For example, the operation *9 * 0.3333333* returns the value *2.9999997*. Word uses seven decimal places because 0.3333333 contains seven decimal places.

Pasting the Result

After Word calculates, it places the result on the Clipboard and temporarily displays the result in the page-number area at the lower left corner of the document window. To paste the result in the document, place the insertion point where you want the result and choose the Paste command from the Edit menu (or press Command-V).

A Calculation Example

The memo contains four columns of numbers, shown in Figure 12-7. The last three list the number of notes played by musicians in the orchestra.

Week◆	Bo.Longo◆	Raoul.Romero◆	Tanya.Pitchov¶
One◆	62,709◆	55,465◆	64,012¶
Two◆	54,809◆	49,441◆	75,545¶
Three◆	57,669◆	58,710◆	81,003¶
Four◆	62,466◆	60,989◆	1,079¶
Totals:◆	237,653◆	224,605◆	221,639¶

Figure 12-7. *Use the Calculate command to calculate the sums of these columns of numbers.*

Type this part of the memo, and use the Calculate command to total the numbers as follows:

1. Set up the heading-line paragraph by placing center-align tab stops at 1.75, 3.50, and 5.25 inches.

2. Set character formatting to underlined and bold, and then enter the first line shown in Figure 12-7. (The tab characters are visible to show you where to press the Tab key.) Press Return at the end of the line.

3. Remove the tabs on the Ruler, and insert new decimal tabs at 2, 3.75, and 5.50 inches.

4. Turn underline and bold character formatting off and type the next four lines, referring to Figure 12-7 to see where to press Tab. Be sure to press Return at the end of the last line of figures.

5. Turn bold character formatting on and type *Totals*. Turn bold formatting off and then press Tab.

6. To select the first column of numbers, move the pointer to the beginning of the number *62,709*, hold down the Option key, drag the pointer to the end of the number *62,466*, and then release the mouse button and option key.

7. Choose *Calculate* from the Utilities menu to add the column. The result appears in the lower left corner of the document window, and is also placed on the Clipboard.

8. Move the insertion point back to the end of the line you last typed and choose *Paste* from the Edit menu to insert the result below the column of numbers.

9. Press Tab to move to the next column.

10. Select the column of numbers under the name ''Raoul Romero'' as you did in the preceding column, and then choose *Calculate* (or press Command-=) to add the numbers.

11. Move the insertion point back to the end of the document and choose *Paste* from the Edit menu to paste the result at the bottom of the second column.

12. Press Tab to move to the final column of numbers. Select the column, calculate its sum, and paste the result as you did previously. Press Return twice at the end of the line to prepare for entering the rest of the document.

THE GLOSSARY

Many phrases, sentences, and parts of a document recur throughout a document or a series of documents. Rather than type each occurrence, you can use Word's glossary feature to store a repeated piece of text or a graphic and insert that text or graphic wherever you want it.

Creating a Glossary Entry

The first step in creating a glossary entry is to enter the text or graphics you want in a document. Once entered, you select the entry as a block. You can select all text, all graphics, or a mixture of both; the Glossary stores the entire contents of the block, preserving all graphics and character formatting.

With a text block selected, choose *Glossary* from the Edit menu to open the Glossary window, shown in Figure 12-8. The entry list box in the main part of the window shows glossary entries that come with Word. It also shows *New* selected at the top of the list to show that the Glossary is ready to accept a new entry.

To give your selection a name and make it a part of the glossary, type a name in the Name text box. Brevity counts. The shorter your glossary name, the easier it will be to type when you want to recall the glossary entry. Of course, being too brief can cause problems: A name such as "j" or "4" often doesn't remind you of the entry contents. A key word in a phrase, a short word describing a picture, the initials of a name, or the title work well as glossary names.

Once you type the name you want, click on the Define button to add the entry to the Glossary. The entry name appears in the entry list box, and the bottom line of the window shows the contents of the entry. Because it's only a

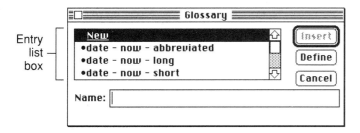

Figure 12-8. *The Glossary window contains a list of glossary entries.*

single line, this description area doesn't show any selected graphics or character formatting. The line displays only the beginning of the selected text and shows each graphic as a small, empty box.

When you're finished working with the Glossary window, click on the Cancel button to close it and return to your document.

An Example

The phrase "Beautiful Music Symphonette of Glamour Valley" occurs often in the rest of the memo. Define it as a glossary entry as follows:

1. Select *Beautiful Music Symphonette of Glamour Valley* as a text block in the first full paragraph of the memo.

2. Choose *Glossary* from the Edit menu to open the Glossary window. *New,* at the top of the entry list, is highlighted.

3. Type *bms* (the initials of the Beautiful Music Symphonette) in the Name text box.

4. Click on the Define button to add the entry to the entry list. The name appears in the entry list, and the contents of the entry appear in the bottom line of the window.

5. Click on the Cancel button to close the window.

Inserting a Glossary Entry in a Document

You can insert a glossary entry in a document in either of two ways:

- Press Command-Delete. The page-number area turns black, indicating that you can type the name of the glossary entry (or enough of the name to distinguish it from other entries). Press Return after you've typed the name. Word inserts the contents of the glossary entry at the insertion-point location, including any graphics and character formatting that are part of the entry.

- Open the Glossary window by choosing the Glossary command in the Edit menu, click on the glossary entry you want in the entry list, and then click on the Insert button (or simply double-click on the glossary name). The window closes and Word inserts the full contents of the glossary entry at the location of the insertion point.

Directly typing a glossary name in a document is the quickest way to insert a glossary entry. Note that Word ignores uppercase and lowercase characters in a glossary name, so you don't need to use the Shift key as you type the name. If you forget a glossary name you need, you can open the Glossary dialog box and read the list of entries. As you select entries in the list, the first part of each entry is displayed at the bottom of the dialog box.

Using Word's Own Glossary Entries

When you open the Glossary window, you can see many entries already in place. These are Word's own glossary entries that you can use to insert special information. The entries preceded by a bullet (•) insert the date, time, and page number in the same way clicking on the icons in a header window does. One of the bulleted entries inserts print-merge brackets, which you'll learn to use in Chapter 23, "Printing Form Letters by Merging Documents." You'll also find an entry for creating an index entry, an advanced feature that helps you create document indexes.

The date and time entries offer two settings: *now* and *print*. If you choose *now*, the date or time you insert is the time read from the Mac's clock at the moment of insertion. It doesn't change when you print or reopen the document later. If you choose *print*, the date or time you insert is updated whenever you print or reopen the document, in the same way that the date or time you create in a header window is updated. Date and time entries also offer different degrees of abbreviation. Experiment by inserting them into a document; you'll find which form you like for different circumstances.

The page-number entry inserts the page number of the page on which it's located. It's updated whenever you print or repaginate the document.

A Glossary Insertion Example

The remaining text of the memo shows "Beautiful Music Symphonette of Glamour Valley" in several places. Use the glossary feature to insert it as follows:

1. Type the rest of the memo shown in Figure 12-1, at the beginning of this chapter, stopping at the beginning of "Beautiful Music Symphonette of Glamour Valley" in the first paragraph following the "Totals" line.

2. Choose *Glossary* from the Edit menu to open the Glossary window.

3. Double-click on *bms* in the glossary list. The window closes, and Word inserts the entry in your document.

4. Continue typing, stopping at the beginning of "Beautiful Music."

5. Press Command-Delete. The page-number area turns black.

6. Type *bms*. It appears in the page-number area.

7. Press Return. Word inserts *Beautiful Music Symphonette of Glamour Valley.*

8. Type the rest of the memo, using the glossary feature to insert the phrase a final time. (It's not important that you enter this text verbatim, so feel free to abridge it if your fingers begin to rebel.)

Saving Glossary Entries

Word retains all the glossary entries you create during a Word session. If you close one document and begin a new one, the glossary entries you created in the earlier document are available to you in the new one. When you close Word at the end of your session, Word asks whether you want to save your glossary changes. If you click on the Yes button, Word stores the glossary entries on disk under the filename "Standard Glossary" along with Word's own glossary entries. If you click on the No button, Word deletes your glossary entries. You won't see them the next time you run Word and open the Glossary.

Deleting and Renaming Glossary Entries

As you add to the entries in the Glossary, you might want to remove some that are no longer useful and rename others that don't work well with their current names. To remove an entry, select its name in the entry list box and then choose *Cut* from the Edit menu. Word asks whether you want to delete the glossary entry; click on the Yes button to remove it from the list.

To rename an entry, select its name from the entry list so it appears in the Name text box, type the new name, and then click on the Define button. The old name disappears from the entry list and the new name replaces it.

Advanced Glossary Features

Word also offers advanced glossary features that you should be aware of in case you'd like to learn more about them. The following are two useful glossary features:

- *Creating more than one glossary.* You can create specialty glossaries that you open only when working with documents that might use the entries in the glossaries. This feature helps you manage the size of the glossary you work with as you write.

- *Adding a glossary entry to a menu.* You can directly insert a glossary entry by simply choosing a command from a menu.

If you'd like to learn more about either of these features, you can find more information in the Glossaries section of *Reference to Microsoft Word*.

You now know how to use the Word Finder DA, the Calculate command, and the glossary feature. In the next chapter you'll learn to use some editing tools that help you edit the text you enter.

Chapter 13

Editing Tools

The best editing tool is an editor who reads your work, corrects your grammar, organization, and spelling, and returns to you a document that says what you really intended it to say. Because most of us can't afford this type of editorial luxury, Word 4 offers editing tools that help the person most sympathetic to your writing—you—make revisions in your text. In this chapter you'll learn to use three editing tools, all of which you'll find on the Utilities menu: the Sort command, the Spelling command, and the Hyphenate command.

SETTING UP WORD

Before you begin working with the examples in this chapter, check to be sure that Word shows full menus and that Page View is turned off:

1. If you haven't done so already, turn your computer on and start Word.

2. Open the Edit menu, and if the Full Menus command appears, choose it to set full menus. If the Short Menus command appears instead of the Full Menus command, full menus are already set, and you can close the menu without choosing any commands.

3. Open the Document menu, and if a check mark appears to the left of the Page View command, choose the Page View command to turn Page View off.

To learn how to hyphenate and sort text and how to check spelling, you'll follow the examples in this chapter to create a report from the director of the Wee Tot Petting Farm, shown in Figure 13-1 on the following page. The trade-specific animal names provide a challenge to Word's spelling checker.

Wee Tot Petting Farm

"Fins, Fur, Feathers, and Finances!"

Date: 6/12/91
To: Limited partners
From: J. Wellington Biddlecomb, General Manager

Dear Partners:

I'd like to take this opportunity to report to you on the burgeoning business here at the Wee Tot Petting Farm; the tykes are tumbling through 'the turnstiles in ever-increasing numbers thanks to our recent improvements.

Many partners have asked me why there were no dividends at the end of last month. The answer is simple: All profits have been reinvested in the facilities at this crucial period. The beginning of the summer is traditionally the time for improvements in the toddler-tactile livestock industry; we have followed suit with spectacular results. The list that follows shows our acquisitions for the month of May followed by favorable comment tallies from the comment box:

Date:	Acquisition:	Favorable Comments:
5/6	3 moomoos	14
5/9	4 oinkoinks	6
5/11	15 cluckclucks	11
5/15	10 quackquacks	18
5/21	2 bowwows	17
5/30	1 hisshiss	0

In order of popularity, our acquisitions are:

Date:	Acquisition:	Favorable Comments:
5/15	10 quackquacks	18
5/21	2 bowwows	17
5/6	3 moomoos	14
5/11	15 cluckclucks	11
5/9	4 oinkoinks	6
5/30	1 hisshiss	0

(continued)

Figure 13-1. *Use Word's Sort, Spelling, and Hyphenate features to edit this sample document.*

Figure 13-1. *continued*

All our bipedal and quadripedal additions have certainly proved their worth. Unfortunately, our lone apedal addition hasn't fared as well, but was still a worthwhile addition—at only $100 for a 14-foot anaconda ($7.14 a foot), we got a great deal! As it turns out, he is proving to be an invaluable resource for getting rid of other unpopular petting animals.

I know that you are proud of the priceless toddler-tactile resource we are creating within our great city. Tell your friends with pride, "I invested $50,000 in the Wee Tot Petting Farm." Their compliments will be additional payback on your investment.

Yours sincerely,

J. Wellington Biddlecomb
General Manager
Wee Tot Petting Farm

SORTING LISTS

Many documents contain lists of names, instructions, or other ordered items. Often the information as you first type it or import it from another source follows no particular order; reading it would be much easier if the list were sorted in alphabetic or numeric order. Sorting is a tedious process perfectly suited to a computer. You can turn the task over to Word by using Word's Sort feature.

An Overview of the Sorting Process

When Word sorts a list, it actually sorts paragraphs, so it's important that you enter each list item as a separate paragraph. Each paragraph is called a *record* (a term borrowed from the world of database software). If you organize information the same way within each record (for example, a list of names with each record showing last name, first name, and phone number), each separate type of information in a record is called a *field* (another term borrowed from database software).

To sort a list of records, first select all the records as a text block. Then choose the Sort command from the Utilities menu. Word sorts all the text records in the block alphabetically and all the number records numerically (by value). To sort a list of records by a field that isn't at the beginning of each record (for example, by a first name that comes in the middle of each record), use columnar selection to select only that field in each record. Then when you use the Sort feature, Word sorts records in alphabetic order by reading the characters in that field, not the characters at the beginning of every record. You'll learn about the details of sorting by field in examples that follow.

Creating Records and Fields

The Sort command works best if you follow these simple rules as you create records in a list:

- Press Return at the end of each record to keep records separated.

- Separate each field within a record by pressing Tab at the end of each field.

Try entering a list of records. Use the text, paragraph marks, and tab stops shown in Figure 13-2 for guidance. The report contains two lists of recently acquired petting-farm animals. If you type the first list, you can copy it and use the Sort feature to reorder it according to the popularity of the animals. When you type the first list, separate each record (an animal purchase)

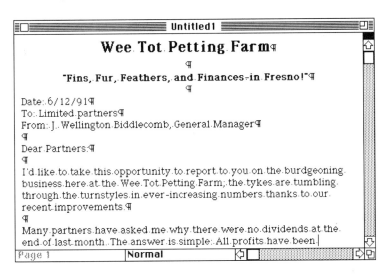

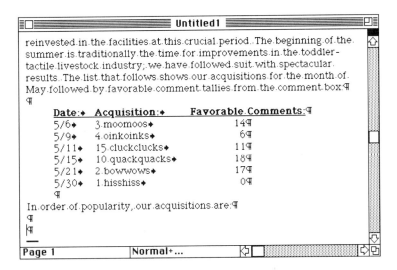

Figure 13-2. *Follow the instructions to enter this text in your sample document.*

with a paragraph mark and each field within a record (date, animal, and number of comments) with a tab. Take the following steps:

1. Enter the title line as 18-point, centered, boldface text in the New York font, and press Return twice.

2. Reduce the size of the text to 12 points, type the second line of the report (''Fins, Fur, ...''), and press Return twice.

3. Change paragraph alignment back to left aligned, and turn boldface off. Enter the remainder of the document shown in Figure 13-2, following the spelling exactly. (Deliberate mistakes are included for the spelling checker to find later.) Stop after you press Return twice at the end of the second full paragraph of text, before you enter the list heading.

4. Move the left indent to the right 0.5 inch.

5. Set left-align tab stops at 1.25 inches and 3 inches.

6. Turn boldface and underline formatting on, and type the heading line for the list: *Date:* (Tab) *Acquisition:* (Tab) *Favorable Comments:* Press Return at the end of the line.

7. Turn boldface and underlining off.

8. Remove the left-align tab stop at the 3-inch mark, and replace it with a decimal tab stop at the 4-inch mark.

9. Enter each line of the list. Press Tab between fields, and press Return at the end of each line.

10. At the end of the last line, press Return twice and move the left margin to the 0 mark.

11. Type *In order of popularity, our acquisitions are:* and press Return twice at the end of the line.

Selecting and Sorting Techniques

Most list sorting is simple—you select the list records as a text block and choose *Sort* from the Utilities menu, and Word sorts the records in alphabetic and numeric order. If you want to sort in a different order or by a selected field, you can use the following special selection and sorting techniques.

Sorting in reverse order

If you want to sort a list in reverse alphabetic and numeric order, select records as you would for forward sorting and then hold down the Shift key while you open the Utilities menu. You'll find that the Sort command has been replaced with *Sort Descending*. Choose *Sort Descending* to sort the selected records in reverse alphabetic and numeric order.

Sorting an entire document

To sort all the paragraphs in a document, first be sure that no text block is selected. Then choose *Sort* or *Sort Descending*; Word sorts all the paragraphs in the document.

Undoing a sort

Immediately after you've sorted a list, you can undo the sort by choosing *Undo* from the Edit menu. If you perform any other editing tasks after you sort, choosing Undo will not undo your sort.

Sorting by a selected field

Some lists contain records that you will want to sort by a field that isn't the first field in the record. For example, in the Petting Farm letter you want to sort the list of animals by the Favorable Comments, which is the last field in each record. If the fields in the record are lined up in columns, you can use columnar selection (which you learned to use in Chapter 12, "Writing Tools") to select only the field on which you want to base your sort. Extend the columnar selection from the first record to the last record in the field list. Once you select a field list, choose *Sort* or *Sort Descending* from the Utilities menu; Word sorts the records according to the selected field.

Try rearranging the list of animals in order of the number of favorable comments each animal received. You'll want to sort by the third field, using reverse order. First duplicate the list:

1. Select the list and its heading line as a text block. Be sure to include the paragraph mark at the end of the last record.

2. Choose *Copy* from the Edit menu.

3. Move the insertion point to the end of the document, and choose *Paste* from the Edit menu to add a copy of the list to the end of the document.

4. Hold down the Option key and drag the pointer down the third column in the copied list (excluding the heading) in order to select the third field for sorting. The result should look like Figure 13-3.

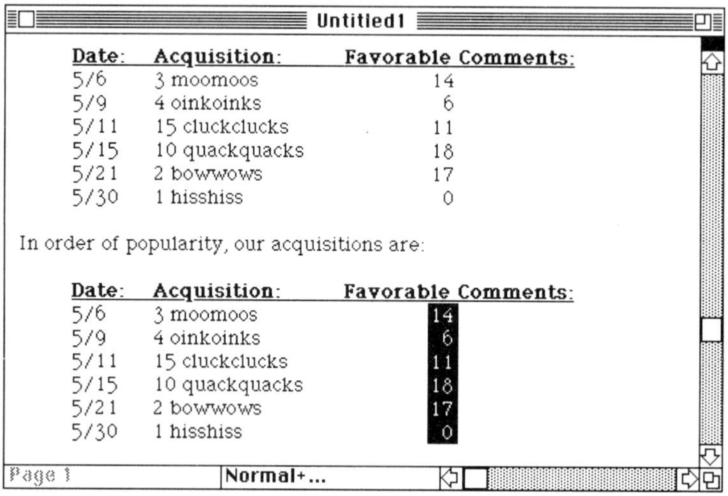

Figure 13-3. *Use extended selection to select the third field of the copied list for sorting.*

5. Hold down the Shift key and open the Utilities menu; *Sort Descending* appears at the bottom of the menu. Choose it to start the sort. Word sorts the records in the list in reverse order by the number of favorable comments.

6. Move the insertion point to the end of the document, press Return, and then type the rest of the document as shown in Figure 13-4.

232

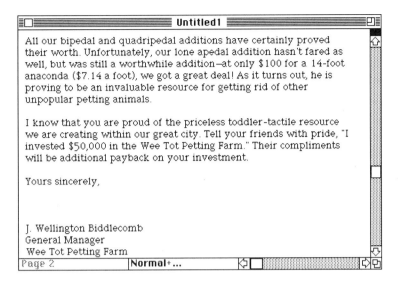

Figure 13-4. *The second half of the report.*

Word's Sort Order

To sort effectively, you should know the character order that Word uses to sort records. When Word sorts in forward alphabetic and numeric order, it follows these rules:

- It ignores commas, quotation marks, tabs, and diacritical marks such as ^ and ~. For example, the list *"baboon" cormorant abacus* is sorted as *abacus "baboon" cormorant.*

- It ignores uppercase and lowercase treatment when sorting unless it sorts two identical letters, one uppercase and the other lowercase. In that instance, it places the uppercase letter before the lowercase letter. For example, Word places *C* before *c* but after *b.*

- International characters such as *ü* and *ë* fall after their unaccented English equivalents. For example, *ü* comes after *u* but before *v.*

- Word sorts numbers by their value instead of alphanumerically. For example, *35* comes before *157* in Word. (In a conventional alphanumeric sort, the 1 at the beginning of 157 would come before the 3 at the beginning of 35.)

■ If you sort numbers that are followed by letters—for example, *25a* and *16c*—Word first sorts the numbers by their value and then sorts the letters alphabetically if any number values match. For example, *25a* comes after *24c* but before *25b*.

Knowing these sorting rules will help you understand how Word sorts your lists.

CHECKING SPELLING

Everybody makes spelling mistakes; if the inexplicable spelling rules of the English language don't trip you up, then straying fingers on the keyboard probably will. When you finish a document, you can use Word to carefully comb through your text for spelling mistakes and typing errors.

An Overview of Spelling Checking

Choosing the Spelling command on the Utilities menu starts Word's spelling checker, which reads through your document (or any portion you have selected), comparing each word it encounters with a list of over 100,000 words stored in its dictionary. If it comes across a word it can't find in its dictionary, it displays the word and asks whether you want to replace it.

You can deal with an unmatched word in several ways. You can replace the word if it's misspelled. If you don't know how to spell a word, you can instruct Word to suggest alternative spellings for you to choose from. If the word is spelled correctly but isn't included in Word's dictionary, you can tell Word to move on without changing the word or, if you use that word often, to add it to a supplemental user dictionary. Once you've placed words in the supplemental dictionary, Word scans both that dictionary and its main dictionary as it runs the rest of the spelling check.

Word's spelling checker does have a limitation: It cannot check for proper usage. If you use a word improperly in a sentence, Word won't notice the problem if the word is in its dictionary. For example, the sentence "It's reel butter" is wrong, but Word won't alert you because "reel" is a word in its dictionary.

Starting a Spelling Check

Before you start a spelling check, you must decide whether to check the entire document or only a portion of it. If you've already checked a document and then added a new section to it, you can save time by checking only the new or revised section. To check a section of a document, first select the section as a text block. If you want to check a single word, select that word as a text block. To check the entire document, select no text blocks.

To start a spelling check, choose *Spelling* from the Utilities menu to open the Spelling dialog box shown in Figure 13-5.

Click on the Start Check button to start the spelling check. If you're checking the entire document, Word reads from the insertion-point location to the end of the document, where it pauses and asks whether you want to continue the check from the beginning of the document. If you click on the Yes button, Word reads from the beginning of the document to the insertion-point location, where it then stops. If you are checking a text block, Word reads from the beginning to the end of the block. The page-number area at the bottom of the document window reports on the check's progress, displaying the percentage of the document or text block that has been checked. You can quit anytime by clicking on the Cancel button or by pressing Command-. (period).

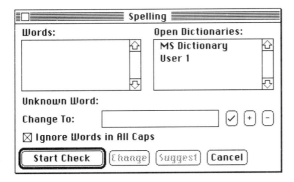

Figure 13-5. *The Spelling dialog box presents the unrecognized words found in a document and offers suggestions for correcting misspelled words.*

Dealing with Unmatched Words

Occasionally Word can match every word in your document to a word in its dictionaries—it finds no misspellings or typing errors. If so, the spelling check ends, and you can go back to work on your document. More often, however, Word finds unmatched words. When it finds one, it stops the check and presents the unmatched word in the Unknown Word area in the center of the Spelling dialog box. It also highlights the unmatched word in the document to let you read it in context. If the Spelling dialog box covers the selected text, drag the box to a new location.

Below the Unknown Word area is the Change To text box. Type a correction for the unmatched word here if you want to change the word. When you click on the Change button, Word replaces the unmatched word with the contents of the Change To text box and then continues the spelling check. If you want to check the spelling of the word you typed in the Change To text box before you insert the word in your document, click on the Check button (✔) next to the text box. If the word isn't in the dictionary, Word displays it in the Unknown Word area. If it's spelled correctly, Word leaves the Unknown Word area blank.

If Word points out a misspelling that you don't know how to correct, click on the Suggest button. Word looks through its dictionaries for words that have similar spellings and displays them in the Words scrolling list. You can scroll through these suggestions if there are more than the window can show at one time. Chances are you'll find the correct spelling of the unmatched word. When you do, choose it to replace the selected word in the document by double-clicking on it, or by clicking on it once and then clicking on the Change button.

When Word presents correctly spelled words as unmatched

Word sometimes displays unmatched words that are spelled correctly; these are usually words unique to a business or profession or proper names that aren't included in Word's main dictionary. (A main dictionary that included all these words would be too large to use with reasonable speed and would be impossible to keep up to date.) You can instruct Word to pass over these words without changing them. You can also set the spelling checker to pass over them without bringing them to your attention.

When Word notifies you of an unmatched word that you know is spelled correctly, you can instruct Word to ignore the word by clicking on the No Change button. (The Start Check button turns into the No Change button as soon as the spelling checker finds an unmatched word.) Word remembers that word for the rest of your Word session and won't flag it as an unmatched word if it encounters it again during a spelling check. Word will not remember the word between sessions, however; if you restart and check spelling again, Word will flag the word when it encounters it again.

One simple way to ignore a set of words during a spelling check is to turn on the Ignore Words in All Caps option in the Spelling dialog box before you start the check. This tells Word to ignore acronyms—words such as ASCII, MIDI, and EBCDIC that are made up of the initial letter of each word in a phrase—during a spelling check. Because many acronyms don't spell out actual words, you can avoid having the spelling checker bring every one of them to your attention.

Working with Supplemental Dictionaries

To keep a list of your own specialized names and words that aren't in Word's own dictionary, you can create a supplemental dictionary that Word will consult during a spelling check. In the Open Dictionaries scrolling list of the Spelling dialog box, you'll find a list of all the dictionaries Word scans when it runs a spelling check. MS Dictionary is Word's main dictionary, and it contains standard American spellings for thousands of words. You can't add words to or delete words from this dictionary, and it is always open so Word can consult it.

Any dictionaries listed below ''MS Dictionary'' are supplemental dictionaries to which you can add words and from which you can delete words. The first time you use Word and open the Spelling dialog box, you'll see a supplemental dictionary named ''User 1'' in the Open Dictionaries scrolling list. Word provides this dictionary for you to create your own set of specialized words. You can also create additional supplemental dictionaries (as you'll learn to do later in this chapter) to hold different sets of words for specialized applications or situations.

Adding words to and removing words from a supplemental dictionary

When Word displays an unmatched word during a spelling check, you can add it to a supplemental dictionary by first clicking on the name of the dictionary in the Open Dictionaries scrolling list. The Words scrolling list changes to show all the words contained in that dictionary. You then click on the Plus (+) button to add the word in the Unmatched Word area to the selected supplemental dictionary. The added word should now appear in the Words scrolling list (which lists words in alphabetic order). If you want to add a word directly to the supplemental dictionary without first finding it in a spelling check as an unmatched word, type the word in the Change To text box and then click on the Plus (+) button.

To remove a word from a supplemental dictionary, click on the name of the dictionary you want from the Open Dictionaries scrolling list, and then select the word you want from the Words scrolling list, or type the word directly into the Change To text box. Then click on the Minus (−) button. Word removes the word from the dictionary.

Creating a new supplemental dictionary

To create a new supplemental dictionary, first open the Spelling dialog box and choose *New* from the Edit menu. Word opens a new dictionary called "User *X*" (in which *X* is the next number in a sequence Word uses to identify supplemental dictionaries) in the Open Dictionaries scrolling list. You can select that dictionary and then add new words to it in the same way you added words to the User 1 dictionary.

To save a supplemental dictionary under a new name, first select the dictionary you want from the Open Dictionaries scrolling list and then choose *Save As* from the File menu. Word opens a Save As dialog box similar to the document Save As dialog box. You can type a new name here and then choose to save the dictionary in any folder or disk. This creates a duplicate dictionary under the new name. To remove the original dictionary stored on disk under the original name, close the Spelling dialog box and use the Delete command in the File menu to delete the dictionary file.

You can at any time instruct Word to save the contents of the dictionary by selecting the name of the dictionary in the Open Dictionaries scrolling list and then choosing *Save* from the File menu. If you add words to or delete words from a dictionary and then quit Word without saving your changes, Word will display a message asking if it should save dictionary changes or quit without saving changes.

Using supplemental dictionaries

When Word checks spelling in a document by using supplemental dictionaries, the checking time increases as you add more words to the dictionaries and as you open more dictionaries for Word to scan in the spelling check. To keep the spell-checking process as efficient as possible, you should maintain small supplemental dictionaries and create a separate dictionary for each related set of words you might use when creating specialized documents. For example, if you frequently write business letters to Putrid Petrochemical Corporation and also run the Perfect Poodle Dog Clip Parlor on the side, you should keep one set of names and corporate words in a petrochemical dictionary and another set of names and words in a dog-clip dictionary. Then when you write a business letter to Putrid Petrochemicals, open only the petrochemical dictionary for spelling checks. When you write a letter to Perfect Poodle customers, open only the dog-clip dictionary. When you write an article about dealing in the world of high-finance petrochemistry and running a poodle-trimming parlor on the side, open both dictionaries simultaneously.

When you open the Spelling dialog box to start a spelling check, you can open any supplemental dictionaries stored in different folders and on different disks by choosing the Open command in the File menu. The name of each dictionary you open appears in the Open Dictionaries scrolling list, and Word scans each dictionary as it conducts the spelling check.

To close an open dictionary so you can speed up the spelling check, click on the dictionary name and then choose *Close* from the File menu.

An Example

Use Word's spelling checker to check the Petting Farm sample document for typing and spelling errors. The animal names in the list won't match any words in Word's main dictionary, so you can add them to a custom dictionary—Petting Farm—for later use. (Delete the dictionary from the disk when you finish this example unless you are in the petting-farm business and might actually make use of the names.) Follow the instructions on the next page.

1. Move the insertion point to the beginning of the document to start the spelling check there.

2. Choose *Spelling* from the Utilities menu to open the Spelling dialog box.

3. Choose *New* from the File menu to open a new supplemental dictionary. It will probably appear in the Open Dictionaries scrolling list as "User 2," but the number might be higher or lower depending on how many other supplemental dictionaries have been opened.

4. Click on the name of the dictionary you created, choose *Save As* from the File menu to open the Save As dialog box, and save the dictionary under the name "Petting Farm." "Petting Farm" replaces the previous dictionary name in the Open Dictionaries scrolling list.

5. Click on the Start Check button to start the spelling check. Word searches until it finds an unmatched word; the first one it finds should be the name "Biddlecomb" (unless you accidentally made typing errors in the document). Word lists the name in the Unknown Word area of the dialog box and also highlights the name in the report.

6. Pass over the name without changing it by clicking on the No Change button. Word continues the spelling check and stops on the next unmatched word: "burdgeoning."

7. Click on the Suggest button. Word offers a single alternative— "burgeoning"—in the Words scrolling list and also displays the word "burgeoning" in the Change To dialog box.

8. Click on the Change button. Word replaces the highlighted word and continues the check. The next unmatched word is "turnstyles."

9. Click on the Suggest button and accept the suggested spelling "turnstiles" to replace the highlighted word. Word continues its spelling check until it encounters "moomoos." It displays "moomoos" in the Unknown Word area and also highlights it in the document.

10. Add "moomoos" to the Petting Farm dictionary by clicking on the Petting Farm name in the Open Dictionaries scrolling list and then clicking on the Plus (+) button. The word "moomoos" appears in the Words scrolling list.

11. Click on the Continue Check button to continue the check. As you encounter the unmatched words "oinkoinks," "cluckclucks," "quackquacks," "bowwows," "hisshiss," "quadripedal," and "apedal," add them to the Petting Farm dictionary by clicking on the Petting Farm name and then clicking on the Plus button. Continue the check after each word addition. Word continues checking until it reaches the end of the document, where it stops the check and displays a message informing you that it has reached the end of the document.

12. Test your new dictionary additions by running a second check. Word passes over all the words you added to the supplemental dictionary. It also ignores "Biddlecomb," not because it's in the dictionary (it's not), but because Word remembers that you didn't change it the last time it appeared. In your next session with Word, the spelling checker will stop when it reaches "Biddlecomb" but will pass over the animal names if the Petting Farm dictionary is open.

CONTROLLING HYPHENATION

Hyphens in text both bind and separate: A hyphen can tie two words together, as it does in the phrase "toddler-tactile," or it can break a word at the end of a line. Unfortunately, when words are repositioned as a result of editing, word-breaking hyphens that you've inserted manually can get in the way. For example, if you break the word "primordial" at the end of a line (so that it reads *primor-dial*) and then insert text to the left of the word, pushing it to the next line, "primor-dial" appears on the next line, still broken by the hyphen.

Different Types of Hyphens

Word offers three types of hyphens to help you avoid this problem:

- The *normal* hyphen, entered by pressing the hyphen key (the key to the right of the 0 key at the top of the keyboard).

- The *soft* hyphen, entered by pressing Command-hyphen (-).

- The *nonbreaking* hyphen, entered by pressing Command-grave accent (`).

The normal hyphen is a standard character that Word treats much like a space. If two parts of a word usually separated by a hyphen fall at the end of a line, Word begins the next line with the second part of the word.

The soft hyphen is an invisible character you can insert to break a word. If the word falls at the end of a line, Word breaks the word at the soft hyphen's location and inserts a hyphen at the break. If revisions move the word to the next line or back to the middle of a line, the hyphen disappears and the word appears undivided. The soft hyphen remains invisible unless further revisions move the word to the end of the line again, where the word is broken and the hyphen reappears.

The nonbreaking hyphen appears as a regular hyphen in text. The only difference is that a word separated by a nonbreaking hyphen will not break if it falls at the end of a line. Use the nonbreaking hyphen on words (such as "V-neck") that you don't want broken between two lines.

You can see the different types of hyphens (visible and invisible) after you enter them in a document by choosing *Show ¶* from the Edit menu. Figure 13-6 shows the types of hyphens. All normal hyphens appear as they usually do; soft hyphens appear with a dot below the hyphen; and nonbreaking hyphens appear with a dot below the hyphen and a tilde (~) above the hyphen.

```
Normal.hyphen:.-¶
Soft.hyphen:.-¶
Nonbreaking.hyphen:.~¶
```

Figure 13-6. *The three types of hyphens are displayed here.*

Automatic Hyphenation

Word does not hyphenate text in a document unless you instruct it to do so. Instead, Word moves any word that doesn't fit at the end of a line to the beginning of the next line. If the moved word was a long word that almost fit in the line, Word ends the line short and moves the long word to the beginning of the next line. If the paragraph is left aligned, you can see a gap left by the moved long word as an especially ragged notch at the right edge of the paragraph. If the paragraph is fully justified, Word fills in the space left by the moved word by rearranging the words and inserting equal space between the words in the line. However, excessive spacing can make reading the line difficult, and the larger the paragraph indents, the worse this problem becomes. Word's automatic-hyphenation feature adjusts for the problem by breaking a large word with a soft hyphen instead of moving the full word to the next line.

To turn on automatic hyphenation, enter text as you do normally and choose *Hyphenate* from the Utilities menu to open the Hyphenate dialog box shown in Figure 13-7. Click on the Start Hyphenation button.

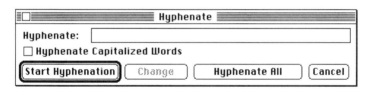

Figure 13-7. *Open the Hyphenate dialog box to start hyphenation and view proposed word breaks.*

When Word automatically hyphenates a document that is not set for full justification, it checks for any large gaps along the right margin. If it finds a large gap, it hyphenates the word that begins the next line, if possible, and moves the first part of that word back to fill in the end of the preceding line. (When Word hyphenates fully justified text, it determines hyphenation as if the text were left justified.)

When hyphenating a word, Word checks its hyphenation list, a file on disk similar to the dictionary file. The hyphenation list contains words broken into acceptable divisions. When Word finds the match for the word it wants to hyphenate, it opens the Hyphenate dialog box and displays the word in the

Hyphenate text box. The word appears broken into syllables with a high-lighted hyphen at the break likely to work best. Word also inserts a dotted vertical line after the last character in the word that will fit on the line.

If you agree with Word's proposed hyphenation, click on the Change button. Word adds a soft hyphen at that location and continues hyphenating. If you don't like the break, click on any of the other possible hyphens, or click between letters where no hyphen appears if you want to break the word there. Click on the Change button to break the word at the location you indicated. If you don't want to break the word at all, click on the No Change button to leave the word undivided. Word moves on to the next word that needs a hyphen. Click on the Cancel button to stop hyphenation.

Hyphenate All

If you trust Word's judgment in hyphenation, click on the Hyphenate All button to start hyphenation. As Word hyphenates, it doesn't stop at each word break to ask you whether the break is acceptable. Instead, it works through the entire document, inserting soft hyphens where it thinks they will work best. To stop the hyphenation process, click on the Cancel button or press Command-. (period). You can, of course, delete any soft hyphens that Word inserts if you think they are inappropriate.

An example

Try hyphenating the Petting Farm report to smooth the ragged right margins:

1. Move the insertion point to the beginning of the document.

2. Choose *Hyphenate* from the Utilities menu to open the Hyphenate dialog box.

3. Click on the Start Hyphenation button to start hyphenating. Word works through the document until it finds its first right-margin gap—the one created by the word ''recent'' in the first paragraph. It displays the word in the Hyphenate text box with a suggested break.

4. Click on the Change button to approve the break and continue hyphenation. Word moves on to ''reinvested.''

5. Click on the Change button to approve the break and continue hyphenation. When Word finishes hyphenating the document, it notifies you in a dialog box. The finished document now has a smoother right margin.

You've now learned about three very useful editing features: sorting, checking spelling, and hyphenating. In the next chapter you will be introduced to a single Word feature: footnotes.[1]

---

[1] See Chapter 14.

Chapter 14

Creating Footnotes

Many documents require footnotes to provide references or comments for statements in the body of the text. Adding these footnotes manually can be a challenging task; if you want the footnotes to appear at the bottom of each page, you must calculate the exact number of lines of body text and footnote text that can fit on each page and then position each footnote accordingly. Creating footnotes in Word 4 is much easier: You simply insert a footnote marker where appropriate, type the text of the footnote, and then continue typing the document. Word does the rest of the work.

In this chapter you'll learn not only how to insert footnotes but how to control footnote numbering or create unnumbered footnotes. You'll learn how to edit existing footnotes—to change their location, content, and formatting—and how to control their placement—at the bottom of the page or at the end of a chapter or document.

SETTING UP WORD

Before you begin working with the examples in this chapter, check to be sure that Word shows full menus and that Page View is turned off:

1. If you haven't done so already, turn your computer on and start Word.

2. Open the Edit menu, and if the Full Menus command appears, choose it to set full menus. If the Short Menus command appears instead of the Full Menus command, full menus are already set, and you can close the menu without choosing any commands.

3. Open the Document menu, and if a check mark appears to the left of the Page View command, choose the Page View command to turn Page View off.

The sample document for this chapter, shown in Figure 14-1, is a scholarly treatise on the footnote by Waldo Ambergris. It includes enough footnotes per square inch to give you plenty of practice.

AN OVERVIEW OF FOOTNOTES

Footnotes are statements that amplify a remark in a document or provide a reference for verification or for further reading. A *footnote marker*, the super-script number or symbol that follows a footnoted statement, informs the reader that a footnote exists for the statement he or she is reading. Footnotes can appear at the bottom of each page or can be collectively placed at the end of a chapter or document (in which case they are called *endnotes*).

Footnotes are usually numbered; each footnote marker is a number that refers to its corresponding footnote. Numbering footnotes adds convenience if your document has a large number of footnotes, and it is essential if you use endnotes. If you use footnotes sparingly, you can use symbols rather than numbers for footnote markers. If you use, for example, an asterisk for the first footnote marker on a page, you can use double, triple, or even quadruple asterisks for additional footnote markers on the same page.

Word separates footnotes appearing at the bottom of the page from the body of the text by inserting a *separator* between the body of the text and the footnotes. The separator is usually a horizontal line about 2 inches in length, but you can create your own separator from any string of characters.

As you add footnotes to a Word document, the footnote area expands from the bottom margin upward into the text area. If the footnote area ex-pands upward far enough to reach a line on which a footnote marker appears in the text area, it must stop expanding—there is no more space on the page for footnotes. If expansion stops and there isn't enough room in the footnote area to include the entire contents of the page's last footnote, Word breaks the text of the footnote and continues it on the next page. It inserts a *continuation separator* on the new page to separate the text area from the extended foot-note. The continuation separator is usually a horizontal line that stretches across the width of the page, but you can create one from any string of

The Footnote in History
by
Waldo Ambergris

Many[1] literary historians have neglected the proper place of the footnote in literary history: Some[2] claim that the footnote is only a parenthetical aside to the mainstream of literary thought; others[3] feel that the footnote should be shunted off the center stage of the written word to languish in the wings, far from the spotlight of literary illuminati. It is my contention[4] that the noble footnote deserves better treatment. To that end I now publish the newsletter "The Bottom[5] Line," which elevates the lowly footnote from the nether regions of literary history to the acme[@] of contemporary addenda. I also present this history, filled with footnote facts.

Why does the footnote deserve an elevated status?[6] Look back with me now to the dimly lit beginnings of the footnote in ancient Rome.

The first recorded reference[7] to a footnote shows us that early Romans used it to support a stone tablet, much as they used the base of a column to support the column.[8] The original text of the footnote was an incantation to the gods asking for textual stability and long

---

[1] Or perhaps only quite a few.
[2] Tools of a structuralist conspiracy.
[3] Academic charlatans.
[4] And also my doctoral thesis.
[5] Made you look!
[@] Trademark of the Acme Corporation. "We go out of our minds so you won't mind going out!"
[6] Why indeed?
[7] Found within a footnote of Style Guides of the Ancient Romans.
[8] The characters at the top of the tablet were called, accordingly, "Capital Letters."

(continued)

Figure 14-1. *Choose the Footnote command to place footnotes in this document.*

Figure 14-1. *continued*

shelf life. Space-conscious stone carvers soon discovered that they could add extra comments by getting rid of the incantation and filling the space with text they forgot to include in the tablet above.[9] This practice soon carried over into the world of papyrus and print. Early attempts at multiple footnotes ran into difficulties when the Roman numerals used to indicate each footnote grew long enough to fill an entire page. This problem was solved by the introduction of the arabic humbering system and the utilization of imaginary numbers. Freed from the constraints of physically imposed brevity, medieval scholars began to explore the limits of the footnote.[10] It was at this time that the copyright and the trademark were invented. In fact, one of the first characters struck by Johannes Gutenberg[11] was the copyright symbol, followed soon after by a smiling Mickey Mouse.[12]

Today, of course, we have computers to help us with footnotes. It has become as easy to enter text in a footnote as it is to enter it in the body of the text, so why not[13] give the footnote its due by subverting the dominant paradigm of the parenthesis and placing all additional comments in footnotes? It is only through concerted effort that we can elevate the footnote to its proper status at the bottom of the page.

---

[9] For a complete discussion of this substitution, read Useless Trivia for the Academic, by Oliver Ibid, Cider Press, 1984.
[10] Op Cit the Elder wrote in his Principia Obscurati of a footnote that lasted for 57 pages. The author's obvious scholarly prestige was boosted even further when readers realized that the body of the text was only two sentences long.
[11] Inventor of the Movable Type, a class of traveling merchants who peddled their wares from town to town.
[12] Trademark of Walt Disney, Inc.
[13] Indeed, why not?

characters. If you want to make it even clearer that the footnote is continued from the previous page, you can add a *continuation notice*—text that Word places at the top of each continued footnote area.

INSERTING A FOOTNOTE

To insert a footnote in a Word document, move the insertion point to the location you want and choose *Footnote* from the Document menu. The Footnote dialog box, shown in Figure 14-2, opens. Here you can select the type of footnote marker you want and choose separators or continuation notices.

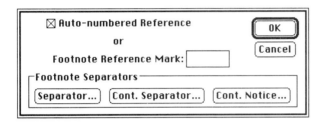

Figure 14-2. *Use the Footnote dialog box to select a type of footnote marker and to change footnote separators.*

If you click on the OK button without making changes in the dialog box, the box closes and Word inserts a numbered footnote marker at the insertion-point location. (Word keeps track of footnote numbers and inserts the correct number for each marker.) Word then opens the *footnote window*, shown in Figure 14-3 on the following page, a partition that appears at the bottom of the document window, forming a split screen. The upper part of the document window is the main text window.

Working with the Footnote Window

The footnote window is separated from the rest of the document by a thick horizontal bar called the *split bar*. You can change the relative sizes of the footnote and main text windows by dragging the split-bar drag box (located at the right end of the split bar).

The footnote window contains all the footnotes you type in a document and has its own vertical scroll bar you can use to scroll through the footnotes. Text in the footnote window does not appear in the body of the document; you

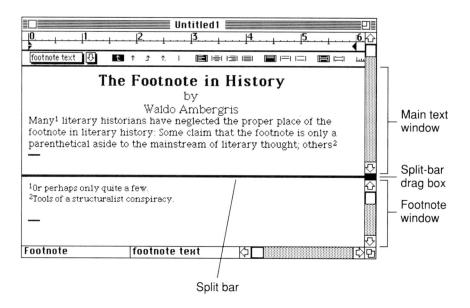

The Footnote in History

Figure 14-3. *The footnote window appears in the lower part of the document window.*

see the footnote (or endnote) text in relation to the page only when you print, use Print Preview, or use Page View.

When you insert a footnote marker in the document, Word places a corresponding marker at the beginning of a new line in the footnote window. The insertion point moves to the footnote window, and you can type the contents of your footnote there. As you type, you can format characters and paragraphs as you do in the body of the text. Note that you can't delete or move a footnote marker in the footnote window; you must alter the marker in the body of the text (as you'll learn to do later in this chapter).

When you finish typing the footnote contents, move the insertion point back to the main text window and click the mouse button so you can continue to type text there; the footnote window remains open. You can move back and forth between windows by using the mouse, or if you prefer using the keyboard you can press keypad 0, which moves the insertion point back to its previous locations. After you've typed a footnote, the previous location is in the main text window, following the footnote marker.

To close the footnote window, you can either drag the split bar all the way to the bottom of the document window or double-click on the split-bar drag box. The footnote window closes, but don't worry—the footnotes are still in memory. To open the footnote window again, you can double-click on a footnote marker or press the key combination Shift-Option-Command-S. Pressing Shift-Option-Command-S also closes the footnote window if the window is open.

An Example

Try entering footnotes in the sample document:

1. Set paragraph formatting to center aligned and character formatting to 18-point boldface. Type the title *The Footnote in History* and press Return.

2. Turn off boldface, reduce the character size to 14 points, and then enter the next two lines: *by* followed by *Waldo Ambergris*. (Press Return at the end of each line.)

3. Set the paragraph formatting to left aligned with double spacing and a blank line before each paragraph. (As the scholarly Waldo Ambergris, you naturally want this treatise to take up as many pages as possible.) Reduce the character size to 12 points and type the first word of the treatise—*Many*—and then stop.

4. Choose *Footnote* from the Document menu. The Footnote dialog box opens.

5. Click on the OK button to close the dialog box and set automatic footnote numbering. A superscript *1* appears following "Many," the footnote window opens, and *1* appears at the beginning of the first line in the footnote window.

6. Type the footnote contents, *Or perhaps only quite a few.*

7. Press keypad 0 to return to the main text window and continue typing the document (as shown in Figure 14-1) up to the end of the word "others." Do not insert footnote 2 shown after "Some" in the sample document. You'll add it later.

8. Choose *Footnote* from the Document menu; click on the OK button in the Footnote dialog box to insert a second numbered footnote. A superscript 2 appears after "others," and *2* appears in the second line of the footnote window.

9. Enter the footnote contents *Tools of a structuralist conspiracy,* and press keypad 0 to return to the main text window.

10. Continue typing the first paragraph. Enter the footnotes you see in the sample document after the words "contention" and "Bottom." Stop after you type the word "acme." (This example doesn't require verbatim text, so you can abridge the body and footnote text if you want.)

Changing the Footnote Marker

Word usually numbers footnotes. To use your own unnumbered footnote marker, type the character you want in the Footnote Reference Mark text box of the Footnote dialog box and click on the OK button. Word inserts that character as a superscript character in the body of the text and then places the character at the beginning of a new footnote line in the footnote window. Try entering the @ symbol as a footnote marker:

1. Choose *Footnote* from the Document menu to open the Footnote dialog box.

2. Type @ in the Footnote Reference Mark box and then click on the OK button. The symbol appears as a superscript character following the word "acme" and again at the beginning of a new line in the footnote window.

3. Enter the footnote contents *Trademark of the Acme Corporation. "We go out of our minds so you won't mind going out!"*

4. Press keypad 0 to return to the main text window and then type the remainder of the document, entering footnotes as they appear in Figure 14-1. Use automatic numbering for the remaining footnotes. (Again, you can abridge any of the text as you type the document, but be sure to fill at least two pages of text so you can work with footnotes on different pages in the examples that follow.)

EDITING A FOOTNOTE

When you enter a footnote in the footnote window, it remains in that window and doesn't appear in the body of the document. The only part of the footnote that appears in the main text window is the footnote marker. It's important to realize that the footnote marker and its footnote are linked; the footnote marker in the main text window controls the existence and location of the footnote in the footnote window. If you cut, copy, or paste the footnote marker in the document, the footnote linked to the marker disappears or moves within the footnote window to correspond to the new location of the footnote marker. It's also important to note that you can't cut, copy, or paste a footnote as a whole entity within the footnote window. You must edit the footnote marker to affect the entire footnote.

Deleting a Footnote

To delete a footnote, move the insertion point to the right side of its footnote marker in the main text window and press Delete. When you delete the marker, its footnote disappears from the footnote window and Word renumbers the markers (if they're numbered) that follow the deleted footnote. If you immediately choose *Undo* from the Edit menu, Word replaces the footnote marker and restores its footnote in the footnote window.

Moving a Footnote

To move a footnote from one location to another, select the footnote marker in the main text window and choose *Cut*. Move the insertion point to the new location and choose *Paste*. The footnote changes its position in the footnote window correspondingly, and Word renumbers the footnotes and markers (if they're numbered) to reflect the new order.

Copying a Footnote

Some footnotes—particularly ''Ibid.'' references—appear frequently in a document. You can use the Copy command to duplicate a repeating footnote. First select the footnote marker in the main text window and then choose *Copy* from the Edit menu. Move the insertion point to the next location at which you need the footnote and choose *Paste*. Word inserts a footnote marker at that location and adds a copy of the original footnote to the footnote window. Word correctly numbers the copy; it doesn't repeat the number of the original footnote.

Searching for a Footnote Marker

To find a specific footnote marker for editing, first scroll through the footnotes in the footnote window until you find the one you want. As you scroll, the main text window scrolls to match the footnotes displayed in the footnote window. When a footnote appears at the top of the footnote window, the main text window displays that footnote's marker and the text surrounding it. You can then move the insertion point back to the main text window to cut, move, or duplicate the footnote marker.

Editing the Contents of a Footnote

You can edit the *contents* of a footnote in the footnote window exactly as you edit text in the main text window—by cutting, pasting, copying, deleting, and formatting. Remember, however, that you can't cut, paste, copy, or delete the footnote marker from within the footnote window.

An Example

After reading the sample document, you decide that the footnote you applied to the word "others" actually applies to the people you described with the word "Some." Move the footnote from "others" to "Some," and then insert a new footnote to describe "others":

1. Scroll the footnote window until footnote 2 appears at the top of the window. The main text window also scrolls to show footnote marker 2.

2. Move the insertion point to the main text window and select the footnote marker "2" as a text block.

3. Choose *Cut* from the Edit menu to cut the footnote marker from the main text. Footnote 2 in the footnote window disappears, and Word renumbers the remaining footnotes accordingly.

4. Move the insertion point to the space following the word "Some" and choose *Paste* from the Edit menu to insert the cut footnote there. The footnote number appears in the body of the text, the footnote itself reappears in the footnote window, and Word renumbers the footnotes.

5. Move the insertion point to the space following the word ''others'' and choose *Footnote* from the Document menu. A footnote marker appears in the body of the text and in the footnote window.

6. Type the footnote contents *Academic charlatans.*

7. Double-click on the split-bar drag box to close the footnote window. The sample document is now complete.

8. Choose *Page View* from the Document menu to turn Page View on, and then look at the results of your work. You see footnotes at the bottom of each page, separated from the body of the text by a short, horizontal line.

CHANGING FOOTNOTE CONVENTIONS

By default, Word places numbered footnotes at the bottom of each page. This works well for most documents, but if you want to follow a different footnote convention, you can easily change Word's settings.

Changing the Separators and the Continuation Notice

To change the horizontal line that separates footnotes from the body of text, choose *Footnote* from the Document menu to open the Footnote dialog box. Click on the Separator button in the lower left corner of the dialog box. A new window, labeled ''Footnote Separator,'' shown in Figure 14-4, appears in the text window.

Replace the horizontal line that appears in the window with your own string of characters. You can enter any characters you think appropriate—

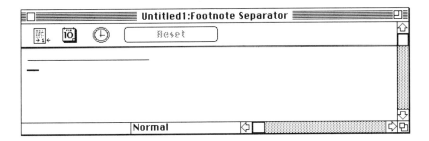

Figure 14-4. *The Footnote Separator window displays the line that separates footnotes from main text. You can change the characters that form the line.*

including the page number, time, and date by clicking on the icons in the upper left quarter of the window—and apply character formatting such as boldface and italic. You can also center the separator and add paragraph borders to it, but keep in mind that short and simple is usually best. Large separators take up space that might be better used for text and footnotes.

After you type the separator characters you want, close the Footnote Separator window by clicking on its close box. If you decide (before you close the window) that you don't like your new separator, click on the Reset button. The separator is reset to its original state. You can then close the window.

To change the continuation separator that appears when a footnote extends over two or more pages or to create a continuation notice, open the Footnote dialog box. Click on either the Cont. Separator button to change the continuation separator or the Cont. Notice button to change the continuation notice. A window similar to the Footnote Separator window opens in the document window. Type the characters you want in the window, and then close the window when you finish.

Changing Footnote Location

To change footnote location, choose *Document* from the Format menu to open the Document dialog box, shown in Figure 14-5. The settings in the Footnotes area (in the lower right quarter of the dialog box) allow you to change the footnote format in a document.

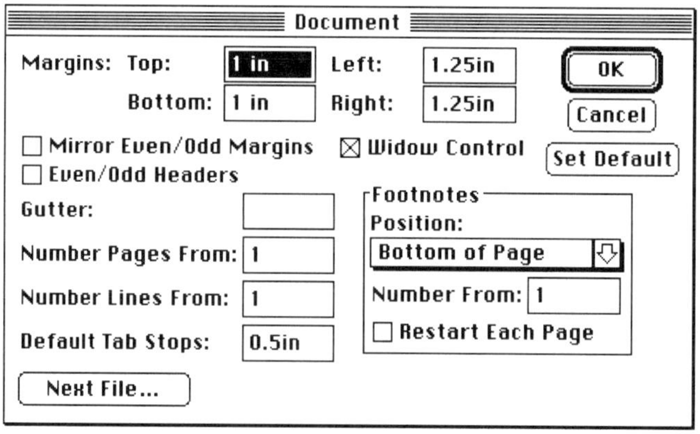

Figure 14-5. *Choose options in the Footnotes area of the Document dialog box to control a document's footnote format.*

The Position list box in the Footnotes area offers four footnote locations:

- *Bottom of Page*. This is the default setting. Word places footnotes at the bottom of each page, building upward from the bottom page margin until the footnotes meet the body of the text. If the last page of a document has only a small amount of text in the body, a large blank space appears between the text body and the footnotes below.

- *Beneath Text*. This setting instructs Word to place footnotes at the bottom of each page, beginning at the bottom of the text body and working downward to the bottom page margin. If the last page of a document has only a small amount of text in the body, the page will contain a large blank space between the end of the last footnote and the bottom page margin.

- *End of Section*. This setting instructs Word to turn footnotes into endnotes by placing them at the end of a document section. (You'll learn to create document sections in Chapter 16, "Section Formatting.") This setting is useful if you use sections to define chapters within a document. In that case, when you print your document, footnotes print at the end of each chapter.

- *End of Document*. This setting instructs Word to turn footnotes into endnotes by placing them at the end of the document.

To select a footnote location, choose one of the settings in the Position list box and then click on the OK button to close the dialog box and change the footnote location.

Setting a New Footnote Starting Number

If a document is a continuation of previous work—perhaps one of many chapters in a book—you might need to number the footnotes beginning with a number other than 1. To set the starting number, open the Document dialog box by choosing *Document* from the Format menu, and change the number in the Number From text box to the starting number you want. Click on the OK button to close the dialog box; Word numbers the footnotes in your document, beginning with the number you entered.

Restarting Footnote Numbering

Word begins numbering on-page footnotes on the first page on which foot-notes appear and continues numbering from one page to the next. To restart the numbering on each page, turn the Restart Each Page option on in the Footnotes area, and click on the OK button to close the dialog box. The foot-note numbering format changes so that numbering restarts at 1 on each page.

By default, Word numbers endnotes that appear at the end of each section sequentially across the section divisions. To change the footnote numbering format so that numbering restarts at the beginning of each section, open the Document dialog box, turn the Restart Each Section option on in the Foot-notes area, and then click on the OK button to close the dialog box.

Try changing the footnote numbering format so that numbering restarts at 1 on each page in the sample document, and then turn the footnotes into endnotes:

1. Turn Page View on (if it's not already on) by choosing *Page View* from the Document menu, and then scroll through the document. Notice that the footnotes are numbered consecutively from the first page through the second page.

2. Choose *Document* from the Format menu to open the Document dialog box.

3. Turn the Restart Each Page option on in the Footnotes area, and then click on the OK button to close the dialog box. When you scroll through the document, notice that the footnote numbers now restart at 1 on the second page.

4. Choose *Document* from the Format menu to reopen the Document dialog box, choose *End of Document* from the Position list box, and click on the OK button to close the dialog box.

5. When you scroll through the document, notice that the footnotes are now collected as endnotes at the end of the last page.

6. Turn Page View off by choosing *Page View*.

You've now learned how to insert and control footnotes in your docu-ments. In the next chapter you'll learn about one of Word's most powerful features: styles.

Chapter 15

Styles Made Simple:
Formatting with Speed and Power

Styles are one of Word 4's most powerful features. Each Word style is a collection of character and paragraph formats that can define the overall look of a paragraph. You can define and name a style and then use it to set the appearance of paragraphs throughout a document. If you change a style definition, you change the appearance of all paragraphs defined by that style, wherever they appear in the document.

In this chapter you'll learn more about styles and how to make them work for you. You'll learn how to define styles and how to apply styles to existing text or to new text as you type. You'll also learn how to redefine existing styles and the text they control and how to move styles from one document to another by using style sheets.

SETTING UP WORD

Before you begin working with the examples in this chapter, check to be sure that Word shows full menus, that Page View is turned off, and that the Ruler is visible:

1. If you haven't done so already, turn your computer on and start Word.

2. Open the Edit menu, and if the Full Menus command appears, choose it to set full menus. If the Short Menus command appears instead of the Full Menus command, full menus are already set, and you can close the menu without choosing any commands.

3. Open the Document menu, and if a check mark appears to the left of the Page View command, choose the Page View command to turn Page View off.

4. Open the Format menu, and if the Show Ruler command appears, choose it to show the Ruler. If Hide Ruler appears, the Ruler is already visible.

Figure 15-1 shows the sample document for this chapter, an article on unicycle racing that includes elements you can control with styles: a title, two levels of section headings, text body, and captions for pictures.

AN OVERVIEW OF STYLES

In the preceding chapters, you set character and paragraph formatting as you typed sample documents, a process that usually involved choosing several commands. For example, to create a title, you centered a paragraph, enlarged the point size of the text, and turned boldface on. When you moved on to the body of the text, you changed to left alignment, smaller point size, and no boldface. Even if you're adept at using keyboard shortcuts, there is a significant pause while you stop to change formatting. Using a single instruction to set the formatting for a title or normal text would be much quicker, and styles enable you to do just that.

Each style is a formatting shortcut; it stores information about combinations of character and paragraph formatting (including tabs) within a paragraph so that you can apply the formatting later, in a single step, to other paragraphs. You can create a style for every type of element in your document and then use the defined style to change formatting whenever you create that type of element.

To define a style, you select an existing paragraph that contains the character and paragraph formatting you want to serve as a model for the style, or you define the formatting you want by choosing options in a dialog box. You then give the style a name; Word stores the defined style under this name. For example, you might create a style named "Section" that shows underlined, italic text with a 0.5-inch indent and then use this defined style to create section headings throughout a document.

Unicycle Racing: The Forgotten Sport

"There's nothing like the smell of bearing grease, the flash of sun on the seat post, and 50 unicyclists straining for the finish line!" Howard Dutilleux is reminiscing, leaning back against the bar railing as he finishes ,another boilermaker. "You'll never see anything like that today—young punks all use two wheels now. Line me up another one, Jimbo...." Rob Formass nods in agreement and adds, "A shame. It's a damn shame." They raise their glasses in leathery hands, salute each other with a loud clink, and toss back their drinks in fond remembrance of better times past. They are the last of a dying breed: professional unicycle racers.

The Beginnings of Unicycle Racing

Although barely remembered now, unicycle racing started with much fanfare at the Auxiliary World's Fair of 1928 in Moscow, Idaho. Billed as a spectacle with "Chills, Thrills, and Spills—With Half the Wheels!," the world's first unicycle race had a purse of $500 to lure hungry unicyclists from around the country. The course, a 7-mile circuit with a steep 500-foot hill, was set up around the fairgrounds. The organizers built an upturned ramp on the descent of the hill so descending unicyclists could leap 15 feet through the air before the main grandstands—a guaranteed audience pleaser!

Picture: The Moscow racecourse, complete with mechanics' pits.

(continued)

Figure 15-1. *Use styles to set and control the elements of this document.*

Figure 15-1. *continued*

A Hit

This first experiment in professional unicycle racing was an immediate success. There were, of course, numerous accidents as unscrupulous unicyclists used their free hands to harass their opponents. A favorite trick was quickly spinning a neighboring unicyclist around 180 degrees so he would start pedaling in the wrong direction. Many cyclists continued pedaling in the wrong direction until they met the pack coming in the opposite direction (or until they came up to the wrong end of the ramp)!

Unicycle Racing Spreads

Unicycle racing soon spread like heat rash under a cheap cycling jersey. Soon the entire Palouse area became the mecca for unicyclists from around the world. Special training camps sprang up, offering specialties like endurance unicycling (the 200-kilometer road race was especially popular at the time) and uphill sprints. Designers began to introduce specialty unicycles: 1935 saw the introduction of both the AeroAce 10-foot unicycle (effective for falling toward the finish line at the last moment) and the Marauder, a competitive unicycle built of solid cast iron. It didn't climb hills well, but its descents were murderous, and nobody wanted to collide with a Marauder. That was indeed the Golden Age of Unicycling.

Picture: The AeroAce and Marauder unicycles, ridden by unicyclist greats Arto DeFeur and Simon Durst.

To apply a style, you first select one or more paragraphs, as you do for paragraph formatting. You then choose the name of the desired style from either the Ruler or a dialog box. The style you apply changes the formatting of any selected paragraphs to match the style's formatting definition. You can also set styles as you type text. When you choose a style during text entry, the style sets your current paragraph and character formatting to the style's formatting. For example, if you define the style named "Section," you can choose it before you begin typing a section heading. When you enter the heading, it appears italicized and underlined, with a 0.5-inch left indent.

Using Automatic Styles

Word comes with predefined styles, called *automatic styles,* that you can apply to any document. The most commonly used automatic style is "Normal," Word's default style. Normal style (if it hasn't been redefined) produces a 12-point New York font with left-aligned paragraph formatting and plain character formatting. Word offers additional automatic styles that control other common elements in documents. For example, when you open the header window, Word applies the automatic style "Header," which includes centered and right-aligned tab stops to help you align page numbers and titles.

Changing Style Definitions

After you apply styles to various document elements, you can redefine the styles to quickly change the formatting of the elements throughout the document. When you redefine a style, all elements controlled by that style change to match the new definition. For example, if every section heading in a document is controlled by the Section style, you can change all the headings at one time by changing the Section style definition. If you change the style to include centered, boldface, and italic formatting, all section headings appear in centered, boldface, italic type. If you didn't use styles, you would need to reformat each section heading individually.

A style definition change can affect more than a single style. Every style, with the exception of Normal, can be based on another style. This means that a style such as Section is defined as "Normal plus italic, underlining, and a 0.5-inch left indent." When you change a base style, all its derivative styles change as well. For example, changing Normal's definition to use the Geneva font instead of New York changes the font to Geneva in all styles that use the Normal style as a base (including a style such as Section). The only exceptions in this example would be derivative styles that specify their own fonts. If you create styles by building on a single base style, you can easily change the properties (such as font or point size) of all the elements in a document by simply changing the base style that acts as the foundation for all the elements.

DEFINING A STYLE

You can define a style in either of two ways: by selecting an example paragraph that already contains the formatting that will make up a style or by creating your own style definition. To define a style by example, first select an example paragraph in a document and then use either the style-selection box in the Ruler or the Define Styles command to capture the paragraph's formatting. To create your own style definition, choose the Define Styles command to open the Define Styles dialog box, where you set all the formats you want to include in the style's definition.

Defining a style by selecting an example paragraph is the fastest and easiest method of defining a style and is useful if you format elements of a document as you write. Once you format a paragraph in a way you think you'll use again, capture its formatting in a style so you can use that style the next time you create a similar element. Defining styles by setting options in the Define Styles dialog box is useful if you plan a document carefully before you begin writing. Define a style for each type of element you plan to include in the document; later, as you write, you can apply your styles to create the elements you want.

Setting a Style by Example

To set a style by selecting an example paragraph, follow the same steps you use when selecting a paragraph for paragraph formatting: You can select a single block of text in the paragraph, select the entire paragraph, or simply move the insertion point into the paragraph. You can also select more than one paragraph, but if you do, Word follows the formatting in the first paragraph in the selection and ignores the formatting in the other paragraphs. (Note that if you select a text block that includes portions of paragraphs, Word considers the paragraphs to be completely selected.)

After you select an example paragraph, use either the Ruler or the Define Styles command to set a style. To use the Ruler, click on the style-selection box on the left side of the Ruler, shown in Figure 15-2. Word highlights the box, indicating that you can replace the style name currently displayed. Replace the name by typing a new style name, and then press Return. If a style doesn't already exist for the name you typed, Word displays a dialog box asking whether you want to define a style based on your selected paragraph. Click on the Define button to set a new style, or click on the Cancel button to escape without setting a style.

Style-selection box

Figure 15-2. *Use the style-selection box to define new styles or to choose from existing styles.*

To set a style by example by using the Define Styles command, choose *Define Styles* from the Format menu to open the Define Styles dialog box, shown in Figure 15-3. In the Style text box, type a name for the style you want to set, and then click on the OK button to close the dialog box and set that style.

Figure 15-3. *Open the Define Styles dialog box to define styles and to apply existing styles to text.*

When you set a style by example by using either of these methods, Word assigns the paragraph and character formatting of your example paragraph to the style name you entered. If your example paragraph contains mixed character formatting, Word determines the character formatting used most often and assigns that formatting to the style you set.

Try setting a style now by using an example paragraph and the Ruler:

1. Set character formatting to 18-point boldface and paragraph formatting to centered, type the title of the sample document, and then press Return.

2. Select the entire first paragraph (the title) as an example paragraph for defining a style.

3. Click on the name in the style-selection box on the Ruler, type the new style name *Title*, and then press Return. A dialog box asks whether you want to define the style "Title" based on your selection.

4. Choose *Define* to close the dialog box and to apply the new style Title.

5. Move the insertion point to the end of the document (to the line immediately below the title) to prepare for further text entry, and reset paragraph formatting to left aligned and character formatting to 12-point plain text.

Setting a Style by Definition

To set a style by defining it yourself, open the Define Styles dialog box by choosing *Define Styles* from the Format menu. Use the parts of the dialog box to create new styles from scratch or (later) to see and edit existing styles.

The styles list box and Style text box

The upper left quarter of the Define Styles dialog box contains the styles list box (a scrolling list box that displays all styles used in the current document) and a Style text box, in which you can type new style names. The styles list box lists style names in alphabetic order and displays a bullet before the name of each automatic style used in the document. You choose the option labeled "New Style" at the top of the list to start a new style.

The Style text box displays the name of the style you select from the styles list, or if you select New Style, it remains blank. To define a new style, choose *New Style* and then type the name of your new style in the Style text box.

The style-description area

The style-description area (directly below the Styles text box) displays the formatting instructions that define both paragraph and character formatting. These instructions form the definition of the selected style.

When you first start a new style, the style-description area is empty except for a style name followed by a plus sign (+). This style name is the *base style* of the new style. Your new style begins with the same formatting instructions as those of the base style, and if you make no changes to it, the new style will look exactly like the base style.

To add formatting instructions to your new style, apply character and paragraph formatting as you would to a document. You can display the Ruler and change indents, alignment, line spacing, tabs, and other paragraph formats. You can choose a new font and point size from the Font menu and a new type style from the Format menu. You can also open either the Paragraph or Character dialog box to choose formatting options there.

Each time you set formatting, a new formatting instruction appears in the style-description area. For example, if you start a new style based on the Normal style, the style-description area first displays ''Normal +.'' When you choose *24 Point* from the Font menu, the style-description area then displays ''Normal + Font: 24 point.'' And when you choose *Bold* from the Format menu, the area displays ''Normal + Font: 24 point, Bold.'' Figure 15-4, on the following page, shows the formatting instructions for a bordered chapter-title style; as you can see, a style definition can contain quite a few formatting instructions.

The Based On text box

Because the base style sets the initial characteristics of your new style, you should choose a base style that looks as much like the new style as possible. One simple way to set a base style is to select a paragraph with an appropriate base style before you open the Define Styles dialog box; Word uses the style of the selected paragraph as the base style for any new styles you create.

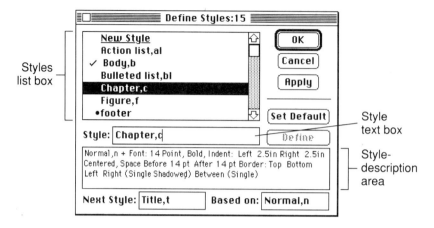

Figure 15-4. *The style-description area displays the definition of the style whose name appears in the Style text box.*

If you want to change the base style while the Define Styles dialog box is open, click on the Based On text box (at the bottom of the dialog box), which shows the name of the current base style; Word highlights the box, indicating that you can change its contents by typing a new style name. Type a new style name and then press Return. The style name you enter becomes the base style for the style defined in the style-description area. You'll see the new base-style name at the beginning of the first line in the style-description area.

The Next Style text box

Whenever you apply a style as you type text, each new paragraph you create by pressing Return follows the style of the last paragraph. There might be times, however, when you don't want to continue applying the same style. For example, when you press Return at the end of a section heading, you might want to return to Normal style. To create such a single-paragraph style, you enter a style name in the Next Style text box at the bottom of the Define Styles dialog box.

If you leave the Next Style text box empty when you define a style, Word inserts the same style's name in the text box. This sets the style so that when you apply it once while typing text, the same style continues each time you press Return. If you type the name of a different style in the Next Style text box and then go on to define the current style, the defined style is set to change when you press Return. For example, you can define the style of a section heading and then set Normal as the next style. When you press Return after typing a heading, Word applies the Normal style to the next paragraph.

The Define and Set Default buttons

Once you set the style name, base style, next style, and formatting instructions for a new style, you can define the new style and add it to the styles list by clicking on the Define button at the right side of the Define Styles dialog box. The style is now available for you to apply as you work in the current document.

Word offers its own set of styles, called *default styles*, whenever you begin a new document. These styles don't include the styles you create in other documents unless you specifically define a style and instruct Word to store it as a default style. To turn one of your own styles into a default style, choose its name from the styles list of the Define Styles dialog box and then click on the Set Default button; Word adds the style to the default list, and the style will be available in every new document you create.

The OK and Cancel buttons

Clicking on the OK button instructs Word to apply the currently selected style to the currently selected paragraph and then close the dialog box. Clicking on the Cancel button closes the dialog box without applying any new styles to the currently selected paragraph.

An example

The sample article includes two different types of section headings: a level-one heading with boldface, double underlining, and a 0.5-inch indent; and a level-two heading with single underlining. The article also includes picture captions with italic text. Define three new styles named Head1, Head2, and Pict for these elements. Take the following steps:

1. Choose *Define Styles* from the Format menu to open the Define Styles dialog box. *New Style* should appear highlighted in the styles list, the Style text box should be empty, and the style-description area should display ''Normal +.''

2. Type the name *Head1* in the Style text box.

3. Choose *Character* from the Format menu to open the Character dialog box.

4. Choose *Double* from the Underline list box to turn double underlining on.

5. Click on the Bold check box to turn boldface on.

6. Click on the OK button to close the Character dialog box. The two formats you set now appear in the style-description area.

7. Drag the left and first-line indent markers to the 0.5-inch mark on the Ruler's measure. The indent change appears in the style-description area. (If the Define Styles dialog box covers the Ruler, drag the dialog box downward.)

8. Choose *Paragraph* from the Format menu to open the Paragraph dialog box.

9. Click on the Keep With Next ¶ check box to turn it on, ensuring that the heading is never split from the text under it by a page break.

10. Click on the OK button to close the Paragraph dialog box. The paragraph formatting you set appears in the style-description area.

11. Type *Normal* in the Next Style text box.

12. Click on the Define button to define Head1 and add it to the styles list.

13. Click on the Apply button to apply Head1 style to the selected paragraph. Because the selected paragraph is the example paragraph for the style definitions that follow, you can then define Head2 with Head1 as its base style.

You've now defined a level-one heading that is boldface, double underlined, set in from body text by 0.5 inch, and won't be separated from following text by page breaks.

Now define a level-two heading:

1. Choose *New Style* from the styles list to define a new style. Notice that the Based On text box shows Head1 as the base style for the new style. This is because the selected paragraph in the document is set to the Head1 style.

2. Type *Head2* in the Style text box to name the new style.

3. Choose *Character* from the Format menu to open the Character dialog box.

4. Choose *Single* from the Underline list box to turn single underlining on, and then click on the OK button to close the dialog box and return to the Define Styles dialog box. The formatting instructions for your new style now include single underlining. Because Head2 style is based on Head1, it also contains boldface, a left indent, and the Keep With Next ¶ option (even though these formats don't appear in the style-description area).

5. Type *Normal* in the Next Style text box.

6. Click on the Define button to define Head2 and add it to the styles list.

Now define the picture-caption style:

1. Choose *Normal* from the styles list, and click on the Apply button to apply Normal style to the selected paragraph.

2. Choose *New Style* from the styles list to start a new style. Normal style appears as the new style's base style.

3. Type the name *Pict* in the Style text box.

4. Choose *Italic* from the Format menu to turn italic formatting on. The style-description area now lists italic character formatting.

5. Click on the Define button to define Pict and add it to the styles list.

6. Click on the Cancel button to close the Define Styles dialog box without applying the current style (Pict) to the currently selected paragraph.

APPLYING A STYLE

After you've defined useful styles for a document, apply them whenever possible to save yourself work in formatting. You can apply a style as you type, or if you prefer, you can type a paragraph (or more) and then return to apply a style to it. However you apply them, try to use styles consistently. If you conscientiously apply the same style to an element whenever it appears in a document, you'll find it very easy to reformat an element throughout a document by simply redefining the element's style.

Identifying a Paragraph's Style

All paragraphs have a style, even if you've never applied any styles in a document (in which case the paragraphs would all follow the Normal style). Before you apply a style to a paragraph, you might want to know its current style. Simply place the insertion point in the paragraph, and then look to the right of the page-number area at the bottom of the document window. The style-name area, shown in Figure 15-5, displays the name of the style that controls the paragraph. If the Ruler is displayed, the style-selection box also displays the name of the current style. By moving the insertion point through a document and watching the style-name area, you can easily see what styles

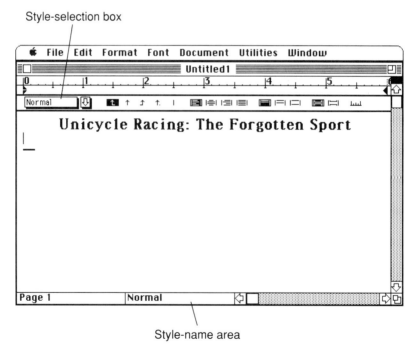

Figure 15-5. *Both the style-name area and the Ruler's style-selection box display the name of the currently selected paragraph.*

274

are applied where. Note also that double-clicking in the style-name area opens the Define Styles dialog box.

Applying Styles During Text Entry

To apply a style to a paragraph as you type, you can click on the Ruler's style-selection box and choose the style you want from the styles list. Word changes the formatting of the paragraph you're typing so that it matches the new style's definition.

If the Ruler is not displayed, you can see a list of styles in the Styles dialog box, shown in Figure 15-6, by choosing *Styles* from the Format menu. The Styles dialog box is a reduced version of the Define Styles dialog box; it includes a styles list box, a style-description area that shows the formatting instructions of the style you choose from the styles list, and three buttons you click on to apply styles and close the dialog box. You can't define styles in the Styles dialog box, but you can apply a style by choosing its name from the styles list and then clicking on the Apply button. Word applies the style and leaves the dialog box open. To apply the style and close the dialog box, click on the OK button; to close the dialog box without applying a style, click on the Cancel button.

If you know all the style names by heart, one of the fastest ways to apply styles is to press Shift-Command-S. The page-number area at the bottom of the document appears highlighted, indicating that you can type a style name. Type the style name and then press Return; Word applies the style.

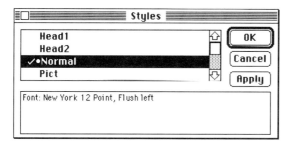

Figure 15-6. *The Styles dialog box lists styles you can apply to selected text.*

Applying Styles to Existing Text

To apply a style to existing text, first select the text as a text block. Word treats the text block as a selection of full paragraphs as it does when you select text for paragraph formatting.

You can apply the style you want in any of three ways: Choose the style from the style-selection box on the Ruler; choose the style from either the Styles dialog box or the Define Styles dialog box; or press Shift-Command-S and type the style name in the style-name area. All the text within the selected paragraphs changes to match the style definition.

Adding Manual Formatting to a Styled Paragraph

After you apply a style to a paragraph, you can go back to the paragraph and change its character or paragraph formatting. Changing the formatting in a paragraph after its style has been set is called *manual formatting*. Although manual formatting changes the appearance of the paragraph, it doesn't change the paragraph's style. Word recognizes manual formatting as an addition to the style's formatting but not as part of the style.

Whenever you add manual formatting to a paragraph, the style-name area at the bottom of the document window adds a plus sign (+) following the style name. If you see a plus sign in the style-name area, you know that the selected paragraph might not appear as it normally does when first formatted by its style.

When you apply a new style to a document paragraph that already contains manual formatting in addition to its style formatting, Word replaces all the manual formatting with the new style's formatting, with one exception: Word *toggles* character emphases in the manually formatted parts of the paragraph; that is, Word allows you to identify the specially formatted characters by maintaining their distinction. For example, if when manually formatting an area of text you italicize several phrases in a paragraph whose text style was set in plain format and then you apply to the paragraph a new style that contains italic formatting, the new style turns all the plain text to italicized text and all the italicized (manually formatted) text to plain text. This ensures that the words you emphasized using italic are still ''emphasized,'' this time by not being italic.

To change text back to a style's original formatting and to remove manual formatting, select the text block and choose *Plain For Style* from the Format menu or press Shift-Command-Spacebar. For example, if you select a text block whose style specifies plain text but the paragraph includes some italic text (through manual formatting), you can choose *Plain For Style* to turn all the text back to plain text, whether or not it's italicized.

An Example

Apply the styles you created earlier—Head1, Head2, and Pict—as you type the rest of the sample article. (It's not important that you type the normal text paragraphs verbatim, but try to keep the paragraphs as long as those in the sample document.)

1. Type the first full paragraph of the document and press Return. (It should be in Normal style; ''Normal'' should appear in the style-name area.)

2. Choose *Head1* from the style-selection box on the Ruler to apply the Head1 style.

3. Type the heading *The Beginnings of Unicycle Racing* and press Return. The heading appears boldface, double underlined, and indented. When you press Return, the style changes to Normal because the Head1 style definition includes Normal as its next style.

4. Type the next paragraph of the article and press Return. It appears in the Normal style.

5. Press Shift-Command-S, type *Pict*, and press Return to apply the Pict style.

6. Type the picture caption *Picture: The Moscow race course, complete with mechanics, pits.* Press Return. The line appears in italic. Notice that when you press Return, the style doesn't change; the Pict style definition doesn't set the next style.

7. Type the rest of the document using the Normal style for the main text, Head1 style for all the headings that have double underlining, Head2 style for all headings that have single underlining, and the Pict style for all picture captions. (You will fill the two pages of text needed for this example before the article ends.)

REFORMATTING WITH STYLES

After you type a document and apply different styles, you can redefine the style of a single element or whole families of elements in the document. By changing a base style, you change all the elements in a document that use derivative styles of that base style; by changing a style that has no derivative styles, you change only the type of element controlled by that style.

Redefining a Style

Redefining a style is much like defining a new style. You can redefine by selecting an example paragraph or by setting your own definition in the Define Styles dialog box.

Redefining by example

To redefine by example, you redefine the style of a paragraph to which you've added manual formatting, thereby including the manual formatting in the redefined style. First select an example paragraph that is already defined by a style and that contains additional manual formatting such as italic, new indents, or additional tab stops. Then display the Ruler if it's not displayed, click on the selected paragraph's style name in the style-selection box, and press Return.

A dialog box opens, asking whether you want to reapply the style to the selection or redefine the style based on the selection. Click on the Redefine button and then click on the OK button to redefine the style, or click on the Cancel button if you decide not to redefine.

Setting your own redefinition

To set your own style redefinition, choose *Define Styles* from the Format menu to open the Define Styles dialog box. Next, select the name of the style you want to redefine from the styles list; its name appears in the Style text box, and its definition appears in the style-description area. Change character and paragraph formatting as you do when you create a new style. To set your new definition, click on the Define button and then click on the OK button, or click on the Cancel button to close the dialog box.

An example

Try changing the appearance of your sample article by redefining its styles. Change the line spacing throughout the document by redefining the Normal style. Change the indention of the headings by redefining the Head1 style:

1. Choose *Define Styles* from the Format menu to open the Define Styles dialog box.

2. Choose *Normal* from the styles list.

3. On the Ruler, click on the double-space icon, the full-justification icon, and the open-line icon. The Normal style definition changes to include full justification with double spacing and an open line before the paragraph.

4. Click on the Define button to redefine Normal with its new formatting. All the lines in the document change to double spaced with full justification, including those in the derivative styles Head1, Head2, Title, and Pict.

5. Choose *Head1* from the styles list.

6. Drag the left and first-line–indent markers from the 0.5 mark to the 0 mark on the Ruler's measure. The Head1 style definition changes to include a left indent of 0 inches.

7. Click on the Define button to set the new Head1 definition. Both level-one and level-two headings move 0.5 inch to the left. Head2 followed the change in Head1 because it is a derivative style of Head1.

8. Click on the Cancel button to close the dialog box without applying a style (you don't want to apply Head1 style to the currently selected paragraph).

9. Save this document under the name ''Unicycles'' for use in the next chapter.

STYLE SHEETS

As you create new styles and add them to the styles list, Word remembers them as a collection of styles called a *style sheet*. Each document you create has its own style sheet. When you save a document, Word saves the style sheet with the document.

Merging Style Sheets

After you've worked to create useful styles for one document, you might want to use them again in another document. For example, you might want to use the title and heading styles in other reports or articles you write. To transfer them to a new document, you need to merge style sheets. First open the document into which you want to transfer the styles. Then choose *Define Styles* from the Format menu to open the Define Styles dialog box. While the Define Styles dialog box is open, choose *Open* from the File menu; Word presents a dialog box almost identical to the Open dialog box that you use to open a document.

Once you open the Open dialog box, you can look through all available documents in the scrolling list and change folders and disks to look for documents there. When you find the name of the document that contains the style sheet you want, double-click on its name, or choose it and click on the Open button. The dialog box closes, and Word merges the style sheet of the document you selected with the style sheet of the currently open document.

When Word merges style sheets, it adds all the styles from the incoming style sheet to the style sheet of the current document. If an incoming style has the same name as a style in the current style sheet, Word replaces the current style with the incoming style. For example, if an open document contains a Normal style that uses the New York font and you bring in styles from a document containing a Normal style that uses the Geneva font, Word replaces the New York Normal style with the Geneva Normal style.

Moving Styles Between Style Sheets

While the Define Styles dialog box is open, you can use the Cut, Copy, and Paste commands in the Edit menu to cut, copy, and paste styles in a style sheet. The commands function as follows.

- *Cut* instructs Word to remove a style selected in the styles list from the style sheet of the current document and place the style in the Clipboard. Use the Cut command to remove styles that you no longer need in a style sheet.

- *Copy* instructs Word to place a copy of the selected style in the Clipboard.

- *Paste* instructs Word to transfer a style from the Clipboard into the style sheet.

To copy a single style from one style sheet to another, first open the document that contains the style you want. Open the Define Styles dialog box, choose the name of the style you want from the styles list, choose *Copy* from the Edit menu, and then close the dialog box. Open the second document, reopen the Define Styles dialog box, and then choose *Paste* from the Edit menu to place a copy of the style in the second document's style sheet.

Printing a Style Sheet

If you want a printed copy of all the styles in a style sheet, choose *Print* from the File menu while the Define Styles dialog box is open. Word displays a standard print dialog box; if you click on the OK button, the box closes and Word prints a list of all the styles in the current style sheet including the formatting instructions for each style. This printed copy can be a useful reminder of all the different elements in a document.

You've now learned how to use styles, one of Word's most powerful and convenient features. In the next chapter you'll learn about section formatting.

Chapter 16

Section Formatting

Not all formatting in Word 4 is applied at the character and paragraph levels; Word also offers *section formatting* so you can control larger portions of a document. In this chapter you'll learn how to divide a document into sections and how to use the different options available for section formatting. You'll learn how to display endnotes, insert line numbers, and control the way a section begins on a page. You'll learn how to change headers and footers from section to section and also how to apply multiple-column text formatting, as you see on the pages of newspapers and magazines.

SETTING UP WORD

Before you begin working with the examples in this chapter, check to be sure that Word shows full menus and that Page View is turned off:

1. If you haven't done so already, turn your computer on and start Word.

2. Open the Edit menu, and if the Full Menus command appears, choose it to set full menus. If the Short Menus command appears instead of the Full Menus command, full menus are already set, and you can close the menu without choosing any commands.

3. Open the Document menu, and if a check mark appears to the left of the Page View command, choose the Page View command to turn Page View off.

Open the article named "Unicycles" that you created and saved in the preceding chapter. After you follow the section formatting examples in this chapter, the document will look like Figure 16-1, on the following pages.

Unicycle Racing: The Forgotten Sport

"There's nothing like the smell of bearing grease, the flash of sun on the seat post, and 50 unicyclists straining for the finish line!" Howard Dutilleux is reminiscing, leaning back against the bar railing as he finishes another boilermaker. "You'll never see anything like that today—young punks all use two wheels now. Line me up another one, Jimbo...." Rob Formass nods in agreement and adds, "A shame. It's a damn shame." They raise their glasses in leathery hands, salute each other with a loud clink, and toss back their drinks in fond remembrance of better times past. They are the last of a dying breed: professional unicycle racers.

The Beginnings of Unicycle Racing

Although barely remembered now, unicycle racing started with much fanfare at the Auxiliary World's Fair of 1928 in Moscow, Idaho. Billed as a spectacle with "Chills, Thrills, and Spills—With Half the Wheels!," the world's first unicycle race had a purse of $500 to lure hungry unicyclists from around the country. The course, a 7-mile circuit with a steep 500-foot hill, was set up around the fairgrounds. The organizers built an upturned ramp on the descent of the hill so descending unicyclists could leap 15 feet through the air before the main grandstands—a guaranteed audience pleaser!

(continued)

Figure 16-1. *Column formatting displays the text in this article in two columns.*

Figure 16-1. *continued*

Picture: The Moscow racecourse, complete with mechanics' pits.

A Hit

This first experiment in professional unicycle racing was an immediate success. There were, of course, numerous accidents as unscrupulous unicyclists used their free hands to harass their opponents. A favorite trick was quickly spinning a neighboring unicyclist around 180 degrees so he would start pedaling in the wrong direction. Many cyclists continued pedaling in the wrong direction until they met the pack coming in the opposite direction (or until they came up to the wrong end of the ramp)!

Unicycle Racing Spreads

Unicycle racing soon spread like heat rash under a cheap cycling jersey. Soon the entire Palouse area became the mecca for unicyclists from around the world. Special training camps sprang up, offering specialties like endurance unicycling (the 200-kilometer road race was especially popular at the time) and uphill sprints. Designers began to introduce specialty unicycles: 1935 saw the introduction of both the AeroAce 10-foot unicycle (effective for falling toward the finish line at the last moment) and the Marauder, a competitive unicycle built of solid cast iron. It didn't climb hills well, but its descents were murderous, and nobody wanted to collide with a Marauder. That was indeed the Golden Age of Unicycling.

CREATING SECTIONS

To apply section formatting effectively, you should first divide a document into separate sections. Although you can apply section formatting to an entire document (wherein Word treats the document as a single section), many section-formatting options aren't truly effective unless you use them on separate and contrasting sections. Within each section, you can create unique headers and footers, set different page-numbering and column-formatting options, and give each section a look completely different from that of the other sections in the same document.

To create a section, simply place the insertion point where you want the new section to begin, and then press Command-Enter. A section marker appears as a double, dotted line across the width of the page. In the same way that a paragraph marker contains all the paragraph formatting for the paragraph that precedes it, a section-break marker contains all the section formatting for the section that precedes it. (The end-of-document mark contains section formatting for the last section in that document.)

Word treats a section marker as a single character (even though it appears as a series of dots) that you can select, copy, paste, and delete. When you copy or move a section marker, you copy or move the section formatting with the marker. When you delete a section marker, all the text preceding the marker follows the section formatting of the next section.

To apply a format to a section, first select the section to be formatted. Do this by placing the insertion point anywhere in the section, by selecting a text block in the section, or by selecting the section marker at the end of the section. To select more than one section for formatting, select a text block that includes text from each section you want to format. The page-number area in the lower left corner of the document window displays both the page number and the section number of the topmost line in the window. Word displays a section number (if the document contains sections) as a capital letter *S* followed by the section number (for example, S1, S2, S3, and so on).

Applying Different Types of Section Formatting

The following are some of the different types of section formatting you can apply to a selected document section.

- *Section starts*—You can start a section on a new page, on a new even-numbered or odd-numbered page, in a new column (if you set more than one column of text), or with or without a break from the text of the preceding section.

- *Page numbers*—You can place an automatic page number (a page number created without using a header or footer) anywhere on a page, you can specify the numbering system of all page numbers (Roman numerals, Arabic numerals, letters, and others), and you can specify sequential page numbering across sections or page numbering that starts anew at the beginning of each section.

- *Columns*—You can instruct Word to format text in one column (the common method of printing), two columns, or any number of columns up to 100. You can format each section with a different number of columns, which is useful for creating newsletters, bulletins, and similar documents.

- *Endnotes*—You can set footnotes to appear following selected sections instead of at the bottom of each page or at the end of the document.

- *Line numbers*—You can instruct Word to number the lines of text on each page, a convenient feature for contracts or similar documents in which readers need to refer to individual lines. You can turn line numbering on or off, set different line-numbering increments in each section, and control the placement of line numbers.

- *Headers and footers*—You can set the distance from the top edge of the page to the top of a header and from the bottom of a footer to the bottom edge of the page. You can also create a special first-page header and footer.

Setting Options in the Section Dialog Box

To set formatting for selected sections, open the Section dialog box, shown in Figure 16-2, on the following page, by choosing *Section* from the Format menu.

The Section dialog box contains list boxes and check boxes you use to set the section formatting you want. When you finish setting your format, click on the OK button to apply the formatting and close the dialog box, or click on

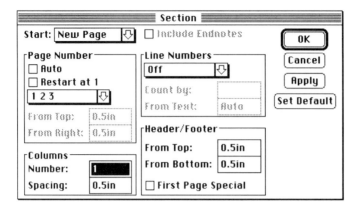

Figure 16-2. *Open the Format Section dialog box to format selected sections.*

the Cancel button to close the dialog box without applying the formatting changes. Click on the Apply button to apply formatting without closing the dialog box; you can see the changes in the document window.

You should already be familiar with two of the areas in the Section dialog box from your work creating headers and footers in Chapter 9, ''Headers and Footers'': the Header/Footer area and the Page Number area. The next section discusses the remaining options in the Section dialog box.

SETTING SECTION-START FORMATS

When you create a new section in a document, Word sets the section to start on a new page by default, even if the previous section didn't fill its final page. You can control the way a section starts by opening the Section dialog box and choosing an option from the Start list box in the upper left corner of the dialog box, shown in Figure 16-3.

The five options in the Start list box function as follows:

- *No Break* instructs Word to start the section as a new paragraph on the same page on which the previous section ended (unless the previous page is full).

- *New Column* instructs Word to start the section at the top of the next column, but only if the selected section and the previous section are formatted with the same number of columns. If both follow a one-column format and you choose this option, Word starts the section at the top of the next page.

■ *New Page* instructs Word to start the section at the top of the next page following the last page of the previous section.

■ *Even Page* instructs Word to start the section at the top of the next even-numbered page (adding a blank, odd-numbered page to the previous section if necessary).

■ *Odd Page* instructs Word to start the section at the top of the next odd-numbered page (adding a blank, even-numbered page to the previous section if necessary).

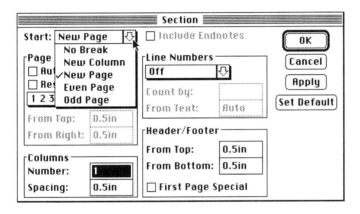

Figure 16-3. *The Start list box offers five section-start formats.*

SETTING COLUMNS

When you apply section formatting to create columns, you create *snaking columns*, which are different from the columns you make by using tab stops or by creating tables. Snaking columns divide each page into parallel vertical strips that Word treats as narrow pages; it fills each column with text and then moves to the top of the next column to continue. If you change, add, or delete text, Word adjusts the text from column to column.

To set columns in a section, select the section and then open the Section dialog box. The bottom of the dialog box contains a Columns area, shown in Figure 16-4, on the following page, in which you can set the number and spacing of columns.

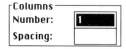

Figure 16-4. *Set the number and spacing of columns in the Columns area of the Section dialog box.*

Set the number of columns by entering a number in the Number box. Two or three columns work well in most documents; you might want to use more columns if you plan to print on wide paper. If you set too many columns for a given page width, the columns will be too narrow, resulting in excessive hyphenation (if you hyphenate your document) or large gaps in text (if you don't hyphenate).

You set the amount of space between columns in the Spacing box. The default setting is 0.5 inch, but you can increase or decrease this width by entering a new value in inches. Again, use good judgment. Spacing too wide leaves no room for text in the columns, and spacing too narrow runs the columns so close together that it becomes difficult to read text.

Mixing Column Formats on the Same Page

Occasionally you might want to mix the number of columns on one page. For example, the Unicycles document shown at the beginning of the chapter includes a title that extends the width of one page (a single column) and appears above text displayed in two columns. To mix column formats, insert a section break where you want to change the number of columns and then choose *No Break* from the Start list box. Because the No Break option continues the new section without a page break, you can set different column formatting in each section to display a different number of columns on the same page.

Divide your sample document into two sections so that you can apply different column formatting to each section:

1. Move the insertion point to the beginning of the line following the title. The line begins, "There's nothing like the smell...."

2. Press Command-Enter to insert a section break.

3. Choose *Section* from the Format menu to open the Section dialog box. (Because the insertion point is in the second section, the Section dialog box shows the formatting of the second section.)

4. Choose *No Break* from the Start list box.

5. Type *2* in the Number box to specify two columns. Leave the Spacing option set at 0.5 inch.

6. Click on the OK button to close the dialog box. The text in the second section of the document appears formatted in a narrow column at the left side of the text window. The right side of the text window is empty.

Viewing Columns

You don't see columns lying side by side in Word's Galley View; instead, you see the text as one continuous column. You can scroll downward to view the entire document. To see the columns formatted side by side, turn Page View on by choosing *Page View* from the Document menu.

Turn Page View on now to see the columns you set in your document. As you move from page to page, you can see the way your text is formatted in columns. You can edit the text and readjust the column width and margins while Page View is turned on. Return now to Galley View to edit your document.

PRINTING ENDNOTES

You can set footnotes to appear as endnotes at the end of each document section. To do so, first set footnotes to appear at the end of each section in the Document dialog box. Once set, the Include Endnotes option becomes available in the Section dialog box. Turning the Include Endnotes option on (it's then turned on by default) sets any footnotes in the section to appear following the text in the section. If you turn the option off, any footnotes in the section then pass on to the next section to appear following the text there, unless that section also has the Include Endnotes option turned off. Word continues to collect footnotes until it encounters a section with the Include Endnotes option turned on. It displays the collected footnotes at the end of that section. If every section passes on the footnotes, Word displays the footnotes at the end of the document.

NUMBERING LINES

Line numbers give the reader a convenient reference to a specific line, as in: "Can we change the phrase on page 43, line 7, to read '$10 per gross' instead of '$10 is gross'?" To add line numbers to a section, place the insertion point within the section, open the Section dialog box, and then set the options in the Line Numbers area, shown in Figure 16-5.

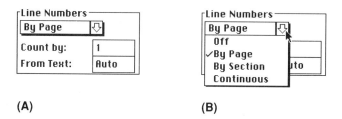

(A)   **(B)**

Figure 16-5. *You can turn the line-numbering feature on and off and control how lines are numbered in the Line Numbers area of the Section dialog box, shown in figure A. Figure B shows the open list box.*

The list box in the Line Numbers area offers four line-numbering options, as follows:

- *Off*—Word does not number lines in the section.

- *By Page*—Word begins numbering lines at the top of each page and starts numbering again from 1 at the top of the next page.

- *By Section*—Word begins numbering lines at the beginning of the section and numbers continuously through the end of the section. Word begins numbering again from 1 at the beginning of the following section (if the following section has the line-numbering option turned on).

- *Continuous*—Word numbers the lines sequentially from one section to the next. For example, if the preceding section ended on line 1527, Word begins numbering the lines in the selected section with 1528.

Choose any option except *Off* to turn line numbering on; choose *Off* to turn line numbering off. Once you add line numbers, you won't see them in your document until you print the document or choose *Print Preview* from the File menu.

If you don't want a line number to appear at the left of every line, you can skip lines by entering a value in the Count by: text box. For example, if you want to see a line number only before every fifth line, enter *5* in the Count by text box.

The From Text text box controls the position of the line numbers in relation to the text line. They usually appear 0.25 inch to the left of each line (0.13 inch in a multiple-column section); any value you enter here instructs Word to move the right edge of the line numbers that far to the left of each line. (Use good judgment; if you enter too large a number, the line numbers disappear off the left edge of the page!)

SETTING HEADERS AND FOOTERS

Whenever you create a new section, Word duplicates any existing headers or footers and inserts them in the new section. Word then *links* the headers and footers of the new section to the headers and footers in the following section. This link keeps the headers and footers consistent throughout the document; whenever you change a header or footer, you change the linked headers and footers in the sections that follow.

For example, if you create a document with a header that reads ''Main Document'' and then divide the document into five sections, every header of the section also reads ''Main Document.'' If you select the first section and change the header to ''Chapter One,'' the headers in all subsequent document sections also change to ''Chapter One.''

To create a section header or footer that isn't linked to the preceding section's header or footer, position the insertion point in the section you want, and then choose *Open Header* or *Open Footer* from the Document menu. The Header or Footer window opens, as shown in Figure 16-6, on the following page, showing the header or footer contents. Change the contents as you want, and then click on the close box to close the window and set the header or footer.

After you change a section header or footer, Word breaks the link between that section and the preceding section so that any changes in the preceding sections won't affect the new header or footer you set. Of course, if the new header or footer is linked to sections that follow, the following headers and footers change to include the revisions.

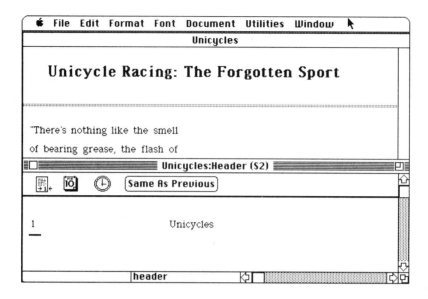

Figure 16-6. *A Header window shows the header for the currently selected document section.*

For example, consider the document from our example. Each of the five sections has a header that reads "Chapter One." If you change the header in the third section to "Chapter Three," you break the link between the second and third sections. The first two sections are still headed by "Chapter One" because the second section is still linked to the first. The third section is headed by "Chapter Three" because it's no longer linked to the second section. And sections four and five are now headed by "Chapter Three" because they're still linked to section three.

You can reestablish a link between sections by opening a Header or Footer window and clicking on the Same As Previous button. After you break the links between a section and the preceding section, the Same As Previous button becomes active. When you click on the button, the contents of the header or footer change to match the preceding section's header or footer, and the link is reestablished between the two sections.

If you set even and odd headers in the Document dialog box (which sets even and odd headers in every section of the document), you should note that a link exists between the odd and even header or footer in a section. The even header or footer displays the contents of the odd header or footer of the section unless you break the link by setting new even header or footer contents.

294

If you click on the Same As Previous button in an Even Header or Even Footer window, you link the header or footer to the even header or footer of the previous section.

One more important linking feature: If you click on the Same As Previous button for a header or footer and there is no previous header or footer, then Word searches back to the preceding section, and continues searching back to the beginning of the document until it finds a header or footer with contents that it can use. It then links to that header or footer.

SETTING DEFAULT SECTION FORMATTING

The Section dialog box includes OK, Cancel, and Apply buttons as the Character and Paragraph dialog boxes do, but it also includes a new button: Set Default. You click on it to set *default section formatting*.

Every time you create a new document, Word sets the default section formatting for the document. You can change the default section formatting, of course, but you always start with the default formatting when you create a new document.

The default section formatting might not be the section formatting you want to use. For example, if you prepare legal documents, you might want to begin with line numbering turned on. To change the default formatting, open the Section dialog box, set the section format options you want, and then click on the Set Default button. Word remembers your settings and uses them whenever you create a new document. It also stores the default settings on disk so that the new default settings remain set even after you quit Word and restart later.

You've now learned how to divide a document into sections and apply section formatting. In the next chapter you'll learn about another type of Word formatting: document formatting.

Chapter 17

Document Formatting

Document formatting in Word 4 controls elements throughout an entire document, spanning any sections created within the document. You've applied document formatting to a limited extent in previous chapters to control footnote locations, set even and odd headers, and control page numbering. In this chapter you'll learn how to control one of the most noticeable aspects of document formatting: margins. You'll also learn how to link separate documents in order to number the pages consecutively from document to document.

SETTING UP WORD

Before you begin working with the examples in this chapter, check to be sure that Word shows full menus and that Page View is turned off:

1. If you haven't done so already, turn your computer on and start Word.

2. Open the Edit menu, and if the Full Menus command appears, choose it to set full menus. If the Short Menus command appears instead of the Full Menus command, full menus are already set, and you can close the menu without choosing any commands.

3. Open the Document menu, and if a check mark appears to the left of the Page View command, choose the Page View command to turn Page View off.

You'll use the Unicycles article once again for the examples in this chapter. Open it now; you should find it saved under the name ''Unicycles.'' Change its format to one column before you begin. You'll change its margins so that the article appears significantly reduced in size on a page, as shown in Figure 17-1.

Unicycle Racing: The Forgotten Sport

"There's nothing like the smell of bearing grease, the flash of sun on the seat post, and 50 unicyclists straining for the finish line!" Howard Dutilleux is reminiscing, leaning back against the bar railing as he finishes another boilermaker. "You'll never see anything like that today—young punks all use two wheels now. Line me up another one, Jimbo...." Rob Formass nods in agreement and adds, "A shame. It's a damn shame." They raise their glasses in leathery hands, salute each other with a loud clink, and toss back their drinks in fond remembrance of better times past. They are the last of a dying breed: the professional unicycle racer.

(continued)

Figure 17-1. *Document formatting increases the size of the margins in this sample document.*

Figure 17-1. *continued*

The Beginnings of Unicycle Racing

Although barely remembered now, unicycle racing started with much fanfare at the Auxiliary World's Fair of 1928 in Moscow, Idaho. Billed as a spectacle with "Chills, Thrills, and Spills—With Half the Wheels!," the world's first unicycle race had a purse of $500 to lure hungry unicyclists from around the country. The course, a 7-mile circuit with a steep 500-foot hill, was set up around the fairgrounds. The organizers built an upturned ramp on the descent of the hill so descending unicyclists could leap 15 feet through the air before the main grandstands—a guaranteed audience pleaser!

Picture: The Moscow racecourse, complete with mechanics' pits.

DOCUMENT FORMATTING OPTIONS

To apply document formatting, choose *Document* from the Format menu to open the Document dialog box shown in Figure 17-2. Set the options in the dialog box to control a document's appearance:

- Setting the Margins options positions your document's top, bottom, left, and right margins. Enter values in the Top, Bottom, Left, and Right text boxes to control the amount of blank space surrounding the text on a page.

- Turning the Mirror Margins option on sets the left and right margins so that they function as inside and outside margins. Use mirror margins for double-sided pages on which the facing pages (an even-numbered page and an odd-numbered page) display outside margins.

- Turning the Even/Odd Headers option on, which you learned to use in Chapter 9, "Headers and Footers," creates a header and a footer for even-numbered pages and a separate header and footer for odd-numbered pages.

- Entering a value in the Gutter text box sets the amount of extra space that appears on the inside margin of each page. Set this option to add extra space to the inside margins to allow for binding.

- Entering values in the page-numbering and line-numbering text boxes sets the beginning page number and beginning line number for any page numbering or line numbering in the document.

- Entering a value in the Default Tab Stops text box sets the distance between default tab stops on the Ruler (the tab stops that appear along the Ruler before you set your own tab stops).

- Turning on the Widow Control option, which you learned to do in Chapter 10, "Creating Pages," lets you avoid separating a single line from the rest of a paragraph when Word paginates a document.

- Setting the options in the Footnotes area, which you learned to do in Chapter 14, "Creating Footnotes," controls the position and numbering of footnotes throughout the document.

■ Clicking on the Next File button links this document with another so that you can continue page numbering from one document to the next.

Most of these options act as independent features, but these options—the margins, the mirror margins, and the gutter—work together to control the size of the text area on a page.

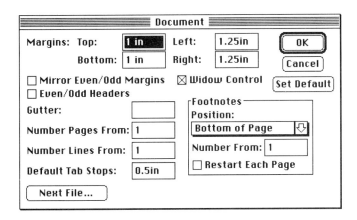

Figure 17-2. *Use the Document dialog box to set document formatting.*

MARGINS

Word uses the margin values you enter to set the amount of space surrounding the body text on each page. The size of the text area equals the size of the page minus the size of the margins. You can change the page size (as you'll learn to do in Chapter 19, "Printing Variations and Document Export") to accommodate many common paper-stock sizes—8½ by 14 inches or 11 by 17 inches, for example. You can set Word's margins for whatever page size you're working with.

For example, Word's default page size is 8.5 inches by 11 inches, the size of a standard (U.S.) sheet of paper, as shown in Figure 17-3 on the following page. Word normally sets left and right margins at 1.25 inches and top and bottom margins at 1 inch. The remaining text area measures 6 inches wide (8.5 inches minus 2.5 inches) and 9 inches high (11 inches minus 2 inches). In Word's default setting, then, you have 6 inches across a page and 9 inches down a page as your work space.

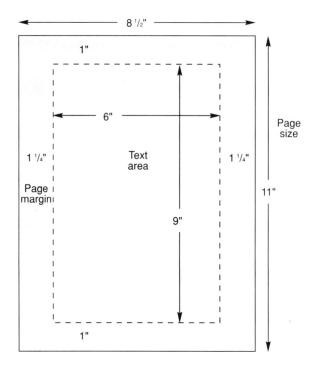

Figure 17-3. *The text area on a sheet of paper equals the page area minus the page margin area.*

Setting Top and Bottom Page Margins

The Margins area of the Document dialog box, shown in Figure 17-4, includes four text boxes in which you can enter values to set the margins you want. Any values you enter there measure margins from the edges of the paper.

The Margins settings determine the area for the body text of the document. Headers and footers usually appear above and below the top and bottom margins. If you set *flexible* margins (as Word does by default), Word moves

Figure 17-4. *Enter values in the Margins area of the Document dialog box to set the document's margins.*

the top or bottom margin of the body text toward the center of the page to accommodate a lengthy header or footer. For example, if you set a flexible top margin of 1 inch and then create a header that descends 1.5 inches from the top of the page, Word moves the top margin downward to avoid overlapping the body text and the header text. If you want to set a top margin that remains at a constant distance from the top of the page regardless of the size of the header, set a *fixed* margin by entering a negative number in the Top text box. And if you want to set a bottom margin that remains at a constant distance from the bottom of the page, enter a negative number in the Bottom text box. Word uses the absolute value of the negative number to set the fixed margin. Be aware, however, that if you create a 1.5-inch header in a document with a fixed 1-inch top margin, the header text will overlap the body text.

Fixed margins are useful if you want to create a sidebar header as in an organizational letterhead that includes a list of board members' names extending down the left margin of the page. You can create this type of letterhead by entering the long list as a header with its left and right indents both set to the left of the body text's indents (to form a column). You then set a fixed margin (such as −1) in the Top text box so that the header and the body text can overlap vertically. When you turn Page View on or print the document, the long list appears to the left of the body text.

Setting Left and Right Page Margins

To set left and right page margins in the Document dialog box, enter their values in inches in the Left and Right text boxes. Always enter positive values in these boxes.

When you change left and right margins, the Ruler shows the new constraints of the text area. The left-margin marker always remains at the 0 mark on the Ruler's measure, showing the edge of the left margin. The right-margin marker, shown in Figure 17-5 on the following page, as a dotted vertical line, moves to the left or right to show the total width of the text area. (Because the right-indent marker usually sits on top of the right-margin marker, you must move the right-indent marker aside to see the right-margin marker.)

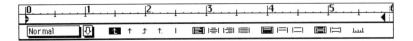

Figure 17-5. *The Ruler shows the width of the text area. The left-margin marker always remains at the 0 mark, and the right-margin marker moves to the left or right to show the edge of the right margin. (Notice that the right-indent marker has been moved slightly to reveal the right-margin marker.)*

You can also set left and right margins by using the Ruler. Click on the Scale icon on the Ruler to turn page scale on, as shown in Figure 17-6. The margin markers appear as brackets on the left and right sides of the Ruler, indicating the actual margin measure from the left and right page edges. To change the margins, simply drag the brackets to new locations along the measure. When you've finished, click on the Scale icon again to return the Ruler to normal.

Left-margin bracket   Right-margin bracket

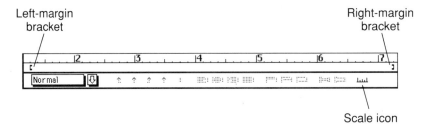

Scale icon

Figure 17-6. *The Ruler in page scale shows the actual margin measures from the left and right edges of the page.*

Try changing the left, right, top, and bottom margins of the Unicycles article so that each increases in size by 1 inch. Use the Document dialog box to set the top and bottom margins and the Ruler to set the left and right margins:

1. Choose *Show Ruler* from the Format menu to display the Ruler if it isn't visible.

2. Choose *Document* from the Format menu to open the Document dialog box.

3. Type *2* in the Top and Bottom text boxes of the Margins area to increase the top and bottom margins to 2 inches.

4. Click on the OK button to close the dialog box and set the new margins. If you scroll through the text on the page, you'll notice

that the first page break now appears higher on the page than it did previously because there are now 2 inches less vertical text space on each page.

5. Click on the Scale icon to set the Ruler in page scale. The margin brackets appear on the Ruler.

6. Drag the left margin bracket from the 1.25-inch mark to the 2.25-inch mark and the right margin bracket from the 7.25-inch mark to the 6.25-inch mark. The text of the document narrows in width to reflect the new text width of 4 inches (6 inches minus 1 inch from each of the two margins).

7. Click on the Scale icon again to return the Ruler to normal scale. The right-margin marker now appears at the 4-inch mark, showing that the text width is now 4 inches.

Setting paragraph indents by using margin markers

As you changed the margin settings in the last example, you probably noticed that the paragraph indents moved with the margins. Indents are set as constant distances from the left and right margins. For example, because the right indent in this example was set at 0 inches from the right margin, when the right margin moved in 1 inch, the right indent moved in with it, maintaining its fixed distance of 0 inches.

Although you normally keep indents within the body text area, you can extend paragraph indents into the margins if you want to display text in the margins. To move a right-indent marker into the right margin, drag the right-indent marker to the right of the right-margin marker. To move a left-indent marker into the left margin, drag its marker to the left of the 0 mark into the negative numbers on the Ruler. (To do so, drag the marker to the left end of the Ruler; the Ruler scrolls left to let you move the marker.) You can also set indents inside the margins by entering negative values in the Indents text boxes in the Paragraph dialog box.

Setting margins when printing with a laser printer

Many laser printers won't print within 0.5 inch of the edge of a sheet of paper. If you set margins to less than 0.5 inch or move the text indents too close to the edge of the paper, you might lose a few characters when you print on a laser printer. Be sure to check your printer's manual to see how close to the edge it will print, or if your manual doesn't specify, experiment.

Creating a Gutter

Whenever you bind printed pages together—whether you have them stitched at a bindery, insert them in a folder, or simply staple them together along one edge—you lose part of the inside edge of each page to the binding. If your text falls too close to the binding, the reader is forced to pry the pages apart to read them. A *gutter* is an extra margin on the inside (binding) edge of each page. By adding a gutter, you ensure that text won't be caught in the binding. To add a gutter, enter a value in the Gutter text box of the Document dialog box to specify the gutter size (in inches) you want. Word adds the gutter space to the inside edge of each page, further reducing the width of the text area.

Creating Mirror Margins

When you print a document on both sides of each sheet of paper and then bind the sheets together (like the pages of this book), your pages require different treatment than when you use only one side of each sheet. The gutter must alternate on odd-numbered and even-numbered pages in order to remain on the inside edge of each sheet, and any unequal left and right margins you set must alternate to maintain their inequality.

Word offers a *mirror margins* feature to accommodate double-sided printing. When you turn the Mirror Even/Odd Margins option on in the Document dialog box, the Left and Right margin text boxes become Inside and Outside text boxes. The Inside box controls the left margin of odd-numbered pages and the right margin of even-numbered pages; the Outside box controls the right margin of odd pages and the left margin of even pages. Word adds to the inside margin of the page any gutter measure you set. Turn the Mirror Even/Odd Margins option on whenever you print a document for reproduction on both sides of a page.

Try setting up mirror margins and a gutter for the Unicycles article as follows:

1. Choose *Document* from the Format menu to open the Document dialog box.

2. Click on the Mirror Even/Odd Margins check box to turn the option on.

3. Type *.5* in the Gutter text box to specify a 0.5-inch gutter.

4. Click on the OK button to close the dialog box and apply your document formatting. Because the gutter eats up another 0.5 inch of the page width, the text width is reduced now to 3.5 inches. The right-margin marker on the Ruler now appears at the 3.5-inch mark.

5. Choose *Print Preview* from the File menu to open the Print Preview window and see the Unicycles article as it appears on the full page.

6. If Word doesn't display two pages in the window, click on the one-page/two-page display icon (the third icon from the top at the left side of the window). Notice that the gutter appears as a shaded vertical strip on the inside edge of each page. Notice also that the gutter appears on the right side of even-numbered pages and on the left side of odd-numbered pages.

7. When you've finished viewing the page layout, click on the Cancel button to close the Print Preview window.

Setting Margins in Print Preview

You can easily set all four page margins in the Print Preview window. First open the Print Preview window, and then click on the margins icon to display the margin edges as four dotted lines on the page, as shown in Figure 17-7 on the following page.

You can move any of the margin lines to reset a margin. To move a margin line, simply drag the margin handle (the small black box at the end of the margin line) to the location you want. As you move the line, you can see the margin's measure at the top of the Print Preview window, shown as a distance in inches from the top or left side of the page. Once you set the margins as you want them, click on the margins icon again to turn the margin-setting mode off. The margin lines disappear, and Word repaginates the document to fit your new margins. Click on the Cancel button to exit the Print Preview window.

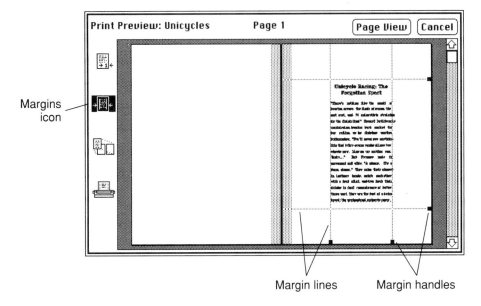

Margins
icon

Margin lines   Margin handles

Figure 17-7. *Set margins in the Print Preview window by clicking on the margins icon and moving the four margin lines.*

SETTING DEFAULT TAB STOPS

Word normally sets default tab stops every half inch along the Ruler. The default tab stops remain in effect until you set your own tab stops (as you learned to do in Chapter 8, "Tabs"). To change the default tab-stop interval, enter a new interval value in inches in the Default Tab Stops text box of the Document dialog box. Word changes the default tab stops on the Ruler to fall at the interval you set.

CONTROLLING PAGE NUMBERING AND LINE NUMBERING

You learned in Chapter 9, "Headers and Footers," to set the starting page number for a document in the Number Pages From text box in the Document dialog box. You can set the starting line number for a document similarly in the Number Lines From text box, which appears below the Number Pages From text box. But in order for the value you enter here to take effect, you must first turn line numbering on in the Section dialog box.

Both the page-number and line-number options in the Document dialog box set page and line numbers only from the beginning of the document. If you divide a document into sections and format page numbering and line numbering to restart numbering at 1, Word overrides the starting number you set in the Document dialog box.

LINKING DOCUMENTS

There might be times when you want to divide a large work into separate documents so the document files don't become unmanageably large, but you also want to number the pages consecutively across the documents. For example, you might write a book as a series of one-chapter documents that you want to print in one batch with consecutive page numbers. If so, you can link the documents for printing.

If you link the first chapter to the second, the second chapter to the third, and so on to the end of the book, then with one print command you can print all the chapters with page numbers that run consecutively from the beginning to the end of the book.

To link one document to another, first open the Document dialog box and click on the Next File button. A dialog box similar to the Open dialog box opens and displays a list of documents. From this dialog box, you can select any documents in any folder and on any drive connected to your Mac. Once you find the document you want to link, choose it by double-clicking on its name. The dialog box disappears, the Next File button becomes a Reset Next File button, and the filename you chose appears next to the button, indicating that the documents are linked.

To break a link between documents, click on the Reset Next File button in the Document dialog box. The filename following it disappears, the button label becomes the Next File button again, and the document is no longer linked to another document.

To create a chain of documents for printing, link the first document to the second document, the second document to the third, and so on until you link the last document. You must also set each document's Number Pages From text box (located in the Document dialog box) to 0. The 0 value tells Word that you don't want to restart page numbering at the beginning of the document but want to continue numbering from the previous document. You set a value of 1 (or higher) in the first document of the chain to set the initial starting number for the entire work.

To print a chain of linked documents, open the first document, and then choose the Print command to print the entire document. When Word finishes printing the first document, it prints the second linked document, then the third, and so on. Note that you can link documents that are located on different disks. When you print, Word asks you to insert the disk when it's time to print the documents it contains.

You've now learned how to apply document formatting to set margins and default tab stops and to link documents. In the next chapter you'll learn how to create document templates.

Chapter 18

Creating Templates

Many of the documents you create with Word 4—letters, reports, memos, and others—share a common foundation. For example, each letter you write might follow the same formatting and include the same closing text and letterhead. Each report you write might use the same styles and follow the same document and section formatting. If you find yourself setting up the same formatting and entering the same text for a common type of document, you can save time by creating a *document template* for that type of document.

A document template can contain standard formatting, styles, and common text that you apply again and again to new documents. In this chapter you'll learn how to create a document template, how to save it and lock it so it isn't easily changed, how to use a template when creating a new document, and how to edit a template once it's been locked. You'll also learn how to create a companion glossary for the template.

SETTING UP WORD

Before you begin working with the examples in this chapter, check to be sure that Word shows full menus and that Page View is turned off:

1. If you haven't done so already, turn your computer on and start Word.

2. Open the Edit menu, and if the Full Menus command appears, choose it to set full menus. If the Short Menus command appears instead of the Full Menus command, full menus is already set, and you can close the menu without choosing any commands.

3. Open the Document menu, and if a check mark appears to the left of the Page View command, choose the Page View command to turn Page View off.

The sample document for this chapter is a business letter—specifically, an acceptance letter from *The Perfect Poodle,* a magazine for dog groomers. You'll create a template and a companion glossary for the letter and use them both to quickly create the acceptance letter.

AN OVERVIEW OF DOCUMENT TEMPLATES

A document template is a stripped-down version of a standard document—a document foundation for you to build on as you create a new document. To create a template, you first open a new document. (A document template starts as a standard document.) Then you set formatting and add standard text elements: You choose a font and type size, create appropriate styles, and set margins, indents, and any other formatting appropriate for the type of document. You can also add to the template text elements such as a letterhead, headers and footers, or a standard opening. Next you save the document template (you're really saving the foundation of a standard document), close the file, and lock the document template file so that you can't accidentally change the template or delete it.

Once you've created a document template, you can open it whenever you begin a new document of that type. You can add to or change the contents of the template—edit existing text, add new text, and even change formatting where necessary—to create a new document based on the template, but you won't be able to save the changes in the actual template file. Because the template file is locked, Word won't write over it with your new document, erasing the template. Instead, Word opens the Save dialog box, asks you for a new filename, and saves your document under the new name, keeping the template file intact for another use.

Templates are not forever fixed, however. You can edit a template by unlocking it from the desktop, opening it, making any changes you want, saving it, and then relocking it from the desktop. The only difference between a template and a regular document is that the template is locked; by returning to the desktop to lock and unlock the template, you can change it as often as necessary.

The Perfect Poodle
A Magazine for Dog Groomers
523 Boulevard Street, Nadir Heights, NJ   05934

5/10/91

Mr. Avron Thillmuller
518 Larval Way
Zzyzzx, NV   84702

Dear Mr. Thillmuller:

We'd like to thank you for your recent submission, <u>Poodle Perms:</u>
<u>Pathway to Prosperity or Perilous Profits?</u>, which we read with
interest. We liked what we read. In fact, we loved what we read and
would like to publish your article! Enclosed is our standard author's
contract. We think you'll find our rate of 2 cents per word to be
extremely fair, given the market for poodle-clipping pieces. We look
forward to hearing from you!

Yours   sincerely,

Pesco Artilladero
Managing Editor

Figure 18-1. *A document template lets you create a letter like this one in a matter of seconds.*

SETTING TEMPLATE FORMATTING

When you open a new document to create a template, first consider the different types of formatting you can set for that document type, beginning with character formatting and working up to document formatting. If you're creating a template for a complex type of document, such as a contract or an article, you might also want to include a set of styles. Then when you save the template, you save the styles and formatting with it so they will be available when you use the template to start a new document.

Character Formatting

One of your first formatting decisions will be choosing a font and type size for the main text in the template. Some documents benefit from a large, legible font; others work best with a small, compact font. You also need to decide whether the majority of the text in your document requires a type style other than plain text (boldface, for example).

Once you make your decisions, the best way to set character formatting in the template is to open the Define Styles dialog box, choose the Normal style, and redefine the style by setting the character formatting you want. If you don't redefine the Normal style and instead simply apply character formatting to the beginning of your document, then you'll be setting the formatting only for the first paragraph of the document. If, as you add new paragraphs, you change the formatting, your original formatting will not resume. If you redefine the Normal style, you can quickly return to your original formatting by reapplying the Normal style.

Paragraph Formatting

Paragraph formatting determines the spacing between lines of text and paragraphs in the document, the size of indents, and other characteristics such as tab stops and paragraph borders. Consider carefully how dense you want text to appear in your document, and then set the line spacing, open paragraph lines, and indents accordingly. If you plan to apply fancy formatting such as paragraph borders for the majority of paragraphs in your document, set that as well.

Like character formatting, paragraph formatting for a template works best if you redefine the Normal style to include the formatting you want.

Keep in mind that if you intend to use many different types of paragraph formatting in the template, you can always define more styles.

Section Formatting

Most documents don't require special section formatting, so you won't need to set anything new. However, if you plan to number lines, position headers and footers, use multiple columns, or change page numbering, you must open the Section dialog box to set the formatting appropriately. Section formatting is not a part of a style definition, so you don't need to include it in the Normal style definition. When you save the template, you'll save the section formatting with it.

Document Formatting

Most documents don't require special document formatting either. But if you want to change margins, footnotes, page numbering, or line numbering, you need to set document formatting. You can also set the page size of your document if you plan to use legal paper, envelopes, or paper sizes other than the standard 8½-by-11-inch sheet. (You'll learn how to set page dimensions in the next chapter.) Like section formatting, document formatting and page-size settings are saved not in a style but with the template.

Creating a Style Sheet

When you change the Normal style definition to include the character and paragraph formatting you want for the majority of your document text, you start a style sheet for your document. If the document has a simple setup, you might not need to format any further. However, if you anticipate including elements such as headers, titles, picture captions, and quoted text, you should create styles for each of those elements so they're available when you begin a new document from the template.

You can define new styles directly in the Define Styles dialog box if you know exactly what you want, but you might prefer to enter actual samples of different elements in your document and then format them. When you finish formatting, use the sample paragraphs to define the styles you need, and then go back and delete the sample paragraphs.

An Example

Try starting the template for the Perfect Poodle business letter. Because it's a simple business letter, you don't need to create a style sheet. You simply redefine the Normal style to apply to the main paragraphs in the letter.

1. Choose *New* from the File menu to open a new document window.

2. Choose *Define Styles* from the Format menu to open the Define Styles window.

3. Choose *Show Ruler* from the Format menu to display the Ruler.

4. Click on the name Normal in the Styles list.

5. Click on the open-line icon on the Ruler to add a blank line before each paragraph.

6. Click on the Define button to apply your definition to the Normal style, and then click on the Cancel button to close the Define Styles windows.

You've now defined the Normal style to precede each paragraph with a blank line. You don't need to change character formatting because you intend to use Word's default 12-point New York font for the body of your letter, and you don't need to change document and section formatting because their default settings work fine for your purposes.

ADDING STANDARD TEXT

Most documents of a particular type include sections of text that are common to every document in that category. For example, a memo probably includes lines beginning with *From:*, *To:*, and *Cc:*. A letter might include the letterhead and a standard opening. And a contract might include a standard sign-off section.

You can include this common text in your template so it will be available whenever you begin a new document. Include text that appears in most, but not necessarily all, of your documents of that type; it's much easier to delete text that you don't need than it is to enter it from scratch.

For multi-page documents, consider adding a header, footer, or both to the document template. Be sure that you don't include changing text in a header or footer—for example, there's no point in including the title of the document in a header if the title changes with every document you create. Instead, insert only standard text, such as the page number and date, and leave out specifics. Or you can type X's in place of changing text to remind you to insert that information before you print the document.

An Example

Return now to your sample template to enter the standard text shown in Figure 18-2. Notice that you change formatting to enter the letterhead, the address, the salutation, and the closing. Because you don't need to apply this formatting in any other place in the document, you don't need to create a specific style for each element.

1. Set paragraph alignment to centered, turn off the open-line option, set the character size to 18 points, and then turn the outline type style on. Then type the name of your magazine: *The Perfect Poodle*.

2. Press Return to begin a new paragraph, reduce the character size to 14 points, turn the outline type style off, turn the italic type style on, and type *A Magazine for Dog Groomers*.

3. Press Return to begin a new paragraph, reduce the character size to 12 points, return the type style to plain text, and then type *523 Boulevard Street, Nadir Heights, NJ 05934*.

4. Press Return four times to add vertical space below the address you entered.

5. Set paragraph alignment to left aligned and move the left and first-line indents to the 3-inch mark on the Ruler's measure.

6. Choose *Glossary* from the Edit menu to open the Glossary window, and then double-click on the glossary entry *date-print-short*, which inserts the date below the address. The current date will always print when you print a document created from this template.

7. Press Return twice to insert a blank line and begin a new paragraph, and then set the left and first-line indents back to the 0 mark on the Ruler.

The Perfect Poodle
A Magazine for Dog Groomers
523 Boulevard Street, Nadir Heights, NJ   05934

5/10/91

Xx Xxxxxxxx Xxxx
Xxx Xxxxxx Xx
Xxxxxxxxxxx, XX XXXXX

Dear Xx Xxxx:

Yours sincerely,

Pesco Artilladero
Managing Editor

Figure 18-2. *The letter document template includes a letterhead, an address, a salutation, a blank line where you add text, and a closing.*

8. Type *Xx Xxxxxxx Xxxx* as the first line of the address. This is a row of X's that will reserve a place in the template, retain the formatting you set there, and remind you that you need to replace it with the addressee's real name when you create a letter. Press Return.

9. Type *Xxx Xxxxxx Xx* as the second line of the address to reserve a place for the street address. Press Return.

10. Type *Xxxxxxxxxxx, XX XXXXX* as the third line of the address to reserve a place for the city, state, and zip code. Press Return.

11. Choose *Normal* from the style-selection box in the Ruler, and then reapply the Normal style to the new paragraph. The Normal style includes the open-line space in its formatting.

12. Type *Dear Xx Xxxx:* as the salutation line, and press Return to start the first paragraph of the body text.

13. Press Return again to move on to the closing. You leave behind a blank line for text entry when you use the template.

14. Move the left and first-line indents to the 3-inch mark, type *Yours sincerely,* and press Return four times to add space to accommodate a signature.

15. Type *Pesco Artilladero* and press Return.

16. Turn the open-line option off, and type *Managing Editor.*

SAVING AND LOCKING THE TEMPLATE

To save a document template, simply choose *Save As* from the File menu, name the template in the Save As dialog box, and then click on the Save button. To lock the template's file, you must leave Word and return to the Mac desktop to choose the commands in the Finder menus there.

If you run your Mac using MultiFinder, you can return to the desktop without quitting Word by clicking on the icon located in the upper right corner of the screen or by choosing *Finder* from the Apple menu. If you run your Mac without using MultiFinder, you must quit Word to return to the desktop.

Once you're back in the desktop, you need to find your template file. You might have to open a few folders if you saved it in a folder (or in a folder within a folder). When you find the file, click on its icon or name to select it. Then choose *Get Info* from the File menu to open the Info dialog box, shown in Figure 18-3.

The Info dialog box displays information about the selected file, including its size, location in the folder, date of creation, and more. A text field appears at the bottom of the dialog box, where you can enter additional information or comments about the file, if you want. The Locked option check box appears in the upper right corner of the dialog box. Click on it to turn the option on, and then close the dialog box by clicking on its close box.

As long as a file's Locked option is turned on, the file is protected from alteration or deletion. If you try to drag the file into the Trashcan, the Finder will notify you that the file is locked and will return the file to its folder. If you open a locked document in Word, Word notifies you in the page-number area that the document is locked and will not allow you to save any changes to the document under the same filename.

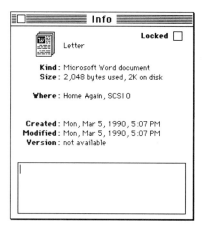

Figure 18-3. *The Info dialog box displays information about a file selected from the desktop and provides an area for entering commentary text and an option for locking the file.*

Storing Templates

You can use templates easily if you can find them quickly. One way to keep templates conveniently at hand is to create a special folder (named ''Templates'' or something similar) and place all your document template files in the folder. You might also want to store any companion glossaries or special spelling dictionaries for the documents in the folder.

An Example

Now that you've finished your document template, try saving it and locking it as follows:

1. Choose *Save As* from the File menu to open the Save As dialog box. Type the filename *Letter* in the Save Current Document As text box, and click on the Save button to save the template.

2. Close the template document window by clicking on its close box.

3. Move to the Macintosh desktop. If you're running MultiFinder, do this by choosing *Finder* from the Apple menu. If you're not running MultiFinder, do this by choosing *Quit* from the File menu to quit Word.

4. Find the icon labeled ''Letter'' on the desktop. Click on the icon or name to select the file.

5. Choose *Get Info* from the File menu to open the file's Info dialog box.

6. Click on the Locked check box in the upper right corner of the dialog box to turn the Locked option on.

7. Close the Get Info dialog box by clicking on its close box.

8. Return to Word. If you're running MultiFinder, do this by choosing *Microsoft Word* from the Apple menu. If you're not running MultiFinder, do this by starting Word again.

CREATING A COMPANION GLOSSARY

If you have common sections of text that don't appear in the majority of your documents, consider creating a companion glossary for your template. For example, let's say you own a musical-instrument store that leases instruments, and you use Word to draw up each lease by using a document template named ''Lease.'' Although the template includes standard sections about matters such as a damage deposit, it doesn't include individualized clauses (for example, a clause about cleaning swabs for woodwind instruments, another clause about water spray bottles for trombones, or a clause about separate bow rental for stringed instruments).

To simplify and speed the entering of the clauses, you can create a companion glossary, in this case named "Lease Glossary," that includes an entry for each of the common clauses, stored under the names "swab," "spray," and "bow." When you draw up a new lease, you begin by opening the Lease template. You then open the Lease Glossary and use it to add any of the standard clauses you need. You finish by typing custom text, such as the name of the customer and the rental rates.

Creating a New Glossary

To create a new glossary, you first open the Glossary window and then choose *New* from the File menu. When Word asks whether you want to delete all nonstandard glossary entries, click on the Yes button to strip the new glossary to the barest minimum. Then begin adding glossary items to the custom glossary as you learned to do in Chapter 12, "Writing Tools." When you've finished, choose *Save As* from the File menu to open the Save As dialog box, type a name for your new companion glossary, and then save it.

A companion glossary isn't saved as part of the current document; it's saved as a separate file. Be sure to save the companion glossary in the same folder as you save the document template so the glossary will be close at hand if you need it. Give the glossary the same name as your template, and add "Glossary" at the end of the name so you can easily identify the file. Because you keep the glossary file unlocked, you don't need to anticipate every entry you'll ever need when you first create the glossary. You can add entries to it whenever you come across a piece of text you think you'll use often.

An Example

Try creating a companion glossary that contains two entries for the Letter template. Include one paragraph that rejects a submitted article and another paragraph that accepts an article:

1. Move the insertion point to the middle of the template, at the beginning of the blank line between the salutation and the closing.

2. Type the following paragraph of rejection:
   We'd like to thank you for your recent submission, Xxxxx Xxx Xxxx-xxx, which we read with interest. Unfortunately, we cannot print your article at this time because we are already committed to printing articles of equally high quality. We are returning your article to you and wish you the best of luck with future submissions.

3. Press Return.

4. Select the entire paragraph as a text block.

5. Choose *Glossary* from the Edit menu to open the Glossary window.

6. Choose *New* from the File menu to open a new glossary. When Word displays a message asking whether you want to delete all nonstandard glossary items from the new glossary, click on the Yes button.

7. Type *reject* in the Name text box, and click on the Define button to enter the paragraph in the glossary under the name ''reject.'' Click on the Cancel button to close the Glossary window.

8. Press Delete to delete the selected paragraph rejection.

9. Type the following paragraph of acceptance:
   We'd like to thank you for your recent submission, Xxxxx Xxx Xxxx-xxx, which we read with interest. We liked what we read. In fact, we loved what we read and would like to publish your article! Enclosed is our standard author's contract. We think you'll find our rate of 2 cents per word to be extremely fair, given the market for poodle-clipping pieces. We look forward to hearing from you!

10. Press Return.

11. Select the entire paragraph as a text block.

12. Choose *Glossary* from the Edit menu to open the Glossary window.

13. Type *accept* in the Name text box, and click on the Define button to enter the paragraph in the glossary under the name ''accept.''

14. Choose *Save As* from the File menu to open the Save As window.

15. Choose the same folder you used to save the letter template, type the name *Letter Glossary*, and then click on the Save button to save your new companion glossary.

16. Click on the Cancel button to close the Glossary window.

17. Close the template window by clicking on its close box. When Word displays a message asking whether you want to save changes, click on the No button.

USING A TEMPLATE TO CREATE A NEW DOCUMENT

Once you've created document templates, you can open one whenever you want to start a new document based on that template. When Word opens a template, it opens a document window as it does for any other document. But because the template is a locked document, Word notifies you by displaying the message ''Locked File'' in the page-number area.

To create a document from a template, enter new text by applying styles from the template's style sheet. If the template has a companion glossary, you can open it and apply its entries as well. (To open a glossary, you open the Glossary window and choose *Open* from the File menu.) If you need to change the template's standard text or any of its formatting, you can edit it as much as you want—none of your changes will affect the original template. And don't forget about headers and footers! If the template has them, it's a good idea to check to be sure they don't need revision.

When you've finished the document, you can save it by choosing either *Save* or *Save As* from the File menu. Because the template is a locked document, Word will not write over the original template file. It opens the Save As dialog box as it would for a new document. Fill in a new name for the document (Word won't let you save it under the same name as the template), and click on the Save button to save the document.

When you save a document created from a template, the document becomes independent of the template; you can close it, open it again at any time, make changes, save changes, and print the document.

An Example

Try using your sample template and companion glossary now. You've just received an article from Avron Thillmuller about the hazards of chemicals used in poodle parlors to perm dogs' hair, and you've decided to publish it. The template and companion glossary make it easy to compose the letter:

1. Choose *Open* from the File menu, and use the Open dialog box to open the "Letter" document template. It appears on the screen in its own document window.

2. Choose *Glossary* from the Edit menu to open the Glossary window.

3. Choose *Open* from the File menu, and use the Open dialog box to open "Letter Glossary." Doing so adds all entries in "Letter Glossary" to the current glossary.

4. Click on the Cancel button to close the Glossary window.

5. Move the insertion point to the beginning of the blank line between the salutation and the closing.

6. Press Command-Delete to prepare for a glossary entry. The page-number area at the bottom of the document window displays the prompt "Name." Type *accept* and press Return. The paragraph of acceptance appears in the middle of the letter.

7. Press Delete to delete the blank line following the paragraph.

8. Select the first line of the address (*Xx Xxxxxxxx Xxxx*), and replace it with *Mr. Avron Thillmuller*.

9. Select the second line of the address (*Xxx Xxxxxx Xx*), and replace it with *518 Larval Way*.

10. Select the third line of the address (*Xxxxxxxxxxx, XX   XXXXX*), and replace it with *Zzyzzx, NV 84702*.

11. Select *Xx Xxxx* in the line *Dear Xx Xxxx,* and replace it with *Mr. Thillmuller*.

12. Select *Xxxxx Xxx Xxxxxxx* in the first line of the acceptance paragraph, and replace it with *Poodle Perms: Pathway to Prosperity or Perilous Profits?*.

13. Choose *Save As* from the File menu to save your new letter. Word opens the Save As dialog box.

14. Type the name *Thillmuller*, and click on the Save button to save the document.

15. Print the letter by choosing *Print* from the File menu and clicking on the OK button in the Print dialog box.

Now that you've finished, you probably realize that creating a template and a companion glossary involved more work than would have been required to simply type the letter from scratch. This is true when creating a single document, but imagine sending out one or two response letters a day and you can see that the template can save a lot of time and work over a few days. To be efficient, use templates only for documents you plan to create over and over again.

EDITING A TEMPLATE

You might need to revise your templates from time to time. You might find ways to improve their layout, or you might want to add or change standard text. If so, simply return to the desktop and unlock the template file in the same way you locked it—by opening the Info dialog box and clicking on the Locked check box. Once the template is unlocked, you can open it in Word, make any changes you want, and then save it. You then return to the desktop and relock the template file to avoid writing over it when you use it to create and save new documents.

You've now learned how to form a document template by creating common document elements in a regular document and then locking the file. In the next chapter you'll learn how to use some of Word's printing options to set page sizes, print on laser printers, and prepare text for printing with page-layout programs.

Chapter 19

Printing Variations and Document Export

Printing most Word documents is a straightforward task: You choose *Print* from the File menu, click on the OK button in the Page Setup dialog box, and then wait for the document to emerge from your printer on 8½-by-11-inch paper. It's the occasional odd document—the one that must be printed on odd-size paper or with a different printer—that makes you appreciate some of Word's special printing features.

This chapter is devoted to describing printing features that you might not normally use. The first section discusses printing on pages of different sizes and rotating the page so that text can print horizontally across the length or width of the page. The next section describes how to print the contents of a glossary or a style sheet and how to print hidden text within a document. The next section offers tips for polishing the look of laser-printed documents. And the final section steps outside the Word program to show you how to prepare your Word documents to export to PageMaker, the most popular Macintosh page-layout program.

SETTING UP WORD

Before you begin working with the examples in this chapter, check to be sure that Word shows full menus and that Page View is turned off:

1. If you haven't done so already, turn your computer on and start Word.

2. Open the Edit menu, and if the Full Menus command appears, choose it to set full menus. If the Short Menus command appears instead of the Full Menus command, full menus are already set, and you can close the menu without choosing any commands.

3. Open the Document menu, and if a check mark appears to the left of the Page View command, choose the Page View command to turn Page View off.

The sample document for this chapter is an envelope label. You'll re-create it in the first section of this chapter by changing page size to accommodate an envelope.

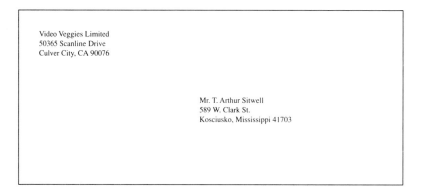

Video Veggies Limited
50365 Scanline Drive
Culver City, CA 90076

Mr. T. Arthur Sitwell
589 W. Clark St.
Kosciusko, Mississippi 41703

Figure 19-1. *You set a custom page size to print an address on an envelope.*

SETTING PAGE SIZE AND ORIENTATION

Not every document you need can be printed on 8½-by-11-inch paper. Lawyers, for example, print documents on legal-size sheets of paper, and some European businesses print documents on A4 European standard paper (which measures 8¼ by 11⅔ inches). And most people, at one time or another, need to print an address on an envelope, which can range in size from the smallest thank-you note to the largest Manila mailer.

When you consider page size, your first consideration should be the paper-handling capability of your printer. A standard ImageWriter II printer, for example, cannot accept an 11-by-17-inch tabloid sheet of paper because its roller isn't wide enough. Each type of printer you can connect to the Mac has its own paper restrictions that you need to consider if you're creating a document for printout.

If you decide on a paper size that is one of Word's standard page sizes, you set the page size by choosing the Page Setup command from the File menu and setting options in the Page Setup dialog box. If you decide on a nonstandard paper size, you set the page size by choosing the Preferences command from the Edit menu and setting the page size in the Preferences dialog box.

Setting a Standard Page Size

To change the page size to any of Word's standard page sizes, choose *Page Setup* from the File menu to open the Page Setup dialog box. Because this dialog box is part of the printer driver provided by Apple, the dialog box you see when you choose *Page Setup* will vary depending on the type of printer you select in the Chooser window. (See Chapter 1, "Setting Up Word 4," for more details on choosing a printer in the Chooser window.) Figure 19-2, on the following page, shows two versions of the dialog box.

The Paper area at the top of the Page Setup dialog box contains a set of paper-size options marked with radio buttons. Some of the sizes offered there (depending on the printer) are:

- *US Letter*—the default page size, 8½ by 11 inches
- *US Legal*—8½ by 14 inches
- *A4 Letter*—the European standard page size, 8¼ by 11⅔ inches
- *Tabloid*—11 by 17 inches.

Other page sizes might appear as well, depending on the capabilities of your printer. Your printer manual should describe the page sizes.

To change the page size, simply click on the radio button for the size you want, and then click on the OK button.

```
┌─────────────────────────────────────────────────────────────┐
│ ImageWriter                              v2.7    ╭────────╮   │
│                                                  │   OK   │   │
│ Paper:    ⦿ US Letter        ○ A4 Letter         ╰────────╯   │
│           ○ US Legal         ○ International Fanfold          │
│           ○ Computer Paper   ○ Custom 8.5 by 5 in ╭────────╮  │
│                                                   │ Cancel │  │
│ Orientation    Special Effects: ☐ Tall Adjusted  ╰────────╯  │
│                                 ☐ 50 % Reduction             │
│  [icon][icon]                   ☐ No Gaps Between Pages       │
│                                                              │
│ ╭──────────╮                                                 │
│ │ Document...│  ☐ Set Default                                │
│ ╰──────────╯                                                 │
└─────────────────────────────────────────────────────────────┘
```

(A)

```
┌─────────────────────────────────────────────────────────────┐
│ LaserWriter Page Setup                    5.2   ╭────────╮   │
│                                                 │   OK   │   │
│ Paper: ⦿ US Letter  ○ A4 Letter  ○ Tabloid      ╰────────╯   │
│        ○ US Legal   ○ B5 Letter                 ╭────────╮   │
│                                                 │ Cancel │   │
│  Reduce or [100] %    Printer Effects:          ╰────────╯   │
│  Enlarge:             ⊠ Font Substitution?      ╭────────╮   │
│                       ⊠ Text Smoothing?         │Options │   │
│  Orientation          ⊠ Graphics Smoothing?     ╰────────╯   │
│  [icon][icon]         ⊠ Faster Bitmap Printing? ╭────────╮   │
│                                                 │  Help  │   │
│ ╭──────────╮                                    ╰────────╯   │
│ │ Document...│ ☐ Fractional Widths  ☐ Print PostScript Over Text │
│ ╰──────────╯  ☐ Set Default                                  │
└─────────────────────────────────────────────────────────────┘
```

(B)

Figure 19-2. *The ImageWriter printer Page Setup dialog box is shown in figure A; the LaserWriter printer Page Setup dialog box is shown in figure B. Each displays options appropriate for its printer.*

Setting a Custom Page Size

If you need to set a page size for an odd-size piece of paper such as an envelope, choose *Preferences* from the Edit menu to open the Preferences dialog box, shown in Figure 19-3. The Custom Paper Size area includes two text boxes.

To create a custom page size, type the height and width of your page in inches in the appropriate text box, and then click on the OK button to close the Preferences dialog box.

Once you create a custom page size in the Preferences dialog box, you set the new size in the Page Setup dialog box. This time when you choose *Page Setup* from the File menu to open the Page Setup dialog box, you see a new setting—Custom—in the paper area. Custom is the new size you created in the Preferences dialog box. Click on the Custom option, and then click on the OK button to close the Page Setup dialog box and set the custom page size.

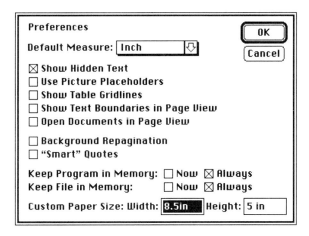

Figure 19-3. *Open the Preferences dialog box and set a custom paper size by entering size values in the Height and Width text boxes.*

Viewing the Page

Once you set a new page size, you can check its dimensions in three ways: Display the Ruler to check its width, turn Page View on and scroll through the document to check both its height and its width, or use Print Preview to view the entire page at one time.

The Ruler

When you set a new page size with a new width, the Ruler adjusts its page-margin markers accordingly. If you click on the Ruler's scale icon to turn page scale on, the Ruler will show the edge of the page if you scroll far enough to the left or right. (To scroll past the left margin hold down the Shift key while using the horizontal scroll bar.)

Page View

When you choose *Page View* from the Document menu, Word shows all four edges of the page if you scroll horizontally and vertically using the scroll bars. Page View shows the text and surrounding white space in full scale.

Print Preview

Choosing *Print Preview* from the File menu opens the Print Preview window, shown in Figure 19-4, which shows the new page in its entirety although reduced in size.

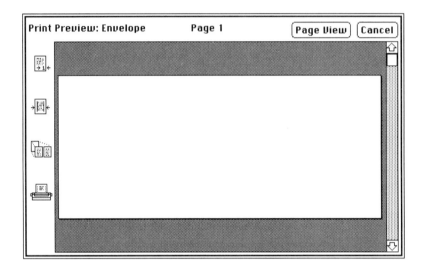

Figure 19-4. *The Print Preview window shows the proportional size of a page. Here the window displays a custom page size for an envelope.*

Changing Page Orientation

Most documents are printed from top to bottom on sheets of paper taller than they are wide. All the sample documents you've created so far have been printed this way—it's Word's default way to print on an 8½-by-11-inch sheet of paper. There might be times, however, when you want to print on a sheet of paper that is wider than it is tall—perhaps for a wide table or many columns of text. No problem; you can simply create a custom page size that is wider than it is tall—for instance, 11 inches wide by 8½ inches high. When you try to feed an 11-inch wide sheet of paper into your printer, however, you might have a problem: Most printers won't accept paper as wide as 11 inches.

The solution to this printer problem is to specify a standard page size, such as 8½ by 11 inches, and then instruct Word to turn the page orientation by 90 degrees so that it prints lines of text down the length of the sheet of paper instead of across the width. This is called changing the *page orientation*.

Word offers two types of page orientation: *portrait* and *landscape*. Portrait orientation is the printer's default page orientation and is so named because, like a portrait of a person, the printed page is taller than it is wide. Landscape orientation is so named because, like most landscape paintings, the page is wider than it is tall.

To set page orientation, you choose *Page Setup* from the File menu to open the Page Setup dialog box. The Orientation area, shown in Figure 19-5, includes two icons: The left icon sets portrait orientation, the right icon sets landscape orientation. Click on the appropriate icon to choose the orientation you want, and then click on the OK button to close the dialog box and set the orientation.

Orientation

Figure 19-5. *Set page orientation in the Orientation area of the Page Setup dialog box.*

When you change the page orientation from portrait to landscape, the Ruler and the text in the document window change to fit the new orientation. In Page View and Print Preview, you can see that the page has been turned by 90 degrees. For example, if you set landscape orientation for an 8½-by-11-inch sheet of paper, the Print Preview window displays an 11-by-8½-inch page, and the Ruler shows margins and page edges set for an 11-inch-wide sheet of paper. Remember that the page is turned sideways only in Word; you still feed the sheet of paper through the printer as you would if page orientation were set to portrait.

When you set page size and orientation for a document and then save the document, Word saves the size and orientation as part of the document. When you reopen the document, it appears in the page size you previously set. Page size and orientation are, in effect, a type of document formatting.

An Example

Try setting page size to accommodate a standard letter envelope that measures 9½ inches wide by 4⅛ inches tall. Because ImageWriter printers can accept an envelope of this width in its normal orientation, you don't need to change orientation unless you plan to print with a laser printer. In that case, you set landscape (sideways) orientation and define the page as 4⅛ inches wide by 9½ inches tall.

1. Choose *Preferences* from the Edit menu to open the Preferences dialog box.

2. If you have an ImageWriter, type *9.5* in the Width text box of the Custom Paper Size area and *4.125* in the Height text box. If you have a LaserWriter, type *4.125* in the Width text box and *9.5* in the Height text box. Then click on the OK button to close the dialog box and set the new custom page size.

3. Choose *Page Setup* from the File menu to open the Page Setup dialog box. The new page size you set should appear in the Paper area as the Custom size.

4. Click on the Custom size radio button to select the custom size. If you have a LaserWriter, click on the landscape-orientation icon (the icon at the right). Then click on the OK button to close the Page Setup dialog box and set the custom size.

5. Show the Ruler if it isn't currently visible, and then scroll the document to the right. The Ruler should show that the right margin has moved out by 1 inch to the 7-inch mark because the page width is now 1 inch wider than Word's default page width of 8.5 inches.

6. Choose *Document* from the Format menu to open the Document dialog box, type *0.5* as top, bottom, left, and right margin settings, and then click on the OK button to close the dialog box. Setting a 0.5-inch margin on all sides ensures that every printer (including a LaserWriter) can print text flush against the margins. If your printer can print closer to the edges, you can set a smaller margin.

7. Reduce the type size to 10 points and then type the return address (the first three lines of the sample document in Figure 19-1). Press Return at the end of each line.

8. Enlarge the type size to 12 points and then press Return five times to insert four blank lines and position the insertion point at the beginning of the fifth line.

9. Move the first-line and left-indent markers to the 4-inch mark on the Ruler.

10. Type the address lines (the second three lines of text in the sample document). Press Return at the end of each line.

11. Choose *Print Preview* from the File menu to view the entire envelope.

Now that your document is finished, you can print it with an ImageWriter printer by inserting the envelope so that it feeds top first into the printer. Advance the envelope as far as necessary, and then choose the Print command from the File menu to print. You print the document with a LaserWriter by feeding the envelope in lengthwise (flap side to your right) and then choosing the Print command. You might need to experiment with the position of the envelope (especially if you use an ImageWriter printer) to print the text exactly where you want it on the envelope. (If you don't have a 9½-by-4⅛-inch envelope, you can print the document on regular 8½-by-11-inch paper to see how the printer positions the text.)

Your ImageWriter might work better if you insert the envelope left side first instead of top first. To find out, change page size and orientation as follows:

1. Choose *Preferences* from the Edit menu to open the Preferences dialog box, type a width of *4.125* and a height of *9.5*, and then click on the OK button to close the dialog box. These are the envelope's dimensions, in inches, if you feed it into your printer lengthwise.

2. Choose *Page Setup* from the File menu to open the Page Setup dialog box, and then click on the Custom setting.

3. Click on the landscape icon (the icon on the right) in the orientation area, and then click on the OK button to close the Page Setup dialog box. Your envelope text should appear the same as it did before you changed both page size and page orientation.

Your document is now set to print on a 9½-inch-by-4⅛-inch envelope inserted lengthwise. Try printing on a standard sheet of paper to check whether the text is positioned correctly before printing on an envelope.

PRINTING DOCUMENT ELEMENTS

A document contains many elements that don't normally appear when you print the document—for example, information about its formatting or hidden text that you inserted. You can print these normally invisible elements by setting Word's special printing options.

Printing Hidden Text

You learned in Chapter 4, "Entering and Formatting Characters," that you can hide text that you don't want to appear on screen. Hidden text remains invisible until you turn the Show Hidden Text option on in the Preferences dialog box. Even after you show hidden text, Word does not normally print the hidden text when you print the document.

To print hidden text, choose *Print* from the File menu to open the Print dialog box. If you turn the Print Hidden Text option on, Word prints all hidden text when it prints the other document text. When the option is turned off, Word prints only the nonhidden text.

Printing Style Sheets

Every document you create has its own style sheet, whether it contains a single style—Normal—or a full list of styles that control the parts of the document. You can normally see the contents of the style sheet only by opening the Styles dialog box or the Define Styles dialog box, or by opening the style-selection box on the Ruler.

If you want to print the style sheet (a convenience if you like to change styles at the keyboard without opening dialog boxes or the style-selection box), first open the Define Styles dialog box (choose *Define Styles* from the Format menu). With the Define Styles dialog box open, choose *Print* from the Edit menu to open the Print dialog box. When you click on the OK button in the Print dialog box, Word prints the current document's style sheet, listing each style by name followed by the style's definition.

Printing Glossaries

You can print the contents of a glossary by opening the Glossary window (choose *Glossary* from the Edit menu) and then opening the glossary you want. Open the Print dialog box by choosing *Print* from the File menu, and then click on the OK button in the Print dialog box. Word prints each glossary entry followed by the contents of the entry.

USING A LASER PRINTER

You might find that you love laser-printer quality but hate the price of a laser printer. To solve the conflict, you can buy an ImageWriter printer to print everyday documents, and when you want to print documents that need the polished look of laser printing, you can save them on a floppy disk and then bring the disk to a printer or copy store that rents time on a Macintosh-based laser printer system. Most rental systems have a copy of Word installed, so printing a document can be simply a matter of running Word, inserting the floppy disk, opening the document, and choosing *Print* from the File menu.

Unfortunately, the document printed by the store's laser printer might not meet your expectations. The line endings and page breaks on your laser-printed document might be different from the ones you set when you created the document on your own Macintosh. And some of the fonts on the page might appear smooth, whereas others might look as jagged as they did on the ImageWriter and your Mac screen. A few tips about laser printing will help you avoid these problems to get the best possible results from the laser printer.

Choosing Fonts for Laser Printing

The Macintosh uses one type of font when it displays characters on its screen, whereas many laser printers use a different type of font to print the same characters on a page. When you print a document with a laser printer, the printer attempts to translate the document's screen fonts into laser-printer fonts, a process that—in some cases—results in smoothly printed characters. In other cases, the printed characters appear as jagged as those you see on your screen. The results depend on the fonts you use in your document. To understand how to choose the best fonts, you need to know more about the two different types of fonts.

Bitmap fonts

Your Macintosh uses *bitmap fonts* when it displays text on screen. A bitmap font contains a picture of each character you can type from the keyboard stored as a pattern of pixels in the computer's memory or on disk. (Pixels are the small dots that form pictures and characters on your screen.) Each bitmap font contains only one point size in a typeface; for example, 12-point New York is one bitmap font, and 14-point New York is another.

When you open the Font menu to choose a font, Word lists the font names that your Mac can find on your system disk. The point sizes listed above the font names show the defined sizes for the font names you choose—defined point sizes appear outlined, undefined point sizes appear in plain text. For example, if your system disk contains fonts for 12-point London and 14-point London, the Font menu shows London as a font name and outlines ''12 point'' and ''14 point'' in the menu to show you that those sizes are defined. Each defined point size of a font forms a separate bitmap font available to your system.

If you choose an undefined point size for a typeface and then type some characters, the characters you see on the screen probably appear very jagged and distorted. This is because the system doesn't have that ''font''; you can't use an undefined type size with good results unless you have a different ''font'' for that size. If the computer tries to stretch or shrink an existing font into a new size (which it must do if you choose a point size for which it has no font), the results can appear very ragged.

When you print a document on an ImageWriter or ImageWriter II printer, your Macintosh sends to the printer the same bitmap fonts it displays on its screen. This is why an ImageWriter-printed document appears exactly like the text you see on the Mac screen, down to the jagged diagonals and curves on letters such as *K* and *C*.

Scalable fonts

Apple LaserWriters (with the exception of the LaserWriter SC) use their own microprocessor and memory, and they use an internal page-description language called *PostScript*. A PostScript laser printer uses *scalable fonts* to draw characters on the page instead of using bitmap fonts like those used by the Mac. Characters in a scalable font are stored in the printer's own memory (or attached disk drive) as a collection of graphic components describing each character—a line at a certain angle, an added curve or serif.

Because the PostScript laser printer knows the components of each letter, it can easily enlarge or shrink characters and still retain their exact appearance. The printer requires only a single font for each typeface; it can create almost any point size from the single font. Scalable fonts also take advantage of the laser printer's high-resolution capability (the ability to draw characters using very tiny pixels, which accurately define curves and diagonal lines) to create much smoother-looking characters than the Mac screen or the ImageWriter printer can create.

Translating Bitmap Fonts into Scalable Fonts

The collection of bitmap fonts available from the Font menu of Word might be completely different from the collection of scalable fonts available in a PostScript laser printer. Some popular bitmap fonts, such as Mobile—a font that produces tiny pictures instead of characters when you press a key—don't exist at all in PostScript. Other bitmap fonts have close PostScript equivalents.

When you print a document that contains different bitmap fonts with a PostScript laser printer, the Macintosh translates each of the fonts in one of three ways:

■ It finds a corresponding scalable font available in the PostScript printer and then uses the scalable font to print the characters. For example, text that you print in the Times bitmap font appears smooth because the PostScript printer has a Times scalable font to correspond.

■ It can't find a matching scalable font in the PostScript printer, so it sends the bitmap font directly to the printer, with jagged results. For example, if you print text in the London font (for which there is no scalable-font equivalent), the printer uses the bitmap font to print the text, so the text appears exactly as jagged as it did on the Macintosh screen.

■ It can't find a matching scalable font in the PostScript printer, but it does find a scalable font that almost matches the bitmap font. It substitutes the scalable font for the bitmap font and adjusts character spacing when necessary to match line breaks. For example, the New York bitmap font closely resembles the Times scalable font, so if you print New York text, it appears in the Times font. Because the Times font is a little narrower than the New York font, the Mac adds some space between words to preserve line breaks.

When you choose fonts for a document you intend to print with a Post-Script laser printer, try to choose a font that you know exists on the laser printer. Almost all PostScript laser printers include at least four scalable fonts: Times, Helvetica, Courier, and Zapf Dingbats. Many laser printers also include additional fonts such as Palatino and Garamond. Before you begin creating your document, read the laser printer manual or check with the person who runs your laser-printer system to find out what fonts are available, and then try to match them.

Your system might not have bitmap fonts that match the scalable fonts you want to use in your laser-printed document. If so, you can often buy the fonts and install them on your system disk. If you can't find the fonts, you can use closely equivalent fonts that come with your Mac. For example, the New York font closely resembles the Times font and the Geneva font closely resembles the Helvetica font. When you print documents with these equivalent fonts, the Mac can substitute the similar scalable font. The only drawback to equivalent fonts is that the spacing between words can often appear awkward.

There are times, of course, when you use a bitmap font that has no equivalent or even similar scalable font. For example, you might like the florid style of the London font or the quirky graphics of the Mobile font. These fonts do print on the laser printer, but they appear jagged.

Printing Graphics with a Laser Printer

You can create graphics, like text, in two forms: bitmap and scalable (which in the graphics world is called *object-oriented* or simply *drawn*). When you create a graphic in the paint layer of SuperPaint, you create a bitmap image— a collection of pixels arrayed in a grid that the computer stores in its memory. When you create a picture in the draw layer of SuperPaint, you create a drawn image—a collection of graphic elements such as lines, circles, polygons, and more—that is stored as a mathematical description of its components instead of as a collection of pixels.

The rule of thumb for laser printing is that you should avoid using bitmap graphics and instead use drawn graphics whenever possible. Not only do drawn graphics appear much smoother than bitmap graphics, but they print much faster, and they're easier to resize if you need to fit them in a smaller or larger space. (You learned to do so in Chapter 5, ''Adding Graphics''.)

Printing an ImageWriter-based
Document on a Laser Printer

To help confound matters a little more for ImageWriter users who intend to print their document on a laser printer, there is a difference in width between characters printed on an ImageWriter printer and characters in the same point size printed on a PostScript laser printer: Laser printer characters are wider, so the laser printer can fit fewer of the same characters in a single line than an ImageWriter can.

To adjust for this difference, Word changes the scale of its document window to match the printing scale of whatever printer driver is selected in the Chooser desk accessory. If the ImageWriter icon is selected, the Ruler's measure extends 6 inches across the top of a normal-size document window. If the LaserWriter icon is selected, the measure extends almost 6.75 inches across the same document window. Figure 19-6, on the following page, shows two views of a document window—one set for an ImageWriter and the other set for a LaserWriter. Because the characters in the document window remain the same size, the LaserWriter-based window displays fewer characters per Ruler inch than the ImageWriter-based window does.

If you prepare documents on the same Macintosh you use when you print documents, this difference in character width will not affect your document. The lines of text you see on your screen are the lines of text that your printer will print. However, if you prepare a document on a Mac set up to print on an ImageWriter and then take the document to another Mac set up to print on a LaserWriter, all the line lengths will be reduced for the LaserWriter and the line breaks and page breaks will move in relation to the reduced line lengths.

If you want to see how your ImageWriter-based document will appear when printed with a PostScript printer, you can trick your own Mac into thinking it's connected to a PostScript printer so that it shows you the line and page breaks. First be sure that your system disk contains the LaserWriter printer driver: Open the System Folder on your disk and look for two files— LaserWriter and Laser Prep. If they're not there, you can find them on one of the disks that came with your Macintosh and copy them to the System Folder.

To preview laser printing, choose *Chooser* from the Apple menu to open the Chooser window, and then choose a laser printer as you learned to do in Chapter 1, "Setting Up Word 4." When you close the window, Word should

(A)

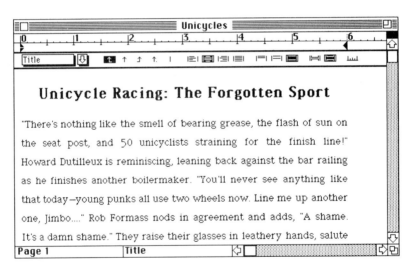

(B)

Figure 19-6. *The document window in figure A shows a document as it appears when the Macintosh is set to print on an ImageWriter printer. The document window in figure B shows the same document as it appears when the Macintosh is set to print on a LaserWriter printer. Notice that the line breaks are different in the two documents.*

display laser-based document windows, which you can easily check by showing the Ruler; the Ruler should be compressed slightly so that you see more of its width in the window than you could before. If it hasn't changed, you might need to choose *Page Setup* from the File menu to open the Page Setup dialog box and then click on the OK button. This tells Word that you've changed printers.

With a laser-based document window, you can edit your document as necessary to work on a laser-based page and then save your document to disk for printing on another system. When you've finished, be sure to use the Chooser to return to the ImageWriter printer (be sure you also reset AppleTalk and the port you use to connect your printer) or you'll have troubles when you try to print with your own system. You might need to open the Page Setup dialog box again to affirm your printer change if Word doesn't change the document window to match.

Setting LaserWriter Printer Effects

Once you've created a document for printout on a PostScript LaserWriter, you can turn special printer effects on that can improve the look of your document. To set the available options, choose *Page Setup* from the File menu to open the LaserWriter Page Setup dialog box. The Printer Effects area offers the following options:

- *Font Substitution.* Leave this option on if you want the Mac to substitute similar scalable fonts for bitmap fonts—such as New York and Geneva—that don't have matching scalable fonts. Turn the option off if you want unmatched bitmap fonts to print as bitmap fonts.

- *Text Smoothing.* This effect smooths out bitmap fonts that are printed as bitmap fonts on the laser printer. This helps smooth curves and diagonals, but it often makes characters appear slightly gooey. Try it to see whether you like it. If you don't, turn the effect off to get jagged but clearly defined bitmap characters.

- *Graphics Smoothing.* This effect smooths out bitmap graphics in the same way Text Smoothing smooths out bitmap fonts. Turn this option on to smooth out bitmap graphics, but turn it off if its effect makes your graphics look gooey.

■ *Faster Bitmap Printing.* This effect speeds bitmap printing so that any bitmap graphics or fonts you use in a document won't slow the printing process as much as they normally would.

Once you've chosen the printer effects you want, click on the OK button to set the options, and then print your document.

EXPORTING WORD DOCUMENTS TO ALDUS PAGEMAKER

Many publications—such as newsletters and pamphlets—contain articles, pictures, and small blocks of text. Articles might begin on one page and continue on another. Pictures might need to be anchored in one spot on the page so they don't move as you edit surrounding text. It is possible to create this kind of publication as a Word document, but it won't be easy—Word wasn't designed to handle such complex publications. You might benefit by using a *page-layout program* such as Aldus PageMaker to pull together the different components of the publication. Page-layout software is specifically designed to assemble text and graphics on a page and print it on a laser printer.

How PageMaker Accepts Word Documents

PageMaker is a program that presents a series of blank pages on the screen and allows you to fill them with blocks of text and graphics. It offers a command named Place that allows you to open any Word document or graphics file. When you use the Place command to open a Word document, PageMaker lets you place the text of the document, called a ''story'' in PageMaker parlance, on the page as a box. If the story contains more text than will fit in a single box, you can place a series of boxes on different pages to contain the overflow; PageMaker links the boxes so the entire story can be edited as a single document.

PageMaker, like Word, lets you create styles to format text throughout a publication. In a typical PageMaker publication, you might create one style for a major headline, another for a subheading, another for body text, another for picture captions, and so on, depending on the type of publication. When you import a Word document, PageMaker reads the styles you assigned to paragraphs within the document; if any style name matches a style name in the PageMaker publication's style sheet, PageMaker can (at the user's option) change the style so it matches the PageMaker style definition. If you apply special formatting within a paragraph, such as boldface or italic, PageMaker imports the formatting without alteration.

Consider an example: You define a Word style named "body" as 12-point New York type with double line spacing, you apply the style to the body of a Word document, and then you enter a paragraph of body text that contains an italicized word. PageMaker in this example also has a style named "body," but it uses 10-point Times type with single line spacing. When you import the Word document into PageMaker, the paragraph appears in Page-Maker's body style—10-point Times type with single line spacing—but it retains the italicized word.

PageMaker does not import all parts of a Word document. It won't import section or document formatting, and it won't import tables into a document. (You'll learn to create tables in Chapter 21, "Creating Tables.") If you include graphics in a document, each graphic is pulled from the document and presented as a separate element on the PageMaker page.

Preparing a Word Document for Export

Many people create documents using Word and then submit them to another person—a newsletter editor, for example—who imports the Word document into PageMaker and places it with other stories and pictures. If you are one of the story writers, you might want to request a style sheet from your editor or newsletter designer so you can apply the same styles (within reason) and style names to your document. As you write, you can define the styles to use whatever formatting is the most legible and understandable for you—applying exact formatting isn't important because it can be changed easily when the story is imported into PageMaker. For example, if the newsletter uses "headline," "subheading," and "text" styles, be sure you use the same style names in your document. However, if the newsletter uses 9-point Times characters in single line spacing for each article, you don't need to use the same formatting for your style—it would make text difficult to read on screen.

Avoid using fancy custom formatting in your document if possible. If you change indents frequently, create columns of numbers, or use many different fonts, the page-layout person will have to reformat them to fit the newsletter. If you do need to add some custom formatting, try to do so by using styles.

For example, if you plan to include a special element such as a quotation, define a new style for it. When the document is imported into PageMaker, any of its styles that aren't matched by a PageMaker style are imported as a new style into PageMaker's style sheet. The page-layout person can then redefine the new style to his or her satisfaction and thereby change all paragraphs defined by the style instead of being forced to format each paragraph individually.

When you finish your document, all you need to do is save it on disk (a floppy disk if you need to send the document to another Macintosh). The rest is up to the PageMaker user—a topic for another book.

You've now learned some printing variations to help you work with different page sizes, to print usually hidden document elements, to improve the quality of laser printing, and to prepare documents for printing in PageMaker. You've also finished the intermediate-level section of this book. In the next section you'll advance to the final level to learn about some of Word's most powerful tools.

SECTION FOUR

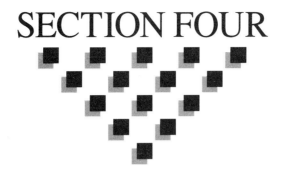

Power Tools

This section introduces you to some of Word 4's most advanced fea-tures. You use them to create easily adjusted tables of information, to print personalized form letters, to display a document in different Word views, including Outline View, and to customize Word by creat-ing your own menus and keyboard shortcuts. The chapters in this section don't go into great detail about these advanced features, which would extend beyond the scope of an introductory book, but they do get you started and might pique your interest to learn even more about Word's power tools.

Chapter 20

Views, Outlines, and Document Windows

This chapter introduces different ways to view a Word document. You'll learn to use Word's Galley View and Page View to see a single document in partial or full formatting. You'll also learn to use the Outline View to create an outline from scratch or to view an outline of an existing document. In the last part of the chapter you'll learn how to open many document windows on the screen at one time and how to split a document window into panes to display two parts of a single document at one time. All these tools make it easier for you to see the contents of a long document and to work with material spread throughout several documents.

SETTING UP WORD

Before you begin working with the examples in this chapter, check to be sure that Word shows full menus and that Page View is turned off:

1. If you haven't done so already, turn your computer on and start Word.

2. Open the Edit menu, and if the Full Menus command appears, choose it to set full menus. If the Short Menus command appears instead of the Full Menus command, full menus are already set, and you can close the menu without choosing any commands.

3. Open the Document menu, and if a check mark appears to the left of the Page View command, choose the Page View command to turn Page View off.

You'll need two documents to work with the examples in this chapter. One is the Unicycles article you created in Chapter 15, "Styles Made Simple." You'll use it to learn about different document views. The second document is an outline you'll create in Outline View that shows the structure of a user's manual for a piece of entertainment software called "Stellar Sawbones," a science-fiction medical adventure program. Figure 20-1 shows the outline document.

DOCUMENT VIEWS

Word offers three different views for any document:

- Galley View

- Page View

- Outline View

Galley View is the view you've used throughout most of this book; it is Word's "normal" view. It shows full character and paragraph formatting but not all the document elements as they appear on the page. For example, it doesn't show footnotes, headers or footers, or the edges of the page. In return for the limited view of the page and document elements, Galley View offers faster display speed—you can scroll through a document more quickly than you can in Page View, and Word doesn't take long pauses to update the screen as you type. Most people use Galley View for entering the text of a document.

You've used Page View in previous chapters to view formatting and document elements that aren't visible in Galley View: headers, footers, footnotes, multiple columns, new page sizes, and the like. Although Page View displays a much more accurate picture of your document as it will print, you give up display speed when you use it. Word takes longer to scroll from page to page in Page View and often pauses in order to form the document elements that will appear on screen as you scroll. Use Page View to view a document after you've entered its text and to make small editing and formatting changes to your final document.

Introduction
Welcome to a world of medical thrills and excitement! As Dr. Thralnor Fefnikal of the Assimilated Lowculture Planetary Association, you will have the opportunity to practice surgery and larceny on unsuspecting denizens of planets throughout the known galaxy. Before you begin your career, take a few minutes to fill in the warranty card.
  The Warranty Card
  Other Digidilly Games
Setting Up
  Computers with the IRS Card
    With Depreciation Accelerators
    With Itemized Raster RAM
    With File Extension
  Computers with the GTI Card
    With Bitstream Injection
    With Radial Disks
    With Molded Graphics Primitives
Playing the Game
  Choosing a Planet
    Ice Planets
    Desert Planets
    Fixer-Upper Planets
  Finding a Patient
    Listening to the Police Scanner
    Waiting Around the Race Track
    The Bad Part of Town
  Your Surgical Tools
    The Laser Scalpel
    The Superglue Sutures
    The Neutrino Nail Clipper
  Malpractice Insurance
    Cut-Rate Firms
    Forging Coverage Certificates
  Intergalactic Flight
    Avoiding Police
    Paying Bribes
    Your Safe Hiding Place
  Scoring

Figure 20-1. *Using Word's Outline View makes creating document outlines easy.*

Outline View isn't intended for page layout or for extensive text editing, but, instead, shows the underlying structure of a document. It displays different levels of headings indented in outline form. Outline View recognizes nine levels of headings and displays them indented at 0.5-inch levels. It also recognizes body text accompanying headings, displaying each block of text indented slightly under its heading.

PAGE VIEW'S SPECIAL FEATURES

As you learned in previous chapters, you choose *Page View* from the Document menu to turn Page View on. Once it's turned on, you see your document as close to the way it will appear when printed as your monitor screen allows. Although you probably won't be able to see an entire page at one time (unless you have a very large monitor), you can scroll to see all parts of the page. In addition to character and paragraph formatting (which you also see in Galley View), you see section and document formatting as you scroll. You see the edges of the page and the page margins you set. You also see footnotes, headers, and footers where they appear on each page. A page break appears not as a dotted line across the width of the document window but as an actual break from one page to another, complete with page edges and top and bottom page margins. If you create multiple columns in a document, you see them side by side in Page View.

Scrolling in Page View works a little differently from the way it does in other views. The bottom of the screen in Page View, shown in Figure 20-2, includes two additional controls: the *page-back icon* and the *page-forward icon*. Click on the page-forward icon to move the view forward to the top of the next page; click on the page-back icon to move the view backward to the top of the preceding page. Use the vertical scroll bar as you do in Galley View to scroll to the top and bottom of each page to see the page edges and any headers, footers, or footnotes there. You can also use the scroll bar to scroll to the preceding or following page.

You use the cursor keys in Page View as you do in Galley View to move up, down, left, and right through the text. When working with multiple columns on a page, you'll find that the insertion point doesn't jump to the right or left to a neighboring column as you use right-arrow or left-arrow cursor keys; the insertion point moves upward or downward to the next line of text in the same column, a useful feature for retaining the thread of text as you

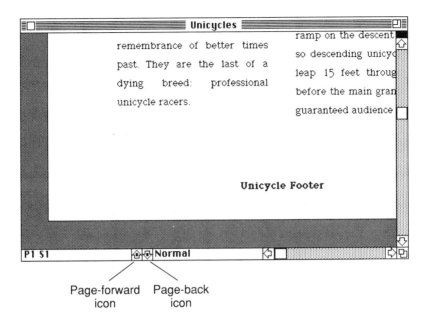

Page-forward icon   Page-back icon

Figure 20-2. *Page View shows all elements of a document, including headers, footers, footnotes, and multiple columns. It also shows the edges of the page.*

entered it. You'll also find that moving the insertion point upward or downward with cursor keys doesn't always move the insertion point upward or downward into a header, footer, or footnote if it exists. To move to any of these document elements, it's best to click on the desired element and then use the cursor keys to move the insertion point.

Editing in Page View has its own conventions. Although you edit body text as you do in Galley View, you don't need to open separate windows to edit headers, footers, and footnotes as you do in Galley View. Because these elements appear on the page, you simply select the text in a header, footer, or footnote where it appears on the page and then change it as you want. If you change a header or footer that's linked to other headers or footers, the text in the linked headers or footers changes accordingly.

Adding headers or footers to a document in Page View is similar to the process of adding them in Galley View: You set the types of footers you want (for example, odd and even, special first page) in the Section and Document dialog boxes and then choose *Open Header* (or the appropriate command) from the Document menu. But instead of opening a special window for the header or footer, Word creates space at the top or bottom of the page and then moves the insertion point there so you can enter the text you want. When you've finished, you simply click elsewhere on the page to move out of the header or footer area.

Adding footnotes to a document in Page View is also similar to the same process in Galley View: You choose *Footnote* from the Document menu to insert a footnote marker. Word then moves the insertion point to the bottom of the page (or to the end of the section or document if you set footnotes to appear there), and you type the contents of the footnote there. To return to the body of the text, you can click on your previous location or choose *Go Back* from the Utilities menu (or, even simpler, press *0* on the numeric keypad).

When you work on a document that has multiple columns in Page View, the Ruler (when displayed) functions differently from the way it does in Galley View. When you move the insertion point to a column, the 0 mark on the Ruler moves to the left margin of the column. For example, if you select the right-hand column of a pair of columns and the column begins halfway across the width of a standard page, the 0 mark on the Ruler moves to the middle of the document window. This convention makes it easier to set indentions in columns.

Word offers an additional Page View tool for working with multiple columns: multiple selection bars. In Galley View, the selection bar is a thin (and invisible) vertical strip, along the left side of the window, in which you can move the pointer to easily select lines, paragraphs, or the entire document. In Page View, Word places a selection bar along the left side of each column so you can select lines and paragraphs within each column. You use the column-selection bars in the same way you use the selection bar in Galley View: Move the insertion point to the left of a line, and click the mouse button to select it; double-click to the left of a paragraph to select it.

A Page View Example

Try viewing the ever-useful Unicycles article in both Galley View and Page View. Set the document to include multiple columns and a footer to see how Page View handles those elements. Follow the steps listed on the next page.

1. Open the document named "Unicycles." It appears on the screen in Galley View.

2. Choose *Section* from the Format menu to open the Section dialog box.

3. Type *2* in the Columns Number text box, and click on the OK button to close the dialog box and set the text in 2 columns.

4. Scroll downward to the end of the document. Notice that the text appears in a single narrow column on the left side of the document window and that page breaks appear as horizontal dotted lines.

5. Choose *Page View* from the Document menu to turn Page View on.

6. Use the vertical scroll bar to scroll upward to the top of the document. You'll now see two columns per page. You'll also see breaks between pages, and when you reach the top of the document, you'll see the top edge of the first page. (Click on the up scroll arrow of the scroll bar to see the top of the page.)

7. Choose *Open Footer* from the Document menu to create a footer. The insertion point jumps to the bottom of the first page, below the body text.

8. Turn on center alignment and boldface, and then type the text *Unicycle Footer*.

9. Click on the page-forward arrow, at the bottom of the document window, to jump the view forward to the second page, and then scroll downward to the bottom of the page. Notice the footer at the bottom of the page. When you created the footer on the first page, Word added it to each additional page.

10. Choose *Show Ruler* from the Format menu to display the Ruler.

11. Move the insertion point into the right-hand column of text. Notice that the 0 mark on the Ruler moves to match the left edge of the column, as shown in Figure 20-3, on the following page.

12. Choose *Page View* from the Document menu to turn Page View off.

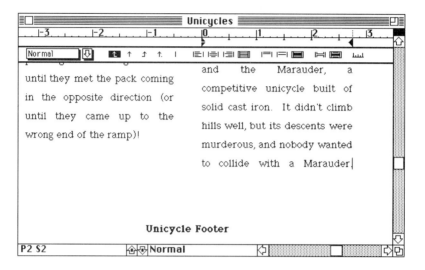

Figure 20-3. *In Page View, the 0 mark on the Ruler shifts to match the insertion point at the edge of the column.*

OUTLINING

An outline is a traditional form for arranging concept descriptions in hierarchical order. Descriptions of main (higher-level) concepts align at the left margin, and descriptions of lesser (lower-level) concepts are indented to the right below the concept they amplify. You can easily discern the main points of an outline by reading only the higher-level-concept descriptions. Outlines make it easy to rearrange concepts in priority order. To promote a lower-level concept to a higher level, you simply move the concept-description line to the left; to demote a concept to a lower level, you move the concept-description line to the right.

Outline View offers many useful features for creating and changing outlines. You can use Outline View to do the following:

- Enter concepts as different levels of headings

- Add associated text (called *body text*) to any heading

- Change a heading's level by moving the heading to the left or right

- Change the order of concepts by moving headings, subheadings, and body text upward or downward in the outline (without using the Cut and Paste commands)

- Hide all subheadings and body text so you can view only the main points of an outline

- Set the display level to hide all body text and any headings below a certain level so that you can view only the selected levels of an outline

You can use Outline View for many tasks, but you might find the following three uses to be particularly helpful:

- Creating an outline from scratch: Use Outline View to create a hierarchical order of headings and to set the basic structure of your document. You then return to any other view to fill in text below each heading.

- Viewing the structure of an existing document: Turn on Outline View for an existing document to show its headings in their hierarchical order and the body text below each heading. By setting the display level to show only important concepts, you can quickly see the overall document structure.

- Scrolling quickly through a document: Turn Outline View on and set it to show only headings at and above a certain level. Doing so ''shortens'' a long document considerably, and you can quickly scroll to the location you want and then switch to another view to see all the text.

Heading Styles

To understand how Outline View works, you should first know that Word offers nine default heading styles that you can apply to your documents. These heading styles are labeled, in order of importance, ''heading 1,'' ''heading 2,'' ''heading 3,'' and so on through ''heading 9.'' When you apply a heading style to a paragraph, it sets formatting appropriate for a heading. For example, the default setting for ''heading 1'' sets 12-point boldfaced and underlined characters in Helvetica. You can change any of these style definitions and set the headings to appear with the type of formatting you want.

When you turn Outline View on, all heading paragraphs change their indentions to show the heading hierarchy within a document. ''Heading 1'' appears flush left, ''heading 2'' is indented 0.5 inch, ''heading 3'' is indented

1 inch, and so on through "heading 9," which is indented 4 inches. Non-heading styles are considered body text and appear indented 0.25 inch to the right below the headings that precede them.

Consider this example: Suppose your document has a level-one heading followed by body text, a level-two heading followed by body text, and a level-three heading followed by body text. When you turn Outline View on, the level-one heading appears flush left, with its body text indented 0.25 inch; the level-two heading appears indented 0.5 inch, with its body text indented 0.75 inch; and the level-three heading appears indented 1 inch, with its body text indented 1.25 inches. Figure 20-4 illustrates this example, displaying a document with three different headings, each followed by body text. The upper view of the document shows Galley View; the lower shows Outline View.

Using Outline View

To turn Outline View on, choose *Outlining* from the Document menu. This is a toggle command that you turn on and off by choosing it. When Outline View is turned on, the *outline icon bar* appears at the top of the document window where the Ruler usually appears. *Outline-selection icons* appear to the left of each paragraph, and paragraphs are indented according to their heading levels. Note that you can't display the Ruler when you're in Outline View; all indentions are set strictly by heading structure and can't be changed by using the Ruler. Figure 20-5, on page 360, shows this chapter's sample document as it appears in Outline View.

You click on the icons in the outline icon bar to perform actions on selected paragraphs. The different groups of icons perform the following actions:

- The *movement icons* move paragraphs upward or downward in the outline or to the left or right to promote or demote them.

- The *demote-to-body-text icon* demotes a heading to body text (the Normal style).

- The *expansion icons* hide or display subheadings and body text below a selected heading.

- The *show-level icons* hide all headings and body text below the level you select.

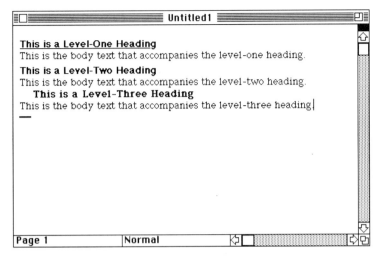

(A)

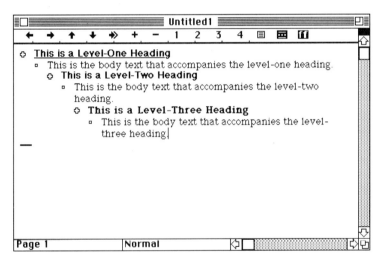

(B)

Figure 20-4. *Outline View changes the indention of heading paragraphs and their accompanying body text. Figure A shows the Galley View of a document; figure B shows the Outline View of the same document. Notice that lower-level headings and their accompanying text are indented farther to the right than upper-level headings.*

- The *show-all icon* shows all headings, subheadings, and body text.

- The *show-body-text icon* shows the full text of each body-text paragraph or reduces the paragraph to a single line of text.

- The *show-formatting icon* shows all the character formatting set in each paragraph or turns character formatting off so that all characters appear in a uniform typeface, point size, and type style.

The outline-selection icon to the left of each paragraph shows a paragraph's status. If the icon is a plus sign, the paragraph is a heading that has subheadings or body text below it. If the icon is a minus sign, the paragraph is a heading that has no subheadings or text. If the icon is a small square, the paragraph is body text. Outline-selection icons also let you drag a paragraph upward, downward, or to the left or right and let you hide or reveal any subheadings or body text associated with a paragraph. You'll learn more about these features later in this chapter.

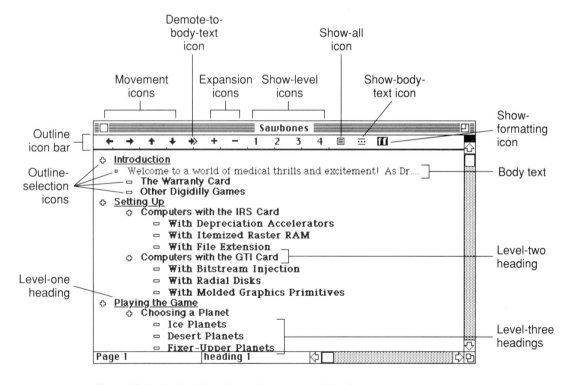

Figure 20-5. *Outline View shows the structure of headings in a document.*

Entering Text

You enter text in Outline View as you do in other views. Any text you enter conforms to the style of the paragraph in which the insertion point is located. There are, however, some small differences in the way you apply styles in Outline View: If you begin a new document in Outline View, the default style of your first paragraph will be "heading 1" instead of "Normal." When you press Return following a heading paragraph, the next paragraph takes the same heading style. In Page View and Galley View, when you press return at the end of a heading-style paragraph, the following paragraph takes the "Normal" style.

Selecting Text

You select text in a paragraph as you do in other views. If you select a text block that includes more than one paragraph, Word selects all the text of any paragraphs in your selected text block. This makes it impossible (fortunately) to promote, demote, or move only part of a paragraph. To select a heading with all its subheadings and associated body text, simply click on its outline-selection icon.

Changing Paragraph Order

To move a paragraph upward or downward in the outline without promoting or demoting it, drag the paragraph's outline-selection icon upward or downward to the new location. If the paragraph is a heading with subheadings and associated body text, the subheadings and body text move with the paragraph.

You can also move a selected paragraph (or paragraphs) upward or downward by clicking on the up-arrow or down-arrow movement icon in the outline icon bar or by pressing the up-arrow or down-arrow cursor key on the keyboard. You might find this new use of the up-arrow and down-arrow cursor keys disconcerting if you regularly use them to move the insertion point upward and downward in Galley View; suddenly, the same keys move paragraphs instead of moving the insertion point. To move the insertion point upward or downward in Outline View, press the 8 key or the 2 key on the numeric keypad.

Promoting or Demoting a Paragraph

To promote or demote a heading paragraph to a new heading level, you drag its outline-selection icon to the left or right. If the heading has subheadings, they are promoted or demoted with the main heading. Associated body text also moves to the left or right to match the new heading positions.

You can also promote or demote heading paragraphs by first selecting them and then clicking on either the promote (left) arrow or demote (right) arrow icon. If you prefer the keyboard, you can promote or demote a selected heading paragraph by pressing the left-arrow or right-arrow cursor key on the keyboard.

To change a heading into body text, you demote it in a different way from the way you demote a heading to a lower-level heading—you click on the demote-to-body-text icon (the right-pointing arrow with the double head). You can also demote a heading to body text by pressing Command–right-arrow cursor key. When you demote a heading to body text, it is associated with the first heading above it.

To promote body text to a heading, first select the body text paragraph or paragraphs, and then click on either the left arrow or right arrow in the outline icon bar or press the left-arrow or right-arrow cursor key.

Whenever you promote or demote a paragraph, you change its style. For example, if you demote a level-two heading to a level-three heading, you change its style from "heading 2" to "heading 3." If you demote a level-one heading to body text, you change its style from "heading 1" to "Normal." Although you might not see the formatting changes that take place with promotion or demotion in Outline View, you will see them when you return to Galley View.

Collapsing or Expanding a Heading

If you don't want to see subheadings or body text beneath a heading, you can *collapse* the text so that only the heading shows. Word adds a thick, dotted bar below the heading to show that the heading has subheadings or body text beneath it, even though the elements are hidden.

To collapse subheadings and body text one level at a time from below a heading, first move the insertion point in the heading and then click on the minus (–) icon in the outline icon bar. You can get the same results by using the keyboard by pressing the minus (–) key on the numeric keypad. Each click on the icon or keypress collapses the lowest visible level of heading or body text beneath the selected heading. For example, if you put the insertion point in a level-one heading that contains level-two, level-three, and level-four subheadings, the first time you click on the minus icon or press the minus key, the level-four headings disappear, collapsing into the level-three headings above them. The next click or press collapses the level-three headings, and the following click or press collapses the level-two headings into the main heading.

To expand a heading that contains collapsed subheadings, move the insertion point into the heading and then either click on the plus (+) icon in the outline icon bar or press the plus (+) key on the numeric keypad. Each click or press expands the next lower level of heading following the selected heading. If you were to expand the heading you collapsed in the last example, the first click or press would reveal the level-two subheadings, the next would show the level-three subheadings, and another would show the level-four subheadings.

To collapse all levels of subheadings and body text with one action, either double-click on the heading's outline-selection icon or select the entire heading, including the paragraph mark, and then press the minus (−) key on the numeric keypad. Double-clicking on the heading's outline-selection icon a second time expands all levels of subheadings. To get the same results by using the keyboard, first select the heading, including the paragraph mark, and then press the plus (+) key on the numeric keypad.

Setting the Display Level

To set the display level of an outline, click on any of the show-level icons in the outline icon bar—1, 2, 3, or 4—or click on the show-all icon at the right of the show-level icons. When you click on a show-level icon, Outline View shows only the headings at and above the level you choose, collapsing lower-level headings and body text into the headings above them. When you click on the show-all icon, Outline View shows all headings and body text.

Showing Formatting and Full Text

When you first turn Outline View on, Word is set to show the full text of each body-text paragraph in the document and to hide any character formatting so all text on the screen appears in uniform typeface, point size, and type style.

If you want to see full character formatting, click on the show-formatting icon (marked "ff") in the outline icon bar. To return to uniform text, click on the show-formatting icon again to turn character formatting off.

You might find that showing the full text of each body-text paragraph bloats the outline so that it's difficult to discern the main ideas contained in its headings. Clicking on the body-text icon (marked with ellipses) truncates each body-text paragraph so that only the first line shows. If a paragraph contains more than one line of text, Word appends an ellipsis at the end of the line to show you that more text exists. To see body-text paragraphs in full, click on the body-text icon a second time.

An Example

Suppose that you are a documentation writer and you have been asked to write a manual for the new medical-adventure computer game "Stellar Sawbones" (published by Digidilly, Inc.). To begin, you create an outline of the material you plan to explain:

1. Open a new document, and choose *Outlining* from the Document menu to turn Outline View on; the outline icon bar appears. The insertion point is in the first paragraph, a "heading 1" paragraph that has a minus (–) icon to its left.

2. Type *Introduction*, and press Return to begin a new paragraph.

3. Type two more paragraphs: *Setting Up* and *Playing the Game*. Each paragraph you type appears as a level-one heading. You have now defined the three major parts of your manual.

4. Now type a level-two subheading under "Introduction." Move the insertion point to the end of the "Introduction" line, and press Return to begin a new paragraph.

5. Drag the new paragraph's outline-selection icon to the right by one position (or click on the right arrow in the outline icon bar) to demote the new paragraph to a level-two heading. Notice that the heading icon to the left of "Introduction" changes to a plus sign to show that the paragraph now has a subheading.

6. Type *The Warranty Card*, press Return, and then type *Other Digidilly Games*. Two subheadings now appear below the heading "Introduction."

7. Now add subheadings below "Setting Up." Move the insertion point to the end of "Setting Up," press Return to begin a new paragraph, and demote it to a level-two heading.

8. Type *Computers with the GTI Card*, press Return, and then demote the new paragraph to a level-three heading.

9. Type three new paragraphs as level-three headings: *With Bitstream Injection*, *With Radial Disks*, and *With Molded Graphics Primitives*.

10. Continue typing outline elements, promoting and demoting paragraphs as necessary until the outline matches that shown in Figure 20-6.

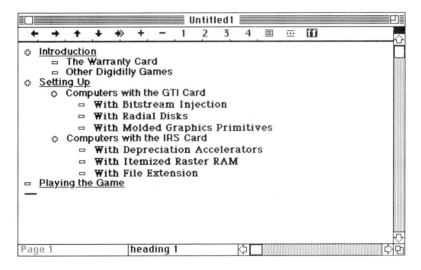

Figure 20-6. *Enter this outline for the example.*

11. Now switch the order of two headings—"Computers with the IRS Card" and "Computers with the GTI Card"—so that the "IRS" heading and all its subheadings appear before the "GTI" heading. Drag the "IRS" outline-selection icon upward until it appears directly above the "GTI" heading, and then drop it there.

12. Type the rest of the outline as you see it in the sample document in Figure 20-1, but leave out the body-text paragraph following "Introduction."

13. To create a body-text paragraph, move the insertion point to the end of "Introduction," press Return, and then demote the new paragraph to body text by clicking on the demote-to-body-text icon in the outline icon bar.

14. To enter the text of the paragraph, first click on the show-body-text icon in the outline icon bar. (This allows each paragraph to show full text so you can see what you're typing.) Then type the text of the paragraph.

15. To view the outline with only level-one and level-two headings, click on the 2 icon on the outline bar. The outline shows only the first two levels of headings with a thick, dotted line below each heading that contains hidden subheadings or body text.

16. Click on the show-all icon to view all the subheadings and body text again.

17. To view the outline with all formatting and with only one line of each body-text paragraph, click on the show-format icon to see formatting and click on the show-body-text paragraph to reduce the body-text paragraph to a single line.

18. Now look at your outline in Galley View. Choose *Outlining* from the Document menu to turn Outline View off. The document appears with headings, subheadings, and body text all in place. All you need to do to write the manual is fill in more (much more!) body text. Good luck!

DOCUMENT WINDOWS

Word lets you open up to 22 documents on the screen at one time to compare text and formatting and to cut, copy, and paste text in and among the documents. Each document you open appears in its own document window; as you open new documents without closing the ones already on the screen, Word displays the document windows in layers, one on top of another, with the most recently opened document on top.

Document windows should look familiar to you—they share most of the features of a standard Macintosh window. You'll find in the upper left corner a zoom box that you can click on to enlarge or reduce the window, in the lower right corner a resize box that you can drag to stretch the window to the size you want, in the upper left corner a close box that you can click on to close the window, and at the top a title bar that you can drag to reposition the window. You'll also find special Word tools such as scroll bars, the page-number area, and the style-name area, that you learned to use in previous chapters of this book.

Setting an Active Document Window

When you open more than one document window in Word, the windows over-lap, usually with the top window completely covering underlying windows. You can move or resize document windows so that you can see more than one window at a time, but if you do, only one window is active—the window on top if they overlap, the window you worked on most recently if they don't overlap. Only the active window has an insertion point and an operating scroll bar, so it is the only window in which you can enter text. To make an inactive window active, click on the desired window (if any part of it is visible), or press Option-Command-W to activate each window in turn and bring it out in front of the others.

If you open the Window menu, you'll find that the bottom of the menu lists each document window currently open in Word. Choose the name of any window you want to make active; Word brings it to the top of any other open document windows and makes it the active document window.

Opening a New Window for an Open Document

You can open more than one window for a document by first opening the document as you would normally and then choosing *New Window* from the Window menu. This opens a second document window that shows the same document already displayed in the document window you first opened. Both the original window and the new window show the same document title in the title bar, but Word numbers the windows with title extensions—:1, :2, :3, and so on.

When Word shows the same document in two or more windows, you can use the windows to view different locations in the document simultaneously, or you can set the windows to display their contents in different formats. For example, one window can show a document with its hidden text hidden, and another window can show the same document with its hidden text visible. No matter how many windows you open to show a document, Word still treats their contents as a single document. If you edit the contents of the document in one window, the contents change in all the other windows as well.

Splitting a Window

To compare different sections of the same document without opening a second window, you can split a window in two, creating an upper and lower window within the document window. These two subwindows (which we'll call *panes* for clarity) are separated by a split bar, a horizontal, double line across the width of the text area of the document window. (You used a split bar in Chapter 14, "Creating Footnotes," to split a document window and enter footnotes in the lower pane.)

When you split a window, each resulting pane has its own vertical scroll bar. You can set each pane to show a different view, so you can use a split window to look simultaneously at different locations in a document, using different document views for each pane. For example, one pane can show the Outline View of a document while the second pane shows the Galley View of the same document; or one pane can show the beginning text of a document while the second pane shows the ending text—many pages away—of the same document.

To split a window into panes, find the *split-bar drag box*, a small, black box at the top of the vertical scroll bar. Drag it downward. As you drag, the split bar moves downward in the window. When you've dragged the split bar to the location you want, release it to split the window into panes, as shown in Figure 20-7. You can also split the window into roughly equal panes by double-clicking on the split-bar drag box.

To change the location of the split bar, simply drag the split-bar drag box to a new location. If you drag the box all the way to the top or bottom of the document window and release it, you close one pane and remove the window split. You can also close a split window by double-clicking on the split-bar drag box.

After you split a window into two panes, you can move the insertion point between panes by simply clicking in whatever pane you want. If you want to change the view in a pane, place the insertion point in that pane and

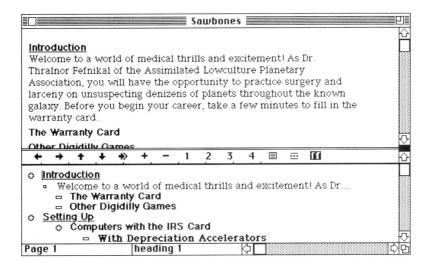

Figure 20-7. *When a window is split into two panes, each pane can show the same document in a different view.*

then set either Page View, Outline View, or Galley View. For example, if both panes show the Galley View, you can move the insertion point to the bottom pane and turn Outline View on by choosing *Outlining* from the Document menu. The top pane shows the document in Galley View (as it did before), and the bottom pane now shows the same document in Outline View.

Word normally allows independent scrolling of each pane to let you see a different section of a document in each pane. However, if you set one pane to show Outline View and the other to show Galley View or Page View, the second pane scrolls to match the location of the Outline View. You can use this idiosyncrasy to your advantage: You can scroll the Outline View pane to find a location you want and then jump to the other view pane (which will be in the same location) to edit or add text. Note that it's the first paragraph of the Outline View pane that sets the document location; other paragraphs that you can see toward the end of the outline might be much farther along in the full document (because of an outline's condensed nature), so they won't appear in the other pane's view.

An Example

Try working with the document you created (the game-manual outline) by splitting its document window. Start with the document in Galley View:

1. Split the window into two panes by double-clicking on the split-bar drag box.

2. Choose *Outlining* from the Document menu. The lower pane (where the insertion point is located) appears in Outline View, and the upper pane remains in Galley View.

3. Scroll the bottom pane upward or downward by one screen. The upper screen scrolls to match. The top line of the Outline View pane controls the view location of the Galley View pane.

4. Close the window split by double-clicking on the scroll-bar drag box. The entire document now appears in Outline View because the document window retains the view of the pane containing the insertion point.

5. Choose *Outlining* from the Document menu to turn Outline View off.

You've now learned how to handle Word's document views—galley, page, and outline—and to control document windows. In the next chapter you'll learn how to use an extremely useful Word feature: tables.

Chapter 21

Creating Tables

If you arrange information in a table, you're guaranteed to draw your reader's eye to it. Unfortunately, tables have traditionally been difficult to create and edit with word processing programs. But this is not true with Microsoft Word. In this chapter you'll learn to create tables by using Word's special table features. You'll begin by inserting a table in a document and setting the table's dimensions. Then you'll learn how to enter and format text, how to move material from one part of the table to another, and how to add and delete rows and columns. In the last section you'll learn how to control the appearance of the table—how to set column widths, align the table rows between the page margins, and add borders.

This chapter does not present an exhaustive discussion of Word's tables. Instead, it provides an introduction that gives you enough working knowledge to create your own tables.

SETTING UP WORD

Before you begin working with the examples in this chapter, check to be sure that Word shows full menus, that Page View is turned off, and that the table gridlines are turned on:

1. If you haven't done so already, turn your computer on and start Word.

2. Open the Edit menu, and if the Full Menus command appears, choose it to set full menus. If the Short Menus command appears instead of the Full Menus command, full menus are already set, and you can close the menu without choosing any commands.

3. Open the Document menu, and if a check mark appears to the left of the Page View command, choose the Page View command to turn Page View off.

4. Choose *Preferences* from the Edit menu to open the Preferences dialog box.

5. If the Show Table Gridlines option isn't turned on, click on its check box to turn it on.

6. Click on the OK button to close the dialog box.

The sample document for this chapter, shown in Figure 21-1, is a single-page letter that solicits subscriptions for a national newspaper. The document includes a table that compares the newspaper's features to those of other newspapers; you'll create the table, enter information, and edit it by using Word's table features.

AN OVERVIEW OF TABLES

In Chapter 8, "Tabs," you learned to arrange information in columns by setting tab stops, a method that works well as long as you don't insert more than a few words of text in each location. Revising column text can be difficult; if you add or delete too much text, entries might jump forward or backward by a tab stop, misaligning information and moving it from the end of one line to the beginning of another. By creating tables in Word, you can avoid these problems.

A table is a grid that divides a page into rows and columns, as shown in Figure 21-2 on page 374. If you're familiar with spreadsheet software such as Microsoft Excel, you'll notice that a table looks like a small spreadsheet. Each location within the table is called a *cell*; you can move the insertion point from cell to cell in a table and enter text or insert graphics in each cell.

Each cell in a table is an independent text-entry area; it has its own margins, indents, and tab stops. You can set character and paragraph formatting within a cell exactly as you do outside the table. You set the width of each cell when you create or modify the table. The height of each cell is determined by its contents; as you enter text and graphics, the cell, along with all the other cells in the same row, extends downward to accommodate the contents of the cell requiring the greatest height.

1/9/91

Dear Friend:

The midwinter doldrums—we all get them! That's why Leander Mylarivek, the man who brought you mail-order pizza, is expanding his services to include home delivery of *The New Midnight Star Tattler*. You might know the *Star Tattler* as the weekly newsmagazine guaranteed to deliver the stories you want, but did you know that it now has double the writing staff to bring even more of these great stories to you? From Mr. Alzorno, our spirit-channeling astrologist/hairdresser columnist, to Zachary Ansadahl, our roving reporter on the lookout for Elvis, we've beat the competition across the board when it comes to giving you the features we *know* you want to read. The table below tells it all:

Number of Features From October through December 1990

	The New Midnight Star Tattler	The Gossip Rag	USA Enquirer	Lifestyles of the Sinful and Wicked
Psychic predictions of natural catastrophes and changing presidential hairstyles	22	19	6	11
Inspiring stories of recovery from drug dependency, psoriasis, or a vague feeling of unrest	35	8	29	13
I-was-there accounts of UFO abductions for interstellar checker tournaments	12	2	4	7
Accurate reports on Elvis's new career as a topless mud wrestler in Motley, Minnesota	49	37	26	47

Well, what are you waiting for—more hours of tedious boredom?! Get out your Visa or MasterCard and call us *now* at the number on the enclosed subscription card. Your copies of the *Star Tattler* will be on their way *immediately!!!!*

Yours sincerely,

James T. Ardentheffer
Subscription Manager

Figure 21-1. *You use Word's table features to create the table in this sales letter.*

Figure 21-2. *A table divides the page into rows and columns of cells.*

After you enter text or insert graphics in a cell, you can easily edit the contents of a cell and move the contents from one cell to another. You edit a cell's contents by moving the insertion point into the cell and editing in the same way you edit regular text. To move the contents of one cell to another, you use the Cut, Copy, and Paste commands. You can also add or delete rows and columns of cells. And you can control the appearance of a table by changing the width of its columns and by adding borders either around groups of cells or around the entire table. When you print the table, only the borders and contents of the table print; the dotted gridlines don't.

Inserting a Table

To insert a table in a document, move the insertion point to the location where you want the table to appear. Choose *Insert Table* from the Document menu to open the Insert Table dialog box, shown in Figure 21-3.

Word's default values create a table that stretches across the width of the page, with two columns across and one row down. To set different table dimensions, change the numbers in the Number of Columns and Number of Rows text boxes.

The Column Width text box controls the width of each column. Its default value is determined by the number of columns you set in the Number of Columns text box. Word divides the distance between the left and right page

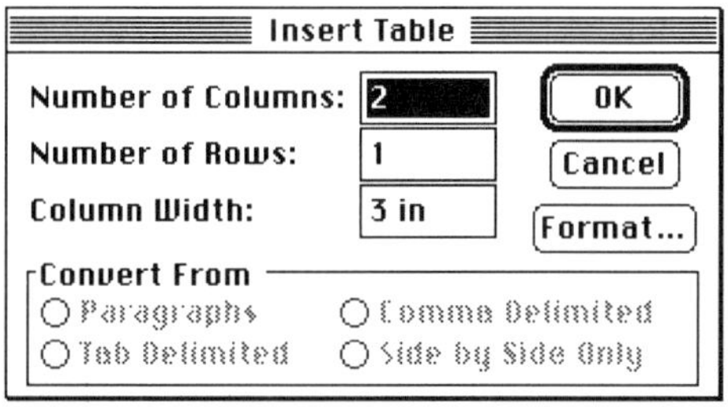

Figure 21-3. *Set the dimensions of a new table in the Insert Table dialog box.*

margins by the number of columns to calculate a column width that will fill the space between margins. For example, if your page has 6 inches of text area between margins (the default Word setting) and you set three columns, Word offers 2 inches as the column width (three columns of 2 inches fill up a 6-inch page width).

To set a column width, enter a value in inches in the Column Width text box. If the width you enter creates columns that don't fill the width of the page, Word inserts the remaining space to the right of the table. If the width is too wide for the page, the right side of the table runs off the page.

The Convert From area at the bottom of the dialog box governs conversion of regular text into a table. If you select a text block and then choose *Insert Table,* you can choose one of the following options:

- *Paragraphs,* which converts each paragraph of the text block into a separate cell

- *Tab Delimited,* which converts each piece of text separated by a tab into a separate cell

- *Comma Delimited,* which converts each piece of text separated by a comma into a separate cell

- *Side by Side Only,* which converts side-by-side paragraphs into separate cells

See Word's *Reference to Microsoft Word* to learn more about these four options.

Click on the buttons on the right side of the Insert Table dialog box to move out of the dialog box. The OK button closes the dialog box and inserts the table, applying the dimensions you set; the Cancel button closes the dialog box without inserting a table; and the Format button opens the Cells dialog box, from which you can control the table's appearance. (You'll learn to use this dialog box later in this chapter.)

An Example

Try including a table in the sample letter:

1. Open a new document. Set paragraph formatting to include a blank line before each paragraph, set the character size to 10 points, and then type the first three paragraphs of the sample letter, ending with the sentence "The table below tells it all." (It isn't important that you enter this text verbatim.) When you finish, press Return to begin a new paragraph.

2. Set paragraph formatting to centered alignment and character formatting to bold, and then type the table's title: *Number of Features from October through December 1990.* Press Return.

3. Set paragraph formatting to left alignment, with no blank line before the paragraph. (Word applies the paragraph formatting of the current paragraph as the paragraph formatting for each cell of the table.)

4. Press Return to add one blank line below the title.

5. Choose *Insert Table* from the Document menu to open the Insert Table dialog box.

6. Set a dimension of five rows by five columns by entering *5* in both the Number of Columns and the Number of Rows text boxes.

7. Press Return to close the dialog box and insert the table. The table appears below the title paragraph, and the insertion point appears in the top left cell.

MOVING THE INSERTION POINT WITHIN A TABLE

Any text you type in a cell fills only that cell—it doesn't extend to adjacent cells. When you reach the right-hand border of the cell, the insertion point jumps to the beginning of a new line within the cell instead of moving to the next cell. To move to another cell by using the mouse, simply click in that cell. The insertion point appears there, and you can begin entering text.

To move the insertion point from cell to cell by using the keyboard, press Tab. Each time you do so, the insertion point jumps one cell to the right unless it's at the end of a row, in which case it jumps to the beginning (left end) of the row below. To jump in the opposite direction, press Shift-Tab. Note that if you press Tab when you're in the lower right cell, Word creates a new row of cells and moves the insertion point to the beginning of the new row. This is an easy way to expand the size of your table.

You can also use the cursor keys to move from cell to cell: If you press the up-arrow cursor key when the insertion point is at the top of the cell or if you press the down-arrow cursor key when the insertion point is at the bottom of the cell, the insertion point moves upward or downward into the adjacent cell. If the insertion point is at the beginning of the first line of the cell's contents, press the left-arrow cursor key to move it to the cell to the left; if the insertion point is at the end of the last line of the cell's contents, press the right-arrow cursor key to move it to the cell to the right.

To leave the table entirely, simply click outside the table. To reenter the table, click in any cell. To leave the table using the keyboard, press the up-arrow or down-arrow cursor key until the insertion point moves out of the table. To reenter the table, use the up-arrow or down-arrow cursor key to move back into the table.

WORKING WITHIN A CELL

After you move the insertion point into a cell, you can enter text and graphics there as you do in other parts of the document. The Ruler shows the indents and margins of the cell you're in. As you type, the text fills in from the left to the right indent and then begins a new line below the current line. If the cell isn't large enough to accommodate the new line, the cell extends downward and all the other cells in the row extend with it to maintain the same height across the entire row.

You can set character formatting within a cell as you do outside the table by choosing different fonts, sizes, and type styles. You can also set paragraph formatting by choosing alignment and spacing and by setting tab stops. To jump from tab stop to tab stop within a cell, press Option-Tab; pressing Tab alone moves the insertion point to the next cell, not to the next tab stop.

Setting Cell Margins and Indents

You set paragraph indents within a cell relative to *cell margins* rather than to page margins. Cell margins are very much like page margins; in the same way in which Word sets page margins to prevent text from running off the edge of the page, Word sets cell margins within each cell to prevent text from running into the border of the cell. These left and right cell margins usually measure only a fraction of an inch. The Ruler shows their location with margin markers, shown in Figure 21-4. The first-line indent and left indent of each paragraph are set relative to the cell's left margin, and the right indent is set relative to the cell's right margin. To set paragraph indents in a cell, select the paragraph(s) you want, and then drag the indent markers on the Ruler or set the indents in the Paragraph dialog box.

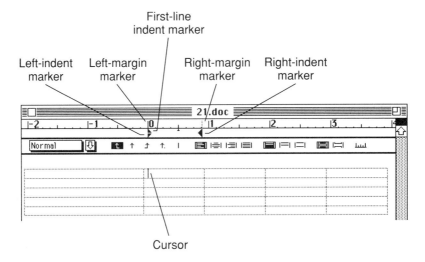

Figure 21-4. *The Ruler shows the margins and indents for the currently selected paragraph in the selected cell. The 0 mark is set at the cell's left margin.*

Editing and Formatting Cell Contents

After you've entered text in a cell, you can edit and format it. First select a text block and then apply editing or formatting commands to alter the text. Your text selection must remain within the cell; if you extend the selection to an adjacent cell, Word selects the entire contents of both cells. Any editing or formatting command you choose affects the entire text block.

An Example

Enter some text in the cells of your sample table. Begin by moving the insertion point to the upper left cell of the table. Then take the following steps:

1. Move to the right by one cell (click in it or press Tab) and type *The New Midnight Star Tattler*. The row expands vertically to accommodate the text.

2. Move to the right by one cell and type *The Gossip Rag*.

3. Move to the right by one cell and type *USA Enquirer*.

4. Move to the right by one cell and type *Lifestyles of the Sinful and Wicked*.

5. Move to the first cell of the next row (click in it or press Tab) and type *Psychic predictions of natural catastrophes and changing presidential hairstyles*.

6. Move through the rest of the cells and type their contents as shown in the sample document in Figure 21-1. (To center the numbers in their cells, turn on centered alignment, and then press Return once before typing each number.)

7. Move to the end of the document (out of the table) and type the rest of the letter.

EDITING AND FORMATTING MULTIPLE CELLS

To edit or format the contents of more than one cell at a time, you must first select all the cells you want:

- To select the entire contents of a single cell, move the pointer into the left margin of the cell (the pointer turns into a right-pointing arrow) and click the mouse button.

- To select a row of cells, move the pointer into the left page margin beside the row you want (the pointer turns into a right-pointing arrow) and double-click the mouse button.

- To select a column of cells, move the pointer to the top border of the top cell in the column you want. When the pointer turns into a small, black, down-pointing arrow, click the mouse button. You can also select a column by moving the pointer anywhere within the column of cells, holding down the Option key and clicking the mouse button.

■ To select a block of cells, drag the pointer from one corner of the block to the opposite corner of the block.

■ To select the entire table, move the pointer anywhere within the table, hold down the Option key, and double-click the mouse button.

After you select a block of cells, you can cut, copy, and paste the cells' contents. If you choose *Cut*, the contents of the cells in the block are cut and placed on the Clipboard, leaving empty cells behind. If you choose *Copy*, the contents of the cells are copied onto the Clipboard, leaving the cell contents intact. To paste the contents of multiple cells from the Clipboard into the table, select a single cell and then choose *Paste*. Word pastes the contents of the Clipboard into the table, using the selected cell as the upper left cell of the block and working to the right and down as it pastes. The pasted cell contents replace any previous cell contents.

Note that if you extend the selection to include part of the table *and* part of the document above or below the table, cutting cell contents also cuts the actual cells along with the contents.

An Example

Format the *Star Tattler's* column so that the text appears in boldface. Begin by selecting the second column from the left. Then take the following steps:

1. Move the pointer to the top of the second column from the left, where the pointer turns into a small, black, down-pointing arrow.

2. Click the mouse button to select the column.

3. Turn bold character formatting on. All the characters in the column appear in boldface.

EDITING A TABLE

After you create a table, you can add or delete cells. To do so, first select a cell or block of cells, and then choose *Table* from the Edit menu to open the Table dialog box, shown in Figure 21-5.

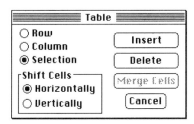

Figure 21-5. *Insert and delete cells in a table by selecting options in the Table dialog box.*

The first three options in the upper left quarter of the dialog box set the type of section in the table that your editing actions affect. If you turn the Row option on, Word works on full rows; if you turn the Column option on, Word works on full columns; and if you turn the Selection option on, Word works only on the selected cells. If you turn the Row option or Column option on when you don't have a full row or column selected, Word extends your selection to include the full row or column. For example, if you select two side-by-side cells in the middle of the table and then turn the Column option on, Word extends the selection to include the full columns containing both cells.

Clicking on the buttons on the right side of the dialog box initiates editing actions. The Insert button inserts a new column if the Column option is on, a new row if the Row option is on, or a new block of cells next to the selected block if the Selection option is on. The Delete button cuts the selected columns if the Column option is on, the selected rows if the Row option is on, or the selected block if the Selection option is on.

The options in the Shift Cells area determine how Word inserts and deletes around a selected cell block. If you turn the Horizontally option on, Word moves existing cells to the right of the selected block to make room for new cells or moves existing cells to the left to fill in a deleted block. If you turn the Vertically option on, Word moves existing cells downward from the selected block to make room for new cells or moves existing cells upward to fill in a deleted block.

FORMATTING A TABLE

To change the appearance of cells within a table, select the cells you want to format, and choose *Cells* from the Format menu to open the Cells dialog box, shown in Figure 21-6.

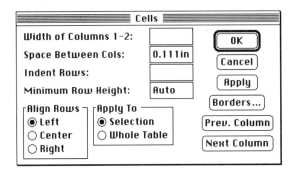

Figure 21-6. *Set cell formatting in the Cells dialog box.*

The first text box in the dialog box is labeled Width of Column(s) *n-n*, where *n-n* are the variable numbers of the columns selected in the table. (If you select only one column, a single number appears.) For example, if you select cells in columns 2 through 4 before you open this dialog box, the text-box label appears as *Width of Columns 2-4*. You set the cell width of all the selected cells in this text box. Enter a value in inches to set the cell width you want.

The Space Between Cols text box sets the cell margins. Any value you enter here in inches determines the cell margins in the selected cells. Word divides the Space Between Cols value by two to set the cell margins. For example, if you enter a value of 0.2 inch in the Space Between Cols text box, Word inserts 0.1 inch of space at both the left and right edges of the cell. Figure 21-7 shows the relationship between cell width and cell margins.

The Indent Rows text box sets an indention for the currently selected rows. This indention moves the rows to the right of the left page margin. Enter a value in inches here to right-indent selected rows.

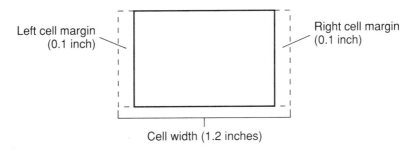

Figure 21-7. *A 1.2-inch cell with a Space Between Cols setting of 0.2 inch has 0.1-inch cell margins.*

Setting Row Alignment

The three options in the Align Rows area of the Cells dialog box align selected rows between the left and right page margins. Turning the Left option on aligns the rows flush against the left page margin; turning the Center option on centers the rows between the left and right page margins; and turning the Right option on aligns the rows flush against the right page margin.

Adding Cell Borders

Click on the Borders button to open the Cell Borders dialog box, shown in Figure 21-8. The Cell Borders dialog box is similar to the Borders dialog box; it offers border-style options along its left side and a border box that you can click on to set border lines where you want them.

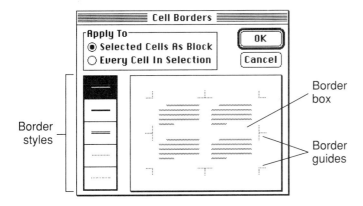

Figure 21-8. *Set cell borders in the Cell Borders dialog box.*

Before you set cell borders, you must first decide how you want to apply the borders to the cells you selected. If you selected more than one cell and want to treat the block of cells as a single block with an outer border surrounding the outer cells and inner borders dividing inner cells, and then turn the Selected Cells As Block option on in the Apply To area of the Cell Borders dialog box. If you want to treat each cell in the block as an individual unit with its own outer borders and no inner borders, and then turn the Every Cell In Selection option on.

To set cell borders, first select a border style from the border-style area at the left side of the dialog box. Click on the border you want, and apply it to any one of the four exterior border sides of the border box by clicking on the side you want. Word adds a border line there using the line style you selected in the border-style area. If you're treating the selected cells as a block, you can add interior lines to the block by clicking in the center of the border box. To remove a line from the border box, click on the line a second time.

Once you've finished setting the borders you want, click on the OK button to close the Cell Borders dialog box and apply the borders, or click on the Cancel button to close the dialog box without effect. When the Border Cells dialog box closes, you return to the Cells dialog box.

Changing the Cell Selection and the Affected Area

Click on the Next Column and Prev. Column buttons to change the selected cells in the table without closing the dialog box. If you click on the Next Column button, Word selects the next single column to the right of the currently selected cell block. If you click on the Prev. Column button, Word selects the next single column to the left of the currently selected cell block. If you move column selection past the right or left end of the table, selection wraps around to the opposite side of the table.

If you've selected a cell block that doesn't encompass entire columns and you want Word to extend cell selection to include any full column that includes a cell in your selected cell block, you can click on the inappropriately named Whole Table option in the Apply To area. To affect only the selected cell block without including full columns if they're not selected, turn the Selection option on instead.

After you set formatting for a selected area, click on the OK button to close the dialog box and apply the formatting to the selection.

Viewing the Table

To view the table without gridlines (which you turned on at the beginning of the chapter), choose *Preferences* from the Edit menu to open the Preferences dialog box. Turn the Show Table Gridlines option off, and click on the OK button to close the dialog box. The table appears as it will print—without gridlines.

An Example

Add borders to your table to improve its readability, and then change column widths to more easily accommodate the text in the first column:

1. Select the entire top row of the table.

2. Choose *Cells* from the Format menu to open the Cells dialog box.

3. Turn the Whole Table option on in the Apply To area so your border settings will affect the whole table. (This option extends selection from each cell in the top row to include full columns reaching all the way to the bottom of the table.)

4. Click on the Borders button to open the Cell Borders dialog box.

5. Click on the thick line in the border-style area (the second option from the top).

6. Click on the four outside borders (left, right, top, and bottom) of the border box to set a thick-line border around the outside of the entire table.

7. Click on the thin line in the border-style area (the first option).

8. Click on the inside of the border box to set thin-line borders between interior cells of the table.

9. Click on the OK button to close the Cell Borders dialog box.

10. Click on the OK button to close the Cells dialog box. The table is now framed with a thick border, and the interior cells are divided by single, thin lines.

11. Select the entire rightmost column of the table.

12. Choose *Cells* from the Format menu to open the Cells dialog box.

13. Type *1* in the Width of Column 5 text box to reduce the cell width of column 5 to 1 inch.

14. Click on the Previous Column button to change the cell selection to column 4.

15. Type 1 in the Width of Column 4 text box.

16. Click on the Previous Column button to move to column 3 and then column 2 and change each of their widths to 1 inch.

17. Click on the Previous Column button to change the cell selection to column 1.

18. Type 2 in the Width of Column 1 text box to set its cell width to 2 inches.

19. Click on the Borders button to open the Cell Borders dialog box.

20. Click on the double line in the border-style area (the third option from the top).

21. Click on the right-hand border of the border box to add a double line to the right border of the first column.

22. Click on the OK button to close the Cell Borders dialog box, and then click on the OK button to close the Cells dialog box. The table now appears with the first column 2 inches wide and the following columns 1 inch wide. The right-hand side of the first column has a double-line border.

23. Select the entire top row of the table.

24. Choose *Cells* from the Format menu to open the Cells dialog box.

25. Click on the Borders button to open the Cell Borders dialog box.

26. Click on the double line in the border-style area if it isn't already selected, and then click on the bottom border of the border box to add a double-line border to the bottom of the top row.

27. Click on the OK button to close the Cell Borders dialog box, and then click on the OK button to close the Cells dialog box. The table

now appears with a double-line border along the bottom of the first row. You've duplicated the table as it appears in Figure 21-1, at the beginning of the chapter.

MORE TABLE FEATURES

The table features you've read about so far are only the basics. If you explore tables more fully in Word's *Reference to Microsoft Word,* you'll find you can do much more, including:

- Convert existing text into a table (including a text file generated by a database program)

- Convert a table into text

- Set table cell widths using the Ruler

- Place tab stops within a cell

- Split a table into two parts

- Insert a page break in the middle of a table

- Set a minimum row height to expand rows with minimal contents

- Merge the contents of several cells into a single cell

- Split a previously merged cell into several separate cells

- Position a table on the page so that text flows around it

- Create irregular tables containing partial rows and columns

You've now learned how to create a simple table and to format its contents and cells. In the next chapter you'll learn how to alter Word itself to create a custom fit between its features and your needs.

Chapter 22

Customizing Word

Word, like clothing, works best with a custom fit. In this chapter you'll learn how to change Word's normal operations so they best fit the way you work with documents. You'll learn not only how to change Word's simple default settings—such as the formatting for new documents or the printer setting—you'll also learn how to change Word's menu commands and the keyboard shortcuts that execute those commands. At the end of the chapter you'll learn how to save your custom Word environments on disk, allowing you to recall them when appropriate for a particular job.

SETTING UP WORD

Before you begin working with the examples in this chapter, check to be sure that Word shows full menus and that Page View is turned off:

1. If you haven't done so already, turn your computer on and start Word.

2. Open the Edit menu, and if the Full Menus command appears, choose it to set full menus. If the Short Menus command appears instead of the Full Menus command, full menus are already set, and you can close the menu without choosing any commands.

3. Open the Document menu, and if a check mark appears to the left of the Page View command, choose the Page View command to turn Page View off.

Instead of working on a sample document in this chapter, you'll work on Word itself.

SETTING DEFAULTS: AN OVERVIEW

When you first start Word and begin to work, Word offers you many settings by default. For example, when you open a new document, its section formatting is normally set so that text appears in a single column. When you display the Ruler, it shows measurements in inches instead of centimeters, points, or picas. As you've learned in previous chapters, these automatic settings are called *default settings*, or *defaults*.

Word offers two types of defaults: *environment defaults* that control your working environment in Word and *document defaults* that set the initial formatting of a new document. The Ruler's unit of measurement is an example of an environment default; the single-column format of a new document is an example of a document default. Defaults act as starting points. You can override any default by setting new options or formatting, in the same way that you change the default New York font in a new document to the Courier font.

Changing Word's Default Settings

Sometimes a Word default setting can be a poor starting point. If you find that you constantly reset the same formatting when you begin a new document, or if you don't like the working environment Word offers, you should consider changing default settings so that Word starts with *your* preferred settings. You've already done this once: At the beginning of this book, you set Word to show full menus instead of short menus, which changed an environment default.

Word has quite a few default settings that you can change. The document defaults include the following:

- *Section formatting.* Open the Section dialog box, shown in Figure 22-1, set any options you want, and then turn them into default settings by clicking on the Set Default button on the right side of the dialog box.

- *Document formatting.* Open the Document window, set any options you want, and then turn them into default settings by clicking on the Set Default button as you did in the Section dialog box.

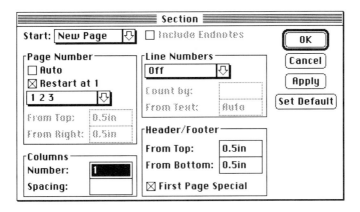

Figure 22-1. *Open the Section dialog box to set the section formatting you usually use. Then click on the Set Default button to turn your section formatting into default section formatting.*

■ *Page setup.* Open the page-setup window for your printer, shown in Figure 22-2, set any options you want—such as page size or orientation—and then turn the Set Default option on at the bottom of the dialog box. Click on the OK button to close the dialog box and set your own page-setup settings as Word's default page-setup settings. If you don't turn the Set Default option on, your page-setup settings will apply only to the currently opened document and won't be saved as document defaults.

```
┌─────────────────────────────────────────────────────────┐
│ ImageWriter                          v2.7   ┌───────┐    │
│                                             │  OK   │    │
│ Paper:  ⦿ US Letter      ○ A4 Letter        └───────┘    │
│         ○ US Legal       ○ International Fanfold ┌───────┐│
│         ○ Computer Paper                        │Cancel ││
│                                                 └───────┘│
│ Orientation   Special Effects: ☐ Tall Adjusted          │
│  ▣  ▣                          ☐ 50 % Reduction          │
│                                ☐ No Gaps Between Pages   │
│                                                          │
│ ┌──────────┐                                             │
│ │Document..│  ☐ Set Default                              │
│ └──────────┘                                             │
└─────────────────────────────────────────────────────────┘
```

Figure 22-2. *To set default page-setup settings, set options in the Page Setup box, turn the Set Default option on, and click on the OK button. (The ImageWriter dialog box is shown here.)*

■ *Default styles.* Whenever you open a new document, Word uses its default style sheet as a base for the new document's style sheet. When you open the document's style sheet, you initially see Word's set of default styles. To add a new default style to the default style sheet, first define a new style as you normally do. Then open the Define Styles dialog box, shown in Figure 22-3, choose the new style name from the styles list, and click on the Set Default button. To redefine a default style, choose the style name from the styles list, change its definition as you want, and then click on the Set Default button.

To delete a style from the default style sheet, choose the style from the styles list, and then choose *Cut* from the Edit menu. Word first displays a message asking whether you want to delete the style. This question refers to the document style sheet, not to the default style sheet; therefore, if you click on the Yes button, Word deletes the style only from the document style sheet. After this deletion, Word displays a message asking whether you want to delete the style from the default style sheet. If you click on the Yes button, Word deletes the style from the default style sheet.

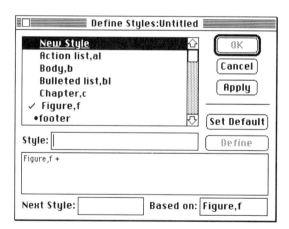

Figure 22-3. *Create and redefine default styles by setting options in the Define Styles dialog box.*

- *The Normal style.* The Normal style in a document's style sheet sets the document's default character and paragraph formatting. To change the formatting of the Normal style, open the Define Styles dialog box, choose the style name from the styles list, redefine the style to your specifications, and then click on the Set Default button. Whenever you begin a new document, Word applies Normal style to the first paragraph using the character and paragraph formatting you defined in your new default Normal style definition.

Once you set new document defaults, Word applies the new settings to any new documents you open. For example, if you add several new default styles to the default style sheet, every new document you open includes those default styles in its own style sheet.

Word also offers several environment defaults that you can change:

- *Chooser settings.* When you open the Chooser window by choosing *Chooser* from the Apple menu, you can choose a new printer and turn AppleTalk on or off. The printer you choose becomes the default printer, and the AppleTalk settings become the default settings.

- *Print settings.* Open the Print dialog box for your printer by choosing *Print* from the File menu. If you change print settings and then click on the OK button, your print settings become the default settings.

- *Preference settings.* Open the Preferences dialog box to choose settings that affect general Word operations. If you change the settings and click on the OK button, these new settings become the default settings. You'll learn more about preference settings in the next section of this chapter.

- *Menu and keyboard shortcut settings.* As you learned when you set full menus in place of short menus, you can change the contents of Word's menus. In later sections of this chapter, you'll learn how to set menus to contain precisely the commands you want and how to change the keyboard shortcuts that activate the menu commands. Any menu or keyboard shortcut changes you make become the default settings for Word.

Note that when you change environment defaults, you don't need to specify them as default settings as you had to do with document defaults.

How Word Saves Changed Default Settings

You've probably noticed that whenever you change defaults—as when you change the default style sheet or turn background pagination on—and then quit Word, Word remembers your new default settings when you restart the program later. To keep track of defaults whenever you quit Word, Word saves all the current default settings in a file named "Word Settings (4)," located in the System Folder of your disk. Word looks for this file whenever you start Word so that it can retrieve the most recent default settings.

Think of Word Settings (4) as a snapshot of Word's default settings at quitting time. When Word restarts, it first looks at the defaults as they're defined in Word Settings (4) in order to re-create the environment as it was when you quit. If you delete the Word Settings (4) file and then restart Word, Word re-creates the file using its own default settings (the defaults you see when you start a new copy of Word). To return to Word defaults after setting your own defaults, simply quit Word, delete Word Settings (4), and then restart.

Saving Separate Sets of Default Settings

A full set of default settings is called a *configuration*, and the file used to store it—such as Word Settings (4)—is called a *configuration file*. If you want to have separate configurations for different situations (for example, one configuration for each different type of document template you have), you can save each configuration in its own configuration file and then open the file when you want to use that configuration. You'll learn how to save and open configurations in the last section of this chapter.

SETTING PREFERENCES

When you choose *Preferences* from the Edit menu, Word opens the Preferences dialog box, shown in Figure 22-4, in which you can set your preferences for some of Word's general operations. You've learned to set several of these preferences in previous chapters—Show Table Gridlines, for example—but some options require explanation, as follows.

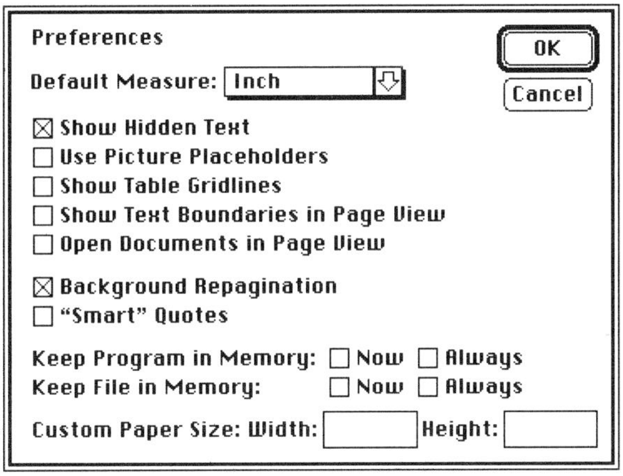

```
┌────────────────────────────────────────────────┐
│  Preferences                         ┌─────────┐ │
│                                      │   OK    │ │
│  Default Measure: │ Inch       │ ⬇  │ └─────────┘ │
│                                      ┌─────────┐ │
│                                      │ Cancel  │ │
│  ⊠ Show Hidden Text                  └─────────┘ │
│  ☐ Use Picture Placeholders                      │
│  ☐ Show Table Gridlines                          │
│  ☐ Show Text Boundaries in Page View             │
│  ☐ Open Documents in Page View                   │
│                                                  │
│  ⊠ Background Repagination                       │
│  ☐ "Smart" Quotes                                │
│                                                  │
│  Keep Program in Memory: ☐ Now ☐ Always          │
│  Keep File in Memory:    ☐ Now ☐ Always          │
│                                                  │
│  Custom Paper Size: Width: │     │ Height: │    ││
└────────────────────────────────────────────────┘
```

Figure 22-4. *Set options in the Preferences dialog box to control the way Word operates.*

■ *Default Measure.* Choose the default unit of measurement by choosing either *Inch*, *Cm* (centimeters), *Points*, or *Picas* from the list box. Word changes the Ruler marks to show distance in the default units and also changes measurement displays, such as the paragraph indent distances shown in the Paragraph window. Setting the default measure in centimeters is especially useful if you're creating documents for printout on European paper; setting measurement to points or picas is convenient if you're accustomed to working with these printers' units of measurement. (There are 6 picas per inch and 12 points per pica.)

Once you choose a default measure, Word assumes that unit of measure when you enter measurement values in dialog boxes without specifying units. For example, if you set the default measurement to picas and enter an indent of 3 in the Paragraph dialog box, Word sets an indent of 3 picas. If you want to enter a measurement in units other than the default units, simply add a unit name after the number: for example, *3 in*, *0.5 cm*, *6 pi*, *12 pt*, and so on.

Note an important exception to default measurement: Measurements of line spacing, character spacing, superscript/subscript position, and character size remain set in points even if the default unit of measurement is inches, centimeters, or picas.

■ *Show Hidden Text.* Turn this option on if you want Word to display text that is formatted as hidden text; turn this option off to hide hidden text. Note that this setting has no control over the printing of hidden text; you still control that in the Print dialog box.

■ *Use Picture Placeholders.* Turn this option on to replace all graphics with gray rectangles. When this option is turned on, it speeds scrolling through a document, a very useful option if you're working with many inserted graphics on a slow Macintosh such as the Mac Plus. Turn this option off to see full graphics instead of placeholder rectangles.

■ *Show Table Gridlines.* Turn this option on to show the gridlines surrounding each cell of a table; turn this option off to hide the gridlines. Note that the gridlines don't print even if Show Table Gridlines is turned on.

■ *Show Text Boundaries in Page View.* Turn this option on to display a dotted rectangle around each text area in a document viewed in Page View. A separate rectangle frames each individual text element on the page—body text, footnotes, the header, the footer, and so on. This option makes each element easy to identify if your document has multiple text elements or if it has many graphics mixed with text. Turn the option off if you don't want to see text boundaries in Page View.

■ *Open Documents in Page View.* Word normally opens every document in Galley View. If you prefer to work in Page View and would like to open your documents in Page View, turn this option on. Turn the option off to have each document open in Galley View.

■ *Background Repagination.* Turn this option on if you want Word to work in the background to repaginate the text in your document; turn the option off to turn background repagination off. Background repagination gives you an accurate and constantly updated view of page breaks. If you turn it off, page breaks are frozen regardless of text revision. However, turning it off also speeds some Word operations that are slowed by background repagination.

■ *"Smart" Quotes.* Turn this option on to use opening and closing quotation marks rather than standard quotation marks in your text. If the Smart Quotes option is turned on, Word inserts double or single opening quotation marks (" or ') and closing quotation marks (" or ') when you type a double or single standard quotation mark (" or ') from the keyboard. Standard quotation marks appear the same at the opening and closing of a quotation. Opening and closing quotation marks appear differently at the opening and closing of a quotation; each curves inward *toward* the quotation.

Word determines whether to substitute an *opening* or a *closing* quotation mark by following a simple rule: If a space appears to the left of the quotation mark, it turns the mark into an opening quotation mark; if no space appears to the left of the mark, it turns the mark into a closing quotation mark. You can also enter opening and closing quotation marks specifically from the keyboard by pressing Option-[(for "), Option-] (for '), Shift-Option-[(for "), and Shift-Option-] (for '). If you export a Word file as a text-only file to a non-Mac computer system, the opening and closing quotation marks might appear as strange characters or might not appear at all. If you plan to export text to other computer environments, it's best to leave Smart Quotes turned off so that you enter standard double and single quotation marks.

■ *Keep Program in Memory.* Microsoft Word is segmented into sections so that it can function on Macs that have limited memory. When you first run Word, only the main part of the program is loaded. Other parts of the program don't load until they're needed, which is why the Mac pauses and the disk-drive light flashes when you use a feature such as Page View. When you're finished using a feature, the Mac might pause again later to load a new segment of Word, which replaces the segment that contains the feature you used.

If the Keep Program in Memory option is turned off (that is, neither Now nor Always is turned on), Word loads only a segment of the program at a time in order to conserve Macintosh memory. If you turn either the Now or Always option on, Word loads as much of the program into memory as the Mac has memory available. This reduces the swapping of portions of the program and speeds Word's operation. If you turn the Now option on by itself, Word loads as much of the program as it can into memory, but only for this session. The next time you run Word, it will once again load only a segment of the program at a time. If you turn the Always option on, Word loads as much of the program as possible each time you run Word.

- *Keep File in Memory.* A long document is like the Word program itself: Word loads only as much of it into memory as is necessary and then swaps parts of the document back and forth from the disk—for example, when scrolling through the document or when checking its contents in a spelling check. This swapping slows Word's operations. To keep as much of each document in memory as is possible, turn either the Now option or the Always option on. If only the Now option is turned on, Word stores full documents in memory for only the current session with Word. If the Always option is turned on, Word loads as much of a document as is possible at all times.

  Remember that turning on either the Keep File in Memory option or the Keep Program in Memory option speeds operation, but eats up memory. If you're running MultiFinder and want to run other programs simultaneously with Word, you might need to turn these options off to save enough memory for the other programs to run.

- *Custom Paper Size.* Enter the width and height of any custom paper size in the Width and Height text boxes. The size appears as an option in the Page Setup dialog box.

Once you set the preferences you want, click on the OK button to apply them. Click on the Cancel button to close the box with no effect. When you quit Word, Word stores your preferences as defaults in the Word Settings (4) file and applies them when you restart Word.

CUSTOMIZING MENUS

You can control the contents of Word's menus in any of three ways:

- Choose the Full Menus command or the Short Menus command to display full or short menus.

- Choose the Add To Menu command or the Remove From Menu command to add or remove a menu command.

- Choose *Commands* from the Edit menu to open the Commands dialog box and select from a list of all commands.

Each method described here offers progressively more control over Word's menus.

Full and Short Menus

You learned at the beginning of this book that Word offers two sets of menus: *short menus*, which contain a limited set of commands, and *full menus*, which offer much more of Word's powers through a full command set. You display either menu set by choosing either the *Short Menus* command or the *Full Menus* command from the Edit menu.

The contents of Word's full menus are flexible; you can add or remove commands from full menus by choosing the Add To Menu command or the Remove From Menu command or by opening the Commands dialog box and setting options there. The contents of the short menus are fixed, however; they contain the same commands regardless of changes you make to the full menus.

The Add To Menu and Remove From Menu Commands

Word offers two keyboard combination commands that aren't available in any of its menus: Add To Menu (Option-Command-+) and Remove From Menu (Option-Command- –). If you press Option-Command-+ to execute the Add To Menu command, the pointer turns into a plus sign. Use the plus-sign pointer to set an option or execute a command that isn't normally available as a menu command. Word then turns your action into a menu command, which it places in a menu of its own choosing.

Consider an example: Press Option-Command-+ to turn the pointer into a plus sign, pull down the Format menu, choose *Character* to open the Character dialog box, and choose Hidden to set the hidden text type style. Word adds

Hidden Text to the Format menu so you can choose Hidden Text from a menu without opening the Characters dialog box. Another example: You can press the Add To Menu key combination and then click on the double-line-spacing icon on the Ruler. Word adds *Double Space* to the Format menu.

One very practical application of adding commands to menus is to add commonly used document names to a menu. For example, if you create a set of document templates (as you learned to do in Chapter 18, "Creating Templates"), you can add each document name to a menu so that you can choose the name directly from the menu to open the template instead of first opening the Open dialog box. To add document names to a menu, press the key combination Option-Command-+ and then choose *Open* from the File menu to open the Open dialog box. Find the name of the template you want and double-click on it; Word adds the document's name to a menu.

Whenever you add a command by using the Add To Menu command, Word chooses the menu in which the command will appear. When you add a document name, a style, or a glossary entry to a menu, Word creates a new menu—Work—which appears at the right end of the menu bar.

To remove a command from a menu, first press Option-Command- –, which turns the pointer into a minus sign. Then use the pointer to choose the command you want to remove. Word removes the command from the menu.

An example

Try adding and removing a menu command:

1. Press Option-Command-+ to turn the pointer into a plus sign.

2. Choose *Open* from the File menu to open the Open dialog box.

3. Find the Unicycles article you created in Chapter 15, "Styles Made Simple: Formatting with Speed and Power" (or any other document if you can't find Unicycles), and double-click on its name. The dialog box closes, the pointer reverts to its usual form, and a new menu—Work—appears at the right end of the menu bar.

4. Open the Work menu to see its only command—Unicycles—and then choose the command. Word opens the Unicycles file.

5. Close the Unicycles document window.

6. Press Option-Command- – to turn the pointer into a minus sign.

7. Choose *Unicycles* from the Work menu. Word removes Unicycles from the Work menu, and because the menu is now empty, it removes the menu from the menu bar. The pointer, which is now a minus sign, reverts to its usual form.

The Commands Dialog Box

From the Commands dialog box, you can add and remove commands and key combinations and save and open configuration files. Choose *Commands* from the Edit menu to open the Commands dialog box, shown in Figure 22-5.

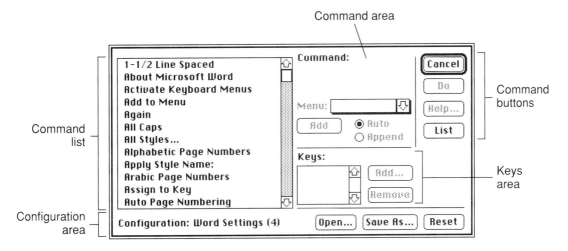

Figure 22-5. *Open the Commands dialog box to add and remove commands and keyboard combinations and to save and open configuration files.*

The dialog box contains the following five areas:

■ The command list, which lists all commands available in Word, including those listed as options in dialog boxes or as icons on the Ruler or similar areas. You'll even find some commands—such as Open Documents With Ruler—that don't appear anywhere else in Word.

■ The Command area, which allows you to choose a menu and then add the command to or remove it from the selected menu.

401

- The Keys area, which allows you to set one or more key combinations for a selected command or to remove a key combination from a selected command. You'll learn to set options in this area later in this chapter.

- The Configuration area, which allows you to save all your default settings in a configuration file or to open a configuration file to reset all of Word's default settings. You'll learn to set options in this area later in this chapter.

- The command buttons, along the right side of the dialog box, which execute your orders in the Commands dialog box.

Selecting a command from the command list

To select a command from the command list, simply click on the command's name. The Command area displays the name of the selected command, and the Menu list box displays the name of the menu where the command already exists or where Word suggests you add the command. If you choose a command that has a colon at the end of its name, you must further define the command. Word adds a list box, a text box, or a combo box to the Command area so you can do so.

For example, if you choose the *Open File Name:* command, Word adds an Open File button to the Command area. You click on it to open an Open dialog box, where you can choose the name of the file you want to open with this command. For another example, if you choose the Change Font command, Word adds a list box that offers the name of each available font. You can choose the font that you want this command to set.

You might find some commands in the command list that you haven't seen before and that aren't documented in *Reference to Microsoft Word*. If you're curious about a command, you can choose it and click on the Help button. A message box appears with help text that describes the command's function. To try the command, choose it and then click on the Do button. The dialog box closes and Word executes the command.

Adding and removing a command in the command area

Once you select and define a command that isn't already in a menu, Word displays the name of the menu it recommends in the Menu list box and places an Add button below the Menu list box. You can choose a different menu for the selected command by selecting a menu name from the Menu list box, and you can set the command's position in the menu by clicking on the two radio buttons to the right of the Add button. If you turn the Auto option on, Word inserts the command in a predetermined location in Word's suggested menu, even if you've selected a different menu. If you turn the Append option on, Word adds the command to the end of whatever menu you choose in the Menu list box.

Once you set a command to appear in a menu and at the menu location you want, click on the Add button to add the command.

To remove a command from a menu, first choose the command from the command list. The Menu list box displays the menu in which the command is located, and Word places a Remove button below the list box. Click on the Remove button to remove the command from the menu.

When you've finished working in the dialog box, click on the Cancel button to exit.

An example

Try adding a command that places a single shadow paragraph border around selected paragraphs:

1. Choose *Commands* from the Edit menu to open the Commands dialog box.

2. Choose *Paragraph Border:* from the commands list. *Paragraph Border:* appears at the top of the Command area, and a list box appears below it.

3. Open the list box and choose *TLBR Single Shadow Paragraph Border.* (TLBR stands for top-left bottom-right, indicating the direction of the shadow's shift.) The Command area now shows *TLBR Single Sha...* as the current paragraph border option, and the Menu list box shows Format as the suggested menu for the command location.

4. Click on the Add button. Word adds the TLBR Single Shadow Paragraph Border command to the Format menu.

5. Click on the Cancel button to close the Commands dialog box.

6. Open a new document if you don't already have one open.

7. Choose *TLBR Single Shadow Paragraph Border* from the Format menu. Word adds a shadow border to the first paragraph.

8. Choose *Commands* from the Edit menu to reopen the Commands dialog box.

9. Choose *Paragraph Border:* from the commands list, choose *TLBR Single Shadow Paragraph Border* in the Command area, and then click on the Delete button to delete the command from the Format menu.

10. Click on the Cancel button to close the Commands dialog box.

A Word of Caution

When you change menu commands, it is possible to remove crucial commands such as *Quit* and *Commands* so that you box yourself in without escape. If you find that you've changed commands so you can't quit Word, you might need to restart your Macintosh by turning it off or by rebooting. If you do restart in this way, be sure to discard the Word Settings (4) file from the System Folder before you restart Word; this resets Word to its original Microsoft defaults and returns the menus to short menus.

CHANGING KEY COMBINATIONS

Most menu commands have a keyboard shortcut that you can use to execute the command, a convenience to help you keep your fingers on the keyboard while typing. You might find that some of the commands you use often don't have a keyboard shortcut, or if they do, it isn't a convenient shortcut. If so, you can either use the Assign to Key command (a keyboard command) or open the Commands dialog box to assign new keyboard shortcuts and to change the key combinations assigned to existing shortcuts.

Using the Assign to Key Command

The Assign to Key command is very similar to the Add to Menu command: You execute it with the key combination Option–Command–keypad+. (''keypad+'' is the plus-sign character on the numeric keypad.) Once you execute the command, the pointer turns into a cloverleaf (the same as the one on the Command key), and you either choose a menu command or click on an option or icon that executes a command. Word then displays a message asking you to type the keystroke for the command. Press any of Word's allowed key combinations (discussed later in this chapter). Word assigns the combination to the command, enabling you to press those keys and execute the command from the keyboard.

If you try to assign a key combination that is already assigned to another command, Word displays a message asking whether it's okay to remove the combination from the other command. If you click on the Yes button, Word reassigns the combination to your selected command. If you click on the Cancel button, Word keeps the original assignment.

Although you can't have more than one command per key combination, you can assign more than one key combination to a single command. To assign additional key combinations to a command, use the Assign to Key command to set each assignment.

Allowable key combinations

You'll find a complete list of Word's allowable key combinations in the Menus section of *Reference to Microsoft Word*. In general, allowable key combinations combine the Command, Shift, and Option modifier keys with the main keyboard keys, the numeric keypad keys, and the function keys (if your keyboard has them). Note that whenever you use a main keyboard key in combination with modifier keys, you must include the Command key. For example, you can use Shift-Command-N, Option-Command-P, or Shift-Option-Command-X, but you can't use Shift-Option-X or Option-P.

If you use function keys or keypad keys in a key combination, you don't need to include the Command key in the combination. For example, you can use Shift-F1 or Option–keypad 1 as allowable key combinations.

You can use the Control key (if your keyboard has one) as a modifier key in addition to the other standard modifier keys. For example, Control-F1 is an acceptable key combination. And you can use the Control key with a keyboard key without including the Command key in the combination. For example, the key combination Control-P is acceptable.

Using the Commands Dialog Box

The Keys area of the Commands dialog box offers even more control over key combinations. Whenever you select a command in the command list, the keys list (the list box in the Keys area) displays any key combinations assigned to the command. If you want to remove any one of the combinations, choose the combination in the keys list, and then click on the Remove button to the right of the list.

If you want to add a key combination, click on the Add button to the right of the list. Word prompts you for a key combination as it did when you used the Assign to Key command. Press the key combination you want; Word adds it to the keys list and assigns the key combination to the command. As before, you must use allowable key combinations when you assign a key combination, and you can assign many key combinations to a single command.

An Example

Try using the Assign to Key command to add a keyboard shortcut to the Show Clipboard command. Then remove the keyboard shortcut in the Commands dialog box:

1. Press Option–Command–keypad + to turn the pointer into a clover symbol.

2. Choose *Show Clipboard* from the Window menu.

3. When Word displays a message asking you to type the key combination for the Show Clipboard command, press Shift-Option-Command-C (for Clipboard). Word assigns the key combination to the Show Clipboard command.

4. Open the Window menu. Notice that the Show Clipboard command now shows a keyboard shortcut after its name. Close the menu without choosing any commands.

5. Press Shift-Option-Command-C. Word opens the Clipboard window. Click on its close box to close it.

6. Choose *Commands* from the Edit menu to open the Commands dialog box.

7. Choose *Show Clipboard* from the command list. The keys list in the Keys area displays the key combination assigned to the command.

8. Choose the key combination in the keys list, and then click on the Remove button. Word removes the key combination from the command.

9. Click on the Cancel button to close the Commands dialog box.

10. Press Shift-Option-Command-C. Nothing happens because the key combination is no longer assigned to a command.

SAVING AND OPENING CONFIGURATION FILES

So far in this chapter, you've learned how to set defaults and how Word saves these defaults in the Word Settings (4) file when you quit Word. You might want to create more than one configuration file so several people working with one copy of Word on one Macintosh can use different configurations for different types of documents. For example, you might find that the configuration you set for producing a publication such as a club newsletter doesn't have the commands and defaults you need for writing a completely different type of document such as a business report. If so, you can create a configuration for each type of document and save it using the Commands dialog box.

Saving a Configuration

To create and save a new configuration, begin with any existing configuration such as the Word Settings (4) configuration, and modify it to your satisfaction. Save the new configuration by opening the Commands dialog box and clicking on the Save As button in the Configuration area. This opens a standard Save As dialog box in which you name the configuration. Click on the OK button to close the box and save the configuration.

Once you save a configuration, it becomes the active configuration. Word displays its name following *Configuration:* in the Configuration area. Any further changes you make in default settings modify the active configuration. If you quit Word, Word saves all changes to the current configuration under its given filename. Thus, if you create a personal configuration and save it under your name—''Ozo Benton,'' for example—Ozo Benton becomes the active configuration. If you choose to use Smart Quotes and Picture Placeholders and then quit Word, Word resaves the Ozo Benton configuration so that it includes your new printer choice.

Opening a Configuration

You open a configuration file in the Commands window by clicking on the Open button in the Configuration area. Word opens a standard Open window, where you can find the name of the configuration file you want and double-click on it to open it. When you open a new configuration file, Word changes default settings, menu contents, and key combinations to match the new configuration. The newly opened configuration becomes the active configuration, and any further changes you make in the working environment alter that configuration.

Resetting a Configuration

If you make configuration changes that you decide you don't like, you can reset a configuration to its state as it was last saved; simply click on the Reset button in the Commands dialog box. If you want to return to Word's original configuration (with Microsoft's original defaults), hold down Shift and click on the Reset button.

Setting the Default Configuration

Whenever you start Word, Word looks for the file named Word Settings (4) in the System Folder and loads its configuration. If you create another configuration file that you want Word to load when it starts, you can replace Word Settings (4) with that file. To do so, first quit Word so you can use the desktop. Open the System Folder and drag the Word Settings (4) file into the Trashcan. Rename your own configuration file, ''Word Settings (4),'' and then move it into the System Folder if it isn't already located there. Whenever you restart Word, it uses the new configuration you stored under the name ''Word Settings (4).''

   You now know how to customize Word for your own working conditions by setting default formatting and preferences, adding and removing commands from menus, assigning key combinations, and creating configuration files. If you take time to read the sections of *Reference to Microsoft Word* that discuss defaults, menus, and the Commands command, you'll discover further uses for creating configurations. In the next chapter you'll learn how to create your own form letters.

Chapter 23

Printing Form Letters by Merging Documents

Form letters are an integral part of life in the twentieth century. They call us directly by name, and they inform, implore, and cajole us. Now you can use Word to create form letters of your own—this chapter shows you how. You'll learn how to create a main document, inserting instructions where you want text to change to individualize your letters. You'll then learn how to create a data document that stores the changing text and how to use the Print Merge command to merge both documents to create a run of form letters. The last part of the chapter offers some ideas for other print-merging possibilities.

SETTING UP WORD

Before you begin working with the examples in this chapter, check to be sure that Word shows full menus, that Page View is turned off, and that table gridlines are turned on:

1. If you haven't done so already, turn your computer on and start Word.

2. Open the Edit menu, and if the Full Menus command appears, choose it to set full menus. If the Short Menus command appears instead of the Full Menus command, full menus are already set, and you can close the menu without choosing any commands.

3. Open the Document menu, and if a check mark appears to the left of the Page View command, choose the Page View command to turn Page View off.

4. Choose *Preferences* from the Edit menu to open the Preferences dialog box.

5. Turn the Show Table Gridlines option on, and then click on the OK button to close the Preferences dialog box.

The four sample documents shown in Figure 23-1 are brief form letters that were created by using Word's print-merging features. The examples in this chapter demonstrate how to create a main document and a data document and then how to merge the two to print the four sample letters.

AN OVERVIEW OF PRINT MERGING

Creating form letters with Word requires a three-step process called print merging. The three steps include:

- Creating a main document

- Creating a data document

- Choosing *Print Merge* from the File menu to merge the two documents and create a run of form letters

The *main document* contains the fixed text of the letter. Fixed text doesn't change from one letter to the next—it usually makes up the main body of information within the letter. You show Word where to insert changing text (such as names and addresses) in the main document by inserting a *field instruction* for each element of changing text.

The *data document* contains a set of *records* that Word uses to insert the changing text in the main document. Each record in the data document contains the information for one version of the form letter. The information within each record is separated into discrete parts called *fields*. Each piece of changing text in the main document corresponds to one field in a record.

(A)

Society for the Prevention of Mail-Order Solicitation
8320 Prosthetic Drive, Suite 1342A
City of Industry, CA 90189

10/1/91

Mr. Rumford Twolips
1365 Tuba Street
Enumclaw, WA 98097

Dear Mr. Twolips:

Aren't you tired of getting pleas for money in your mailbox? Don't
you cringe every time you see the mailman headed for your mailbox
at 1365 Tuba Street? Well, we're on your side! Please send us a
donation of $25 to the address above, and we'll do our best to rid the
mails of pesky solicitations! Thank you, and have the best of days!

Fervently yours,

Ortholian Pip
Chairman

(B)

Society for the Prevention of Mail-Order Solicitation
8320 Prosthetic Drive, Suite 1342A
City of Industry, CA 90189

10/1/91

Ms. Frannie Blander
834 Gotta Drive
Ishpeming, MI 47209

Dear Ms. Blander:

Aren't you tired of getting pleas for money in your mailbox? Don't
you cringe every time you see the mailman headed for your mailbox
at 834 Gotta Drive? Well, we're on your side! Please send us a
donation of $35 to the address above, and we'll do our best to rid the
mails of pesky solicitations! Thank you, and have the best of days!

Fervently yours,

Ortholian Pip
Chairman

(continued)

Figure 23-1. *Word merges two documents to create this run of four form letters.*

Figure 23-1. *continued*

(C)

Society for the Prevention of Mail-Order Solicitation
8320 Prosthetic Drive, Suite 1342A
City of Industry, CA 90189

10/1/91

Rev. Ollie Bortalk
12 Wildside Walk, Apt. #2
Thibodaux, LA

Dear Rev. Bortalk:

Aren't you tired of getting pleas for money in your mailbox? Don't you cringe every time you see the mailman headed for your mailbox at 12 Wildside Walk, Apt. #2? Well, we're on your side! Please send us a donation of $10 to the address above, and we'll do our best to rid the mails of pesky solicitations! Thank you, and have the best of days!

Fervently yours,

Ortholian Pip
Chairman

(D)

Society for the Prevention of Mail-Order Solicitation
8320 Prosthetic Drive, Suite 1342A
City of Industry, CA 90189

10/1/91

Dr. Jane Smith
4321 Main Street
Anytown, PA 29303

Dear Dr. Smith:

Aren't you tired of getting pleas for money in your mailbox? Don't you cringe every time you see the mailman headed for your mailbox at 4321 Main Street? Well, we're on your side! Please send us a donation of $100 to the address above, and we'll do our best to rid the mails of pesky solicitations! Thank you, and have the best of days!

Fervently yours,

Ortholian Pip
Chairman

After you create both the main document and the data document and save them on disk, you move to the main document and choose *Print Merge* from the File menu. Word inserts the data from the fields of the first record of the data document into the field instruction locations of the main document and then prints the letter. Then Word replaces this data with data from the fields of the second record of the data document and prints a second letter. It continues to work through all the records of the data document, printing letters until no more data records remain.

CREATING A MAIN DOCUMENT

To create a main document, you need to know how to insert *instructions* in the document. You insert a *data instruction* at the beginning of the document to prepare it for print merging and to identify it as a main document. As you type the rest of your document, you insert *field instructions* wherever you want Word to insert changing text.

Instructions

An instruction is a command to Word that you can insert in the text of a main document. When you print the main document by using Print Merge, Word reads the instruction and executes it as it creates a form letter. To identify text in a document as an instruction, you enclose it in special *instruction characters,* one on each end of the instruction text. Figure 23-2 shows a typical instruction.

Figure 23-2. *An instruction in a main document requires two instruction characters to enclose instruction text.*

To enter an instruction, you first insert a left instruction character by pressing Option-\ (backslash). You then type the instruction text and close the instruction by pressing Shift-Option-\ to enter a right instruction character.

You can also enter an instruction by using the Glossary to insert a glossary entry named "print merge," which places the left and right instruction characters in your document and positions the insertion point between them. You can type the instruction text and then use the mouse or the cursor keys to move outside the instruction characters.

Note that you can also close an instruction by pressing Return instead of inserting a right instruction character. The paragraph mark acts as the right instruction boundary. Use this option when you enter an instruction on a line by itself and you don't want Word to print a blank line there. This is necessary because Word never prints instructions; it only executes their commands. Some instructions, such as data instructions, don't ask Word to print anything in their location. If you insert such an instruction enclosed within two instruction characters in a line and then end the line with a paragraph mark, Word follows the instruction and then reads the paragraph mark, creating a blank line. If the instruction ends with a paragraph mark instead of an instruction character, Word interprets the paragraph mark as the close of the instruction instead of as a paragraph mark, so it doesn't print a blank line.

The Data Instruction

The data instruction is an instruction that tells Word to look for a data document and then retrieve information from that document during print merging. You must insert a single data instruction in the first paragraph of the main document, in a location that precedes any field instructions. You can insert the data instruction within the text of the first paragraph, or you can enter it on its own line, before any text paragraphs. If you enter the data instruction on its own line, be sure to close the instruction with a paragraph mark instead of a right instruction character so that an extra blank line doesn't appear at the beginning of the document. The data instruction itself does not appear in the document.

To create a data instruction on its own line, move the insertion point to the very beginning of the document, and then press Option-\ (backslash) to insert the left instruction character. Type *DATA*, press the space bar once, type the name of the data document you plan to use with this main document, and then close the instruction by pressing Shift-Option-\ to insert a right instruction character or by pressing Return to insert a paragraph mark. For example,

<<DATA Addresses>> is a data instruction that tells Word to look for data in a document named Addresses when print merging. If you don't insert a data instruction at the beginning of the main document, Word won't know where to find the data to fill the field instructions.

Field Instructions

A field instruction tells Word to pull a particular field of information from a record in the data document. A field instruction's text lists only the name of the data field. To insert a field instruction, move the insertion point to a location where you want to insert changing text and then press Option-\ to insert the left instruction character. Type a suitable field name (a single word that reminds you of the changing text to be inserted) as the instruction text, and then press Shift-Option-\ to close the instruction with a right instruction character. For example, <<name>> and <<address>> work well as field instructions that describe a name and an address to be inserted in a form letter.

You can use the same field instruction in more than one place if you want Word to insert the same data in more than one place. For example, if you want to insert a person's first name in the top of the form letter and then insert it again in the body of the letter, use the same field instruction for both places—perhaps a field instruction such as <<firstname>>.

An Example

Create the main document for the sample form letter, following the screen shown in Figure 23-3, on the following page, as a guide. The field instructions you insert supply the name and address of the recipient and an estimate (a field named *estsum*) of the amount the recipient can donate. Take the following steps:

1. Open a new document.

2. Press Option-\ to insert a left instruction character.

3. Type the instruction text *DATA Addresses* and press Return to close the instruction with a paragraph mark. You've now inserted a data instruction that tells Word to look for the data document named ''Addresses.'' The paragraph mark closes the instruction, ensuring that it won't leave a blank line there.

4. Set paragraph formatting to centered alignment.

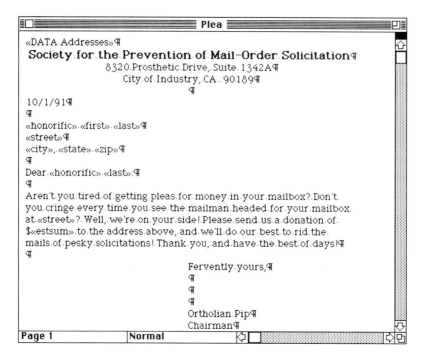

Figure 23-3. *This main document shows the instructions necessary for print merging.*

5. Use boldface 14-point New York characters to enter *Society for the Prevention of Mail-Order Solicitation*. Press Return.

6. Turn bold formatting off, reduce the character size to 12 points, and then type the next two lines of text.

7. Press Return twice to insert a blank line and to begin a new paragraph below that.

8. Set paragraph formatting to left alignment.

9. Enter the rest of the document as it appears in Figure 23-3. Be sure to enclose field instructions in instruction marks, and be sure that you spell the field names exactly as they appear in the figure. You should also take care to insert spaces before and after instructions as they appear in the figure; when you print form letters, these spaces separate inserted data from surrounding text so that they don't run together. When you type the closing (the line that starts

with "Fervently yours,"), set a 3-inch left indent to move the closing to the center of the page.

10. Save the document under the name "Plea."

CREATING A DATA DOCUMENT

A data document is made up of information arranged as records and fields. The first record in the document is the *header record,* a record that lists the field name for each field in the records that follow it. The records that follow are called *data records.* Each field within a data record contains the text for a field instruction with the same name in the main document. Each record contains all the fields necessary to fill all the field instructions in the main document.

Arranging Records in a Table

Records in a Word data document are often arranged so that each record forms a single paragraph, separated from other records by a paragraph mark. Fields within the records are separated from other fields by a comma or by a tab. This method of creating records has a big drawback: If you use field data that contains commas, Word might read a comma as a field separator instead of as a part of a field.

Fortunately, Word offers a more exact alternative to create and store records—you can arrange them in a table. Each row of a table is a record, and each cell in a row contains a separate field of the record. You can enter text in a cell without regard for commas and other potentially confusing punctuation, and because formatting in a data document doesn't transfer to the main document when you merge documents, you don't need to worry about the appearance of the table; you can create as many field columns (within limits) as you need.

To prepare a new data document that contains a table of records, first count the number of *different* fields listed in field instructions in the main document. Keep in mind that you might use the same field several times in the main document; if so, count that field only once. For example, the sample main document you created contains eight fields even though there are 11 field instructions. The "honorific," "last," and "street" fields are all used twice.

Choose *Insert Table* from the Document window to insert a table, and when Word displays a dialog box asking for the number of columns, enter the number of fields you counted. (If you create a main document that has more than 35 fields, you won't be able to create a table wide enough to accommodate the fields. In that case, you'll need to arrange records in paragraphs with fields separated by commas or tabs.) Leave the number of rows set to 1.

The header record

The first record in a data document *must* be a header record so that Word knows the field name for each field in the records that follow it. These field names must exactly match the names you used in the field instructions in the main document; otherwise, Word won't be able to find the information it needs in the data document. As an example, the header record for an address data document might appear as follows:

firstname	lastname	street	city	state

After you type the last field name in the header record, press Tab to add a new row to the table. Note that Word doesn't insert any of the names from the header record into the main document during print merging—it moves to the data records to find the actual insertion data.

Data records

When you enter data records below the header record, it's important that the fields match the column location of the appropriate field name in the header above. If you don't have the necessary information to fill in a field, you can leave the cell in that location blank and move on to the next one. For example, if you didn't know Mark Time's street address, you'd leave the address field blank and move on to the next field:

Mark	Time		Scranton	PA

During a print merge, Word would read the third field as empty and insert nothing at its corresponding field instruction in the main document.

It's not necessary that the order of fields in the data document match the order of field instructions in the main document. For example, a main document might ask for data items in the order "firstname," "lastname," "street," "firstname." If the data document lists them in records that follow the order "lastname," "firstname," and "street," it makes no difference because the field names act as identifiers for the information. Word still retrieves the information it needs and inserts it in the proper field instruction locations.

Once you've finished creating the data document, you must save it under the name you listed in the data field of the main document. If you don't save the document, or if you save it under a different name, Word won't be able to find it for print merging. You should also save the data document in the same folder in which you saved the main document so that Word won't have any trouble finding the data document during the print merge.

An Example

Create and save a data document for the main document you created earlier, using a table to arrange records. For this example, you'll reduce character size so text will fit easily in the narrow cells of the eight-column table. (Or you can use a larger type size if you increase the width of the table to be wider than the screen. Because you don't print the data document, it doesn't matter how wide it is.) Take the following steps:

1. Open a new document and reduce the character size to 9 points.

2. Choose *Insert Table* from the Document menu to open the Insert Table window.

3. Type *8* in the Number of Columns text box and click on the OK button to close the window and to insert an 8-column-wide-by-1-row-high table in the new document.

4. Click in the first cell of the table to begin entering records.

5. Enter the header record as it's shown in Figure 23-4 (on the following page) in the first line of the document. Be sure that the spelling of each field name exactly matches the spelling you used in the main document field instructions. Press Tab to move from cell to cell, and press Tab again at the end of the last cell to begin a new row in the table.

6. Enter the four data records that follow, as shown in Figure 23-4, on the following page. Notice that the zip code is missing in the third data record—the "zip" cell is empty. Press Tab at the end of each record except the last record to begin a new table row.

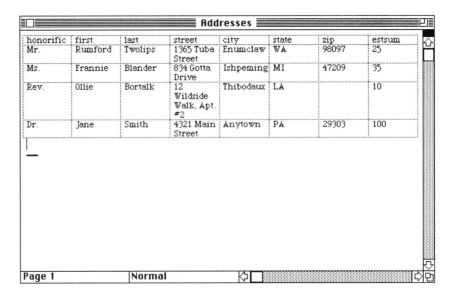

honorific	first	last	street	city	state	zip	estsum
Mr.	Rumford	Twolips	1365 Tuba Street	Enumclaw	WA	98097	25
Ms.	Frannie	Blander	834 Gotta Drive	Ishpeming	MI	47209	35
Rev.	Ollie	Bortalk	12 Wildside Walk, Apt. #2	Thibodaux	LA		10
Dr.	Jane	Smith	4321 Main Street	Anytown	PA	29303	100

Page 1   Normal

Figure 23-4. *This data document supplies the data necessary for print merging.*

7. Save the document under the name ''Addresses,'' the filename you listed in the data instruction of the main document.

8. Close the data document and return to the main document.

USING THE PRINT MERGE COMMAND

After you create a main document and a data document, click in the main document window to be sure it's the active document window. Then choose *Print Merge* from the File menu to open the Print Merge dialog box, shown in Figure 23-5.

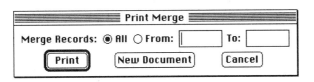

Figure 23-5. *Open the Print Merge dialog box to set preferences for print merging and to start printing form letters.*

420

Setting a Range of Records

When Word prints a run of form letters, it normally uses every record in the data document. To limit the run to a smaller set of records, specify a range of records in the Merge Records area of the Print Merge dialog box. Word counts the records in the data document beginning with the first data record following the header record, counting up to the last record in the document. Enter values for the range of records you want to merge. If you leave the From box empty, Word prints beginning with record number 1. If you leave the To box empty, Word prints through the last record. Turn the All option on if you want Word to merge all records.

Printing Form Letters

To start printing a run of form letters, click on the Print button. The Print Merge dialog box closes, a new document window shows the first form letter Word is ready to print, and the Print dialog box opens. Set printing options as you want them, and then click on the OK button to start printing. Word prints the run of form letters, substituting new data in each version of the main document it prints.

Merging to a New Document

You might want to see the results of your print merge without printing documents. If so, click on the New Document button in the Print Merge dialog box. Instead of sending the merge results to the printer, Word merges the documents and creates a new document named Form Letters1. The new document contains all the form letters created by the print merge, with a New Page section break separating each form letter. The section breaks ensure that each form letter begins on a new page. You can scroll through the document to check for irregularities created by the print merge (such as bad grammar resulting from unexpected word juxtapositions). When you've finished, you can print the whole run simply by printing the Form Letters document.

Tracking Errors

The merge won't work if field instructions in the main document don't correspond to the fields in the data document, if the beginning of your main document doesn't include a data instruction, or if the beginning of your data document doesn't include a header record. If any of these conditions or other irregularities exist, Word displays an error message and stops the merge.

You can choose to continue the merge in spite of the error (Word inserts an error message in the affected form letter), or you can stop to check the main document and the data document. Be sure that the spelling of the names in the field instructions matches that of the field names in the header record and that you included all the necessary instructions and field names. For further explanation of the error message, check the section of *Reference to Microsoft Word* that describes the Print Merge command.

An Example

Use the main document and the data document you created to complete the sample form letters shown in Figure 23-1. For this exercise, place the results in a document instead of printing them.

1. Be sure the main document text window (titled ''Plea'') is the active window. Then choose *Print Merge* from the File menu to open the Print Merge dialog box.

2. Click on the New Document button. The dialog box closes and a new document window titled ''Form Letters1'' appears.

3. Scroll through the Form Letters1 document to see the four form letters you created. They should match the four sample letters in Figure 23-1. Notice that the missing zip code in the third record caused no problems; Word simply inserted no text at the ''zip'' location because it encountered an empty field.

4. If you want to print the form letters, choose *Print* from the File menu, and then click on the OK button to close the Print dialog box.

ADDITIONAL PRINT-MERGE POSSIBILITIES

Word offers several other types of instructions that you can include in a main document. The following are a few of them:

■ ASK is an instruction that tells Word to prompt you for information as it prints each form letter; use it when you want to insert personalized text in each form letter. During the print merge, you can enter text at each ASK instruction location in each letter.

- IF, ENDIF, and ELSE are logical instructions that tell Word to test a field value in a record and then, depending on the results of the test, print or not print a section of text. These instructions can be very useful for adding flexibility to form letters. For example, you can add logical instructions to the sample main document to check the amount of money that the record lists as an estimated donation. If the amount is greater than $25, you might instruct Word to add an extra paragraph that discusses the obligation of generous and well-to-do people to contribute to good causes. If the amount is $25 or less, you can instruct Word to add a paragraph that mentions how every little bit helps.

- INCLUDE is an instruction that tells Word to add the contents of another document to the main document. You can use it in combination with logical instructions to assemble a form letter from many other optionally included documents.

You'll find more information about instructions in the Print Merge section of *Reference to Microsoft Word.*

Creating a Data Document in a Database Program

Creating the data document can be the most arduous part of printing a form letter—you can spend hours at the keyboard typing long lists. Fortunately, many people keep names, addresses, and other print-merge data in a database file. Most database programs offer a report-generation option that finds the addresses you need and sends them into a disk file instead of printing them. It's a happy fact that most database programs separate data items in the disk file by a comma or a tab and that they separate each record with a return (the equivalent of a paragraph mark in Word). This is a data form that Word can use without alteration as data records in a data document.

By spending a little time with your database program, you can create a text-only file with the data you need for printing. To turn it into a data document, open the file in Word, add a header record, resave the file, and then list the file's name in the data instruction in the main document. *Reference to Microsoft Word* describes a technique that uses a header in a second document so you can use the database file without altering it at all.

You've now learned to create your own form letters in Word by using print merging. With some creativity, you might think of new uses for print merging—creating mailing labels, multiple-choice tests, numbered documents, and more.

With this chapter you've reached the end of this book. You now know how to use Word tools that range from simple to complex, from helpful to indispensable. Don't stop here! Word is a vast world of word processing features. The more you explore, the more you'll find of value. Browse through *Reference to Microsoft Word,* look through the commands in the Commands window, talk with other Word users, and experiment—you're sure to find tricks that can make your documents better looking and easier to create.

Appendix

Keyboard Shortcuts

This appendix lists Word's default keyboard shortcuts for single keys and key combinations. Look through the following tables, which list convenient keyboard shortcuts for tasks you might otherwise perform by clicking on icons, setting options in dialog boxes, or choosing menu commands. If you memorize the key combinations most useful to you, you can not only save time but can also issue commands as you type, without moving your hands from the keyboard.

You can, of course, set your own keyboard shortcuts as described in Chapter 22, ''Customizing Word.'' Note that if you have changed keyboard shortcuts, these tables might not be accurate for your personal Word configuration.

ALPHANUMERIC KEYBOARD SHORTCUTS

Use the keys in the main alphanumeric section of the keyboard with these shortcuts.

Press this key	With these modifiers	To execute this command
~	Command	Insert Nonbreaking Hyphen
1	Option-Command	No Paragraph Border
2	Option-Command	Thick-Line Paragraph Border
-	Command	Insert Soft Hyphen
-	Option-Command	Remove from Menu
-	Shift-Command	Subscript 2 points
=	Command	Calculate
=	Option-Command	Add to Menu
=	Shift-Option-Command	Add to Menu
=	Shift-Command	Superscript 3 points
[	Option-Command	Scroll Line Upward
[	Shift-Command	Double Underline
]	Option-Command	Zoom Window
]	Shift-Command	Word Underline
\	Option-Command	Insert Formula
\	Shift-Command	Dotted Underline
;	Option-Command	Move to Next Word
'	Option-Command	More Keyboard Prefix
,	Command	Edit Link (Quickswitch)
,	Option-Command	Move to Next Line
,	Shift-Command	Smaller Font Size
<	Shift-Command	Smaller Font Size
>	Shift-Command	Larger Font Size
.	Command	Cancel
.	Option-Command	Scroll Screen Downward
.	Shift-Command	Larger Font Size
/	Command	Context-Sensitive Help
/	Option-Command	Scroll Line Downward
/	Shift-Command	Strikethru

(continued)

Alphanumeric Keyboard Shortcuts. *continued*

Press this key	With these modifiers	To execute this command
A	Command	Again
A	Option-Command	Find Again
B	Command	Page View
B	Option-Command	Move to Next Paragraph
B	Shift-Command	Bold
C	Command	Copy
C	Option-Command	Copy Text
C	Shift-Command	Centered
D	Command	Character...
D	Option-Command	Copy as Picture
D	Shift-Command	Outline
E	Command	Footnote...
E	Shift-Command	Change Font
F	Command	Find...
F	Option-Command	Delete Forward
F	Shift-Command	First Line Indent
G	Command	Go To...
G	Option-Command	Delete Next Word
H	Command	Change...
H	Option-Command	Extend to Character
H	Shift-Command	Small Caps
I	Command	Print Preview...
I	Shift-Command	Italic
J	Command	Repaginate Now
J	Option-Command	Move to Previous Word
J	Shift-Command	Justified
K	Command	Glossary...
K	Option-Command	Move to Previous Character
K	Shift-Command	All Caps
L	Command	Spelling...
L	Option-Command	Move to Next Character
L	Shift-Command	Flush Left

(continued)

Alphanumeric Keyboard Shortcuts. *continued*

Press this key	With these modifiers	To execute this command
M	Command	Paragraph...
M	Option-Command	Select Whole Document
M	Shift-Command	Unnest Paragraph
N	Command	New File
N	Shift-Command	Nest Paragraph
O	Command	Open...
O	Option-Command	Move to Previous Line
O	Shift-Command	Open Spacing
P	Command	Print...
P	Option-Command	Scroll Screen Upward
P	Shift-Command	Normal Paragraph
Q	Command	Quit
Q	Option-Command	Paste Special Character
Q	Shift-Command	Symbol Font
R	Command	Show/Hide Ruler
R	Option-Command	Find Formats
R	Shift-Command	Flush Right
S	Command	Save
S	Option-Command	Split Window
S	Shift-Command	Change Style
S	Shift-Option-Command	Open Footnote Window
T	Command	Define Styles...
T	Option-Command	Outline Command Prefix
T	Shift-Command	Hanging Indent
U	Shift-Command	Underline
V	Command	Paste
V	Option-Command	Copy Formats
V	Shift-Command	Hidden Text
W	Command	Close
W	Option-Command	Move to Next Window
W	Shift-Command	Shadow

(continued)

Alphanumeric Keyboard Shortcuts. *continued*

Press this key	With these modifiers	To execute this command
X	Command	Cut
X	Option-Command	Move Text
X	Shift-Command	Hidden Text
Y	Command	Show/Hide ¶
Y	Option-Command	Move to Previous Paragraph
Y	Shift-Command	Double Space
Z	Command	Undo
Z	Option-Command	Go Back
Z	Shift-Command	Plain Text
Delete		Backspace
Delete	Command	Insert Glossary Text
Delete	Option-Command	Delete Previous Word
Return		Insert New Paragraph
Return	Command	New Paragraph with Same Style
Return	Option-Command	New Paragraph After Insertion Point
Return	Shift	Insert Line Break
Space bar	Command	Insert Nonbreaking Space
Space bar	Option-Command	Insert Paragraph Above Table Row
Space bar	Shift-Command	Plain for Style
Space bar	Option	Insert Nonbreaking Space
Tab		Insert Tab
Tab	Command	Activate Keyboard Menus
Tab	Option	Insert Tab in Table Cell
Tab	Shift	Move to Previous Cell

NUMERIC-KEYPAD SHORTCUTS

Use the keys on the numeric keypad with the following keyboard shortcuts.

Press this key	With these modifiers	To execute this command
Clear		Numeric Lock
Enter		Insert New Paragraph
Enter	Command	Insert New Section
Enter	Shift	Insert Page Break
*		Scroll Line Downward
-		Extend to Character
+		Scroll Line Upward
+	Option-Command	Assign to Key
		Activate Keyboard Menus
0		Go Back
1		Move to End of Line
1	Command	Move to Next Sentence
1	Option-Command	Move to Last Text Area
2		Move to Next Line
2	Command	Move to Next Paragraph
2	Option-Command	Move Downward One Text Area
3		Scroll Screen Downward
3	Command	Move to End of Document
3	Option-Command	Move to Next Text Area
4		Move to Previous Character
4	Command	Move to Previous Word
4	Option-Command	Move Leftward One Text Area
5	Command	Move to Top of Window
6		Move to Next Character
6	Command	Move to Next Word
6	Option-Command	Move Rightward One Text Area
7		Move to Start of Line
7	Command	Move to Previous Sentence
7	Option-Command	Move to First Text Area
8		Move to Previous Line

(continued)

Numeric-Keypad Shortcuts. *continued*

Press this key	With these modifiers	To execute this command
8	Command	Move to Previous Paragraph
8	Option-Command	Move Upward One Text Area
9		Scroll Screen Upward
9	Command	Move to Start of Document
9	Option-Command	Move to Previous Text Area

CURSOR-KEY SHORTCUTS

Use the cursor keys and the six keys above them (Help, Home, Page Up, Page Down, End, and Del—all found only on the extended keyboard) with these keyboard shortcuts.

Press this key	With these modifiers	To execute this command
Left arrow		Move to Previous Character
Left arrow	Command	Move to Previous Word
Left arrow	Option-Command	Assign to Key
Right arrow		Move to Next Character
Right arrow	Command	Move to Next Word
Up arrow		Move to Previous Line
Up arrow	Command	Move to Previous Paragraph
Down arrow		Move to Next Line
Down arrow	Command	Move to Next Paragraph
Del		Delete Forward
End		Move to Bottom of Window
End	Command	Move to End of Document
Help		Context-Sensitive Help
Home		Move to Top of Window
Home	Command	Move to Start of Document
Page up		Scroll Screen Upward
Page up	Command	Move to Previous Page
Page down		Scroll Screen Downward
Page down	Command	Move to Next Page

FUNCTION-KEY SHORTCUTS

If your keyboard includes a row of function keys, you can use them with the following keyboard shortcuts.

Press this key	With this modifier	To execute this command
F1		Undo
F2		Cut
F2	Option	Edit Link (Quickswitch)
F2	Shift	Move Text
F3		Copy
F3	Option	Update Link
F3	Shift	Copy Text
F4		Paste
F4	Option	Paste Link
F4	Shift	Copy Formats
F5		New File
F5	Shift	New Window
F6		Open...
F6	Shift	Open Any File...
F7		Save
F7	Shift	Save As...
F8		Print...
F8	Shift	Page Setup...
F9		Plain For Style
F9	Option	Hidden Text
F9	Shift	Plain Text
F10		Bold
F10	Option	Small Caps
F10	Shift	All Caps
F11		Italic
F11	Option	Shadow
F11	Shift	Outline
F12		Underline
F12	Command	Word Underline

(continued)

Function-Key Shortcuts. *continued*

Press this key	With these modifiers	To execute this command
F12	Option	Dotted Underline
F12	Shift	Double Underline
F13		Page View
F13	Option	Print Preview...
F13	Shift	Outlining
F14		Character...
F14	Command	Document...
F14	Option	Section...
F14	Shift	Paragraph...
F15		Spelling...
F15	Command	Renumber...
F15	Option	Word Count...
F15	Shift	Hyphenate...

Index

Michael Boom

Michael Boom is the author of three Microsoft Press books: *Learn Word for Windows Now*, *Music Through Midi*, and *The Amiga*. He has worked as a software producer for Electronic Arts and as a music and software development consultant for Commodore-Amiga, Inc. He currently lives in the Bay Area, where he works as a consultant for Sun Microsystems.

The manuscript for this book was prepared and submitted to Microsoft Press in electronic form. Text files were processed and formatted using Microsoft Word.

Principal word processor: Debbie Kem
Principal proofreader: Jean Zimmer
Principal typographer: Lisa Iversen
Interior text designer: Darcie Furlan
Principal illustrator: Rebecca Geisler-Johnson
Cover designer: Rebecca Geisler-Johnson
Cover color separator: Rainier Color Corporation

Text composition by Microsoft Press in Times Roman, with display type in Times Bold, using the Magna composition system and the Linotronic 300 laser imagesetter.

Printed on recycled paper stock.

Other Titles from Microsoft Press

WORD 4 COMPANION
Gena B. Cobb, Allan McGuffey, Judy Mynhier

This up-to-date tutorial and reference—for all levels—includes everything you need to know about Word version 4: from the basics of editing, formatting, and printing a document to more advanced features such as multicolumn formatting, creating form letters, and using style sheets and macros. There are also special techniques for working with numbers and formulas, integrating graphics into a document, and customizing Word's menus. Beginners will find the book an unbeatable source of clear tutorials, and intermediate and advanced user will turn to it for its in-depth information.

864 pages, softcover   7$^{1}/_{2}$ x 9$^{1}/_{4}$ $22.95   Order Code WO4CO

WORKING WITH WORD, 2nd ed.
The Definitive Guide to Microsoft® Word on the Apple® Macintosh®
Chris Kinata and Gordon McComb

When you are ready to go beyond simple word processing with Microsoft Word for the Macintosh, WORKING WITH WORD is *the* book of choice for intermediate to advanced users. Now updated for version 4, it's filled with insider's advice, detailed information, and tutorials on every software feature. Scores of tips—many not in the documentation—add power and range to your use of Microsoft Word, no matter what kind of printed documents you want to create. Topics cover desktop publishing with Word (integrating graphics into a Word document and wrapping text around them, working with lists and multiple columns, creating spreadsheetlike tables); customizing menus and retrieving lost files; linking Word with other applications; programming conditional print merging instructions; including PostScript instructions in Word documents; and optimizing memory management. Also included are blueprints for correspondence, multicolumn newsletters, brochures, and reports.

752 pages, softcover   7$^{3}/_{8}$ x 9$^{1}/_{4}$ $22.95   Order Code WOWO2

QUICK REFERENCE GUIDE TO MICROSOFT® WORD
FOR THE APPLE® MACINTOSH®
Lisa Ann Jacobs

This great little guide, organized alphabetically, is a handy reference to Microsoft Word through version 4. You can look up specific tasks—customizing menus, indexing, underlining text—without knowing the specific Word commands. It's a practical, fast way to understand and use Microsoft Word.

144 pages, softcover   4$^{3}/_{4}$ x 8 $5.95   Order Code QRWOMA

DESKTOP PUBLISHING BY DESIGN
Aldus® PageMaker® edition
Ronnie Shushan and Don Wright

"...a treasure-trove of useful, detailed examples and tips designed to help readers create desktop-published documents that get attention." **PC World**

Named "Best How-To Book for 1990" by the Computer Press Association, DESKTOP PUBLISHING BY DESIGN is filled with helpful information, layout ideas, and inspiration for anyone new to design, publishing, or computers. The authors offer a primer on the use of basic design elements—typeface, page layout, and graphics. And they provide a wide-ranging and imaginative portfolio of promotional flyers and brochures, newsletters and magazines, catalogs, data sheets, and forms that highlight good design and constitute a sourcebook of inventive ideas. You'll also find a series of PageMaker projects (Aldus PageMaker version 3 for the IBM PC or Apple Macintosh) that provide hands-on experience and build confidence while demonstrating how to produce exciting, professional-looking printed pieces. DESKTOP PUBLISHING BY DESIGN is a fact-filled, designed-oriented resource you'll turn to again and again.

408 pages, softcover   8 $^{1}/_{2}$ x 11 $24.95   Order Code DEPUDP

Microsoft Press books are available wherever quality computer books are sold.
Credit card orders can be placed by calling 1-800-MSPRESS. Please refer to BBK.